Soil Balancing

The Albrecht Papers, Volume VII

by William A. Albrecht, Ph.D.
Edited by Charles Walters

Albrecht on Soil Balancing

The Albrecht Papers, Volume VII

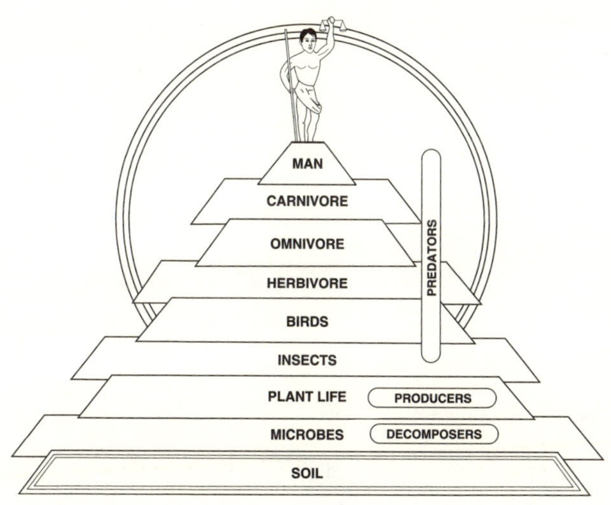

by William A. Albrecht, Ph.D.
Edited by Charles Walters

Acres U.S.A.
Austin, Texas

Albrecht on Soil Balancing

Acres U.S.A.
P.O. Box 91299
Austin, Texas 78709 U.S.A.
(512) 892-4400 • fax (512) 892-4448
info@acresusa.com • www.acresusa.com

Printed in the United States of America

Publisher's Cataloging-in-Publication

Albrecht, William A., 1888-1974; and Charles Walters, editor
Albrecht on soil balancing / William A. Albrecht., Austin, TX, ACRES U.S.A., 2011
xx, 230 pp., 23 cm.
Includes Index
Includes Bibliography
ISBN 978-1-601730-29-9 (trade)

1. Agriculture — crops & soils. 2. Soil management.
3. Soil — plant relationship. 4. Soil fertility 5. Plants — nutrition.
I. Albrecht, William A., 1888-1974 and Charles Walters, 1926-2009
II. Title.

S593.A43 2011 631.4

Dedicated to
Neal Kinsey,

teacher, consultant and long-time messenger
of the Albrecht word as enlarged in the book,
Hands-On Agronomy, and in hundreds of seminars and articles.

Contents

About the Author

Dr. William A. Albrecht, the author of these papers, was chairman of the Department of Soils at the University of Missouri College of Agriculture, where he had been a member of the staff for 43 years. He held four degrees, A.B., B.S. in Agriculture, M.S. and Ph.D., from the University of Illinois. During a vivid and crowded career, he traveled widely and studied soils in the United States, Great Britain, on the European continent, and in Australia.

Born on a farm in central Illinois in an area of highly fertile soil typical of the cornbelt and educated in his native state, Dr. Albrecht grew up with an intense interest in the soil and all things agricultural. These were approached, however, through the avenues of the basic sciences and liberal arts and not primarily through applied practices and their economics.

Teaching experience after completing the liberal arts course, with some thought of the medical profession, as well as an assistantship in botany, gave an early vision of the interrelationships that enrich the facts acquired in various fields when viewed as part of a master design.

These experiences led him into additional undergraduate and graduate work, encouraged by scholarships and fellowships, until he received his doctor's degree in 1919. In the meantime, he joined the research and teaching staff at the University of Missouri.

Both as a writer and speaker, Dr. Albrecht served tirelessly as an interpreter of scientific truth to inquiring minds and persistently stressed the basic importance of understanding and working with nature by applying the natural method to all farming, crop production, livestock raising and soil improvement. He always had a specific focus on the effect of soil characteristics upon the mineral composition of plants and the effect of the mineral composition of plants on animal nutrition and subsequent human health.

Dr. Albrecht strove not to be an ivory tower pontificator trying to master and defeat nature, but to be a leader of true science and understand the wondrous ways of nature so we could harness them for the lasting benefit of all. A man of the soil, William A. Albrecht summed up his philosophy as such, "When wildlife demonstrates the soil as the foundation of its health and numbers, is man, the apex of the biotic pyramid, too far removed from the soil to recognize it as the foundation of his health via nutrition?"

Dr. Albrecht was a true student of the characteristics of soil and wasn't timid about his views — be they to a farmer in the field, an industry group or to a congressional subcommittee.

Respected and recognized by scientists and agricultural leaders from around the world, Dr. Albrecht retired in 1959 and passed from the scene in May 1974 as his 86th birthday approached.

About the Albrecht Papers

When the first volume of these papers was issued, no one could foresee the possibility of recovering and publishing all the papers of this great scientist. For this reason the organization of these papers has not followed Dr. Albrecht's work in a calendar sequence, meaning the order of study and investigation. Instead the papers have been organized into topic themes.

Here the papers have been grouped to best focus attention and allowed to reciprocate the values upon which all of Albrecht's work.

About the Editor

Charles Walters was the founder and executive editor of *Acres U.S.A*, a magazine he started in 1971 to spread the word of eco-agriculture. A recognized leader in the field of raw materials-based economic research and sustainable food and farming systems, this confirmed maverick saw one of his missions as to rescue lost knowledge. Perhaps the most important were the papers of Dr. William A. Albrecht, whose low profile obscured decades of brilliant work in soil science. Albrecht's papers, which Walters rescued from the historical dustbin and published in an initial four volumes, continue to provide a rock-solid foundation for the scientific approach to organic farming. Additional volumes of Albrecht's papers were organized and edited by Walters for later publication—the result is shown here with this book. During his life, Walters penned thousands of article on the technologies of organic and sustainable agriculture and is the author of more than two dozen books (and co-author of several more), including *Eco-Farm: An Acres U.S.A. Primer, Weeds, Control Without Poisons, A Farmer's Guide to the Bottom Line, Dung Beetles, Mainline Farming for Century 21* and many more. Charles Walters generously shared his vision, energy and passion through his writing and public speaking for more than 35 years and made it his lifelong mission to save the family farm and give farmers an operating manual that they couldn't live without. The Albrecht Papers are an important part of this message. Charles Walters passed on in January 2009 at the age of 83.

From the Publisher

A large part of the Acres U.S.A. mission is to preserve and promote the wisdom of those who came before us. Prof. William Albrecht was such a visionary. A collection of his papers was the first publishing entry toward this mission, that book being *The Albrecht Papers*.

Charles Walters, our founder and longtime editor — and my father — sought out Dr. Albrecht not knowing what lessons were there to be learned. The name Albrecht appeared in journals around the world, yet officials at the University of Missouri where the retired professor kept an office discouraged a meeting citing his age, poor hearing, and the like. Charles Walters visited anyway. What came from these meetings, which soon grew into weekly sessions, was a mentor/student dialogue. Albrecht, ever the patient pedagogue, dispensed the logic, elegance and simplicity of his agricultural systems to an eager mind. And Charles Walters, the publisher and writer, picked up the charge and spread the timeless wisdom of William Albrecht around the world to a new generation of farmers and agronomists.

It's hard to say whether Dr. Albrecht's work would have found its way to light through the efforts of others or if without the republication of Albrecht's papers they would have remained just that, papers to eventually fall into the dustbin of history.

Four volumes of *The Albrecht Papers* eventually came forth. Each had a style and character of its own and each brought new lessons from the master soil scientist to life, but only the most disciplined students of the soil tended to seek out and study these dense works.

Late in his career, semi-retired and legally blind, Charles Walters undertook the Herculean task of reading and sorting the hundreds of remaining papers and articles in Albrecht's archives. He completed that task a few years before his death in 2009. What was left to accomplish was the monumental task of converting damaged and faded copies of articles, some 80 years old, into formats compatible with modern publishing and readable by all.

From file cabinets full of faded photocopies came forth several new volumes of *The Albrecht Papers*, each with a specific focus and theme. It is our goal to produce these works in a timely fashion. In your hands is the beautiful collaboration of the visionary research of Professor William Albrecht and the deft editorial eye of Charles Walters. We hope you enjoy this new creation of William Albrecht and Charles Walters.

— *Fred C. Walters*

Foreword

ANY SURVEY OF PAPERS by William A. Albrecht will suggest the reality that none of his findings lend themselves to isolation in neat little compartments. That everything is related to everything else becomes evident every time we enlarge even a single factor.

Thus the lessons on calcium presented as popular papers in Volume III of The Albrecht Papers, grew to become Volume V, *Albrecht on Calcium* when expanded to present scholarly papers and added insight.

The present volume reclaims an Albrecht development that was 50 years ahead of its time, that of the balance equation. The reasons for being of that equation were stated in the "Fringe Soils" article for *Natural Foods and Farming* magazine originally published in January 1965 following on the next page.

I encountered Dr. William A. Albrecht in 1971, a few weeks after launching *Acres U.S.A.* In due time he offered me a correspondence course he was providing to consultants joining Brookside Laboratories, New Knoxville, Ohio.

Following is a reproduced copy of the soil audit report he gave me, and with that presentation came months of lessons so priceless they might as well have been weighed out on a jeweler's scale. As noted earlier, calcium came first because it was the prince — no, the king — of nutrients.

Albrecht's balance equation asks for well-defined, cation nutrient loads of calcium, magnesium, sodium and potassium and the trace elements. "I have to have 65 percent of that clay capacity loaded with calcium, 15 percent with magnesium — I have to have four times as much calcium as magnesium. You see why we ought to lime the soil? We ought to lime to get it up to where it feeds the plant calcium, not to fight acidity."

FRINGE SOILS

It has often been said that "most discoveries are the result of accidents, but only thus for the minds prepared to make them."

The truth of that statement was experienced recently by a consultant at a research laboratory in the Midwest. He was called to observe a case of "core rot" in a field of onions just going into storage. Then, soon afterward, he had a similar request to investigate a farm where nematode attacks had destroyed a field of carrots.

In both cases, the use of soil tests and the subsequent prescription for balanced fertility restored the same successive crops to healthy production on the same fields. The fungus rot and the nematodes were thereby prevented. No cures were used. Instead, healthy rather than "sick" crops were marketed thereafter. Prevention, at no special cost but by an investment in creative powers, was a profitable discovery for the mind prepared for it.

But that mind did not emphasize discovery. Rather it went to work, in practice, to deliver the next onion crop as a healthy one and the next carrot crop as a pest-free one. The consultant replaced the previous crop disasters with restored earnings for the commercial gardeners by rewards for their arduous labor. The gardeners were not put out of the business of growing health-giving foods through fertile soils. They did not have to resort to raising sickly crops of poor food value brought to harvest by means of sprays and other dangerous chemicals.

Both of these discoveries — which illustrated that *"an ounce of prevention" in the form of balanced plant nutrition from fertile soils "is better than a pound of cure"* in the form of dangerous poisons — were made on sandy soils. Those were "fringe" soils. Fringe soils cannot readily produce growth, self-preservation and fecund reproduction, as is the case of soils with more clay holding larger supplies of available nutrient elements and more organic matter to carry into the plants both the ash elements and larger organic nutrient molecules, whose nutritional services we do not yet comprehend fully.

When most virgin soils in the mid-continent were well stocked with humus in their deep surface layers and given annual dust deposits of windblown, less-weathered, nutrient-rich, rock mineral fertility, like loess, we were slow to see failing or sickly crops as evidence of their troubles on "fringe" soils. Soil depletion is putting more and more acres of them under that classification.

It is through such observations by keen-eyed consultants that we are discovering that once-fertile soils are reclassifying themselves into the "fringe" group. Early discovery means prompt remedies. Those can come by prevention, which always surpasses cures. Simultaneously, *prevention of diseases and pests by improved plant nutrition means healthy crops* giving better health to their consumers, whether they be beast or man.

It was nature's habit of using prevention rather than cure which handed down to us the healthy crops and animals which we took over in our agricultural production. We cannot continue in that industry by making more "fringe" soils. Nature still offers opportunities for making discoveries in prevention. The big question is, "Are we preparing our minds to make them through better soils?"

The formal paper giving expression to these findings was presented at the International Society of Soil Scientists the day Hitler marched into Poland in 1939. There were formal papers presented in Russia and Australia, but in a manner of speaking, home base Missouri and Illinois was the font of knowledge.

Central to the Albrecht system which works in northern climes and in the tropics, according to soil consultant Neal Kinsey, is the base exchange and comprehension thereof. When Kinsey completed his course of study under Albrecht, the great professor told him, "Now you're entitled to go out and learn to be a consultant." In hand was an understanding of the exchange equation, a translation of which is a necessary prelude to this volume of *The Albrecht Papers*.

Standing on the shoulders of giants, the steady progress in soil science was able to hand Neal Kinsey, C.J. Fenzau — even this editor — the worksheet now a part of this Foreword. The signal words in this worksheet are total exchange capacity in milliequivalents (m.e.), an index to the amount of colloidal energy used to adsorb and hold to the soil's colloidal mass various amounts of essential nutrients that are positively charged, cations, that is. These are the base metal elements and each has its own atomic weight, that weight is invoked when the multiplier extends the payload to be applied to each acre of soil.

Albrecht's course work explained it this way. "If you have a bushel of shell corn, it will likely weigh around 55 pounds, give or take a little. Well, these cation nutrients have their weight. You won't expect a bushel of bluegrass to weigh the same as a bushel of corn."

The soil audit laboratory measures the amount of energy in soil needed to adsorb the following specific payloads in the top seven inches of soil:

Soil Audit and Inventory Report

Account of **SAMPLE** __________ City __________

State _____

Samples taken by __________ Sent in by __________

Date ________

	Soil Sample No:		Sandy Loam	Sandy Soil	Silty Loam	Clay Loam	Rich Muck
	Total Exchange Capacity (m.e.)		12	5	15	40	100
	pH of Soil Sample (6.2 to 6.5)		6.2	6.3	6.2	6	5.8
	Organic Matter (Percentage)		2.8	1.3	3.2	4.6	72
Anions	Nitrogen: (lbs./acre)		84	68	96	138	216
	Sulfates: (lbs./acre)		186	80	320	480	1000
	Phosphates (as P_2O_5): lbs./acre	Desired Value	250	250	250	300	350
		Value Found	140	180	120	150	175
		Deficit	110	70	130	150	175
Exchangeable Cations	Calcium: lbs./acre	Desired Value	3,120	1,300	3,900	10,400	26,000
		Value Found	3,120	1,280	4,200	10,400	24,800
		Deficit	0	20		0	1,200
	Magnesium: lbs./acre	Desired Value	432	180	540	1,440	3,600
		Value Found	432	180	480	1,248	2,400
		Deficit	0	0	60	192	1,200
	Potassium: lbs./acre	Desired Value	280	117	351	936	2,340
		Value Found	312	195	234	624	780
		Deficit			117	312	1,560
	Sodium: (lbs./acre)		Included under other bases				
	Base Saturation Percent						
	Calcium (60 to 70%)	} 80%	65	64	70	65	62
	Magnesium (10 to 20%)		15	15	13.33	13	10
	Potassium (2 to 5%)		3.33	5	2	2	1
	Other Bases (Variable)		5	6	4.67	5	6
	Exchangeable Hydrogen (10 to 15%)		11.67	10	12	15	21

400 pounds of calcium
240 pounds of magnesium
780 pounds of potassium
20 pounds of exchangeable hydrogen

The unit of measurement is the milliequivalent. If a soil has an exchange capacity of, say 10, then the Albrecht computation becomes 10 × 400, or 4,000 total saturation, less the existing inventory of calcium in the soil, less 35 percent (because only 65 percent — give or take — of the soil colloid should be loaded with calcium), leaving room for magnesium, potassium, etc. Soils vary in their structure, composition, in their base exchange capacity. The sample soil audit and inventory report presented here will enable the student to follow the logic and understand the nuances contained in these papers.

Exchange capacity is influenced by factors too numerous for instant comprehension — soil humus, bacteria, air, even light and moisture. Soil, after all is little more than the manure of rocks reduced to microscopic size.

Students may reasonably ask, why are some soils high in m.e. readings, others low, with sand being excluded? The answer is organic matter or humus. The last two are about three times more effective than clay in constructing m.e. index numbers. Organic matter or humus has properties equal to albeit multiplied three times to clay. Thus its effectiveness.

These notes are more or less an aside. The real meat in this agricultural coconut can be found in the individual papers.

Albrecht met often and long with Friends of the Land. He was a regular guest at Louis Bromfield's Malabar Farm. He was Bromfield's counsel and watched with keen interest Bromfield's progress based on the balance equation. Bromfield had seen most of the world's abused acres. He lived in India and Europe and wrote novels, *The Green Bay Tree, The Rains Came, Mrs. Parkington* and *Early Autumn*. The latter won for him a Pulitzer Prize.

When the world started coming apart in the 1930s, Bromfield came home to Ohio, to a place called Pleasant Valley. Here land had been abused. Bad practices and poor cultivation filled the territory with erosion, gullies and poverty. Bromfield picked up one farm after another using the Albrecht system. Crops did a turn-around. In a practical arena he validated the Albrecht balance equation, proving that insect damage and disease could be controlled with humus, plants and nutrition, and some soil management. In *From My Experience: The Pleasures and Miseries of Life on a Farm*, published in 1955, he gave the world his findings. Insects, he wrote, did not like plants grown in good productive soil.

During the late 1940s, public policy decided to turn farming, a biological procedure, into an industrial procedure. The Malabar experience became eclipsed.

Also eclipsed was E.R. Kuck, the founder Brookside Dairy Farms, another of Albrecht's friends. In fact it was a case of animals telling Kuck about vanished nutrition that launched Brookside Research Laboratories and the worksheet Albrecht used in his post-university days in the correspondence course, Brookside and Albrecht stood almost alone in rejecting the university N, P and K prescription and toxic rescue chemistry.

After plastering the walls of a new calf barn, Kuck noticed that the animals literally ate the plaster off the walls of their stalls. Calves had been scouring at the time. Scouring stopped almost immediately. Kuck, connecting with Albrecht determined that the hungry animals were in fact after the calcium carbonate and the magnesium carbonate in the plastering material. These nutrients had been mined out of the soil of the dairy operation.

Other observations came to the fore at Brookside. Soil and leaf tests revealed a wide variance in treated versus untreated soils. The lessons thus harvested seemed obvious. Kuck issued a request embodying the wisdom of Albrecht. Surely farmers would listen to another farmer even if they rejected the science of a schoolman.

Not so. In December of 1946, Kuck issued a report, *Better Crops with Plant Food*, published by the American Potash Institute. The article was picked up by the farm press and circulated widely. Feedback arrived almost immediately, some 1,000 letters from farmers telling Kuck about their own problems and asking for help. The letters from academia were vitriolic in tone and content. Especially denounced was any role for magnesium in animal nutrition. Moreover, the college people seemed to think no farmer had the right to make such observations telling it the way it was without the imprimatur of a consensus from the collective university.

The calcium-magnesium connection flows through every division — if that word can be permitted — of the Albrecht papers. Albrecht practically demanded that his later-day students more or less memorize a paper by the German professor, Oscar Loew.

Oscar Loew, a German researcher, was perhaps the first to point out that excess magnesium is a poison to the calcium in the nucleus of the plant cell. This may seem odd since magnesium is a close associate in natural chemodynamics with calcium, and the later is a major inorganic element in the human body, magnesium and calcium are alkaline elements, calcium being dominant in terms of sheer bulk.

It is this poison property of magnesium related to calcium that confers a majestic property to the Albrecht equation courtesy of Professor Loew's research.

Many high-pH soils are built expressly from high levels of sodium and potassium, remaining low in calcium. Albrecht never tired of iterating and reiterating this point, for which reason a somewhat weighted consideration often attends scrutiny of cation balances on the soil audit worksheet.

Still, excessive calcium will cause magnesium, phosphorus and minor element deficiency. This assuredly means vegetables without digestive calcium, according to Albrecht. In general it means plants with imbalanced hormone and enzyme systems, ergo poor health — the magnet for bacterial, fungal and insect attack.

Excessive magnesium causes phosphate, potassium and other deficiencies. High magnesium and low calcium permit organic residue to ferment into alcohol, a sterilant to bacteria. The deficits are endless. So are the gems of wisdom contained in the lines and between the lines of the papers in this volume.

It is assumed that readers will have read the earlier volumes of these papers, otherwise it would be necessary to print and reprint, arriving at a volume six or seven times the size of this one. Some readers have commented that it is necessary to read *Eco-Farm, an Acres U.S.A. Primer* before tackling The Albrecht Papers. If not true, the idea would be helpful. For now it is enough to note that generations have come and gone since the age of Albrecht, and many have built on and enlarged his findings. None have embraced the hard work that accounted for the balance equation in the first place.

Admittedly, cation and anion represent a chemist's conceptualization. They do not proscribe due consideration of microorganisms, cosmic forces, or even enlivened rock powders.

Field-ripened crops, or lack thereof, sealed soils that aid and abet germination of seed types that prefer carbon dioxide and the absence of oxygen, all are the product of imbalance. Much the same is true of improper water insoak and capillary return.

Withal, Albrecht seems to say that if it is important to define percentages of nitrogen, potassium and phosphorus, why is it not important to state the percentages of calcium, magnesium and sulfur on a have and needed basis.

— Charles Walters, Editor

CHAPTER 1

Nature's Soil Management

WE ARE MET at the Brookside Research Laboratories, New Knoxville, Ohio on December 11, 1965, Anno Domini. This is an institution of many dedicated folks given to the study of what was once called "Natural Philosophy," or "The love of truth about Nature's Creations and Behaviors." Today that effort in study is called "Research." It includes the mental struggles which have organized our knowledge about matters natural into the many "Sciences."

To mention a few, those are, Zoology, Botany, Microbiology (and others) concerned about forms of life; and also Physics, Chemistry, Geology, Pedalogy, Meteorology (and others) representing the materials and forces manifest on the surface of the earth to support the several strata of living substances with soil as the base and man as the apex of that Biotic Pyramid.

Research at Brookside Laboratories is given to a fuller comprehension of a clear vision that there must be close nutritional interrelations between soils, plants, animals and man; and that those must be naturally understood if man and his agriculture are to manage our soils successfully as guarantee of healthy growth and survival of at least those first three living and supporting strata on the earth, namely, Soil, Microbes and Plants on which all others are predators.

Historical View

The westward march of the pioneer peoples, in the overflow of population from crowded Asia, was directed largely by man's herds and flocks. They did so by selecting grassy roadways growing on, and maintaining,

Nature's heritage of "Living Soils." That stream of multiplying human species flowed westward along the narrower belt of the North Temperate Zone. It branched, as safaris out from there, which now have taken man to both the North and South Poles. Having found them uninhabitable by any agriculture, he is resigned to the threat of a population explosion on the limited, once-productive soil areas on the lone habitable planet of our energy-supplying star, the sun.

That explosive danger comes just when we accept the fact of insufficient land area for more people of whom less and less are farmers, and when we have a formerly fertile soil heritage now nearly squandered under our emphasis on economic and technological management of but decades rather than centuries. Yet, before we came along, there were large areas of land where the soil had been built up by Nature to produce climax crops and to maintain them in place for centuries. As youthful prodigals in soil conservation, we are beginning to repent and return to Nature for more critical research study of the *Living Surface Soil Layer* whereby past populations came about and where in the future only limited ones must establish their survival.

We are met here where a few dedicated minds are turning to concentrated studies of *Nature's Management* of the *Living Soil*. That is not aimed to be merely more of man's bold exhibition of his technologies for collection of speedy economic gain only, but an honest, humble cooperation, complying with the natural requisites of restoring — to some degree — the soil's fuller power to create well-nourished — and thereby healthy — species of microbes, plants, animals and man. Also those must be living in mutual interdependencies for maximum survival of all.

When we examine Nature's soil maintenance (via management), we find but two practices, or two principles, which we have not yet accepted widely as recommendations — even in vision, much less in adopted practices. The first of these is maintaining a generous reserve mixture of unweathered, pulverized silt minerals of the essential inorganic elements; or the periodic application of such to the surface soil by wind or inwash. The second is the maximum regular return to the surface soil of the organic material grown in place. Nature's soil management has not included the application of water-soluble salts of concentrations as high as one percent in solution where She grew forages generally acceptable to grazing animals. Nor were there significant salts in the forest soils where the few browsing animals venture. Under Nature's management the nutrients of the soil are insoluble yet available by way of the weathering forces of the soil microbes and of the plant root contacts. Heterogeneity of the soil presented to searching roots and not a homogeneity, equivalent of a laboratory compounding, is Her requisite for healthy plant growth.

Nature's soils are a complex make-up of the mineral particles from as large as sand-size fragments of rock-mineral mixture to particles of inorganic matter of clay size and newly created clay minerals. Those latter carry even carbon and nitrogen within their chemical structure. Then in addition to the mineral portion, Nature's soils contain organic matter consisting of carbon, hydrogen, oxygen, nitrogen, etc. combined, or chelated, with inorganic matters in all degrees of molecular complexity. They represent many degrees of activity under the microbial struggles to survive by their making a living soil.

Microbes are the wrecking crews and salvage agents to keep nutrient elements and compounds recycled from life above the soil back down into it for another repeat of that circuit through crops. Microbial soil life is Nature's means of conservation of Her creative capital. That lowly flora prepares the table for hungry crop plants by offering them the insoluble yet available soil fertility for their nutrition.

This recycling process by the organic matter, with slight additions of fertility from deeper root penetrations, is reported to represent as much as 90% of the plants' annual needs in the case of some European forests of ages of 100 and 130 years.[1] That the duplicate of such management of soil organic matter has had no consideration for practice on our agricultivated soils in the U.S.A. is evident when one examines the reports of the annual consumption of commercial fertilizer salts. Were we to recycle the organic matter grown on our soils with an efficiency approaching that of the natural forests, and then experience also the natural dust deposits coming out of the Missouri River bottoms — whereby our fertile loess soils were built — at the measured rate of an half-ton per acre per annum, very likely our Corn Belt soils would be productive for at least a century in place of being exhausted to uneconomic levels in a third of that time.[2]

---

[1] *Dr. Franz Hartmann. Zur Frage der Nahrsloffbilanz im Waldboden. Allgemeine Forst-zeitung. Vol. 74. Nos. 7 & 8 1963. Wien. (Austria)*

[2] *G. E. Smith. Sanborn Field. Fifty years of Field Experiments with Crop Rotations, Manure and Fertilizers. Mo. Agr. Exp't Sta. Bul. 458 Dec. 1942*

Soil as Plant Nutrition . . . Only Partially Understood

Pulverized rock-minerals, weathering in the soil by acid-clay contact, give up their positively charged (cationic) elements to be adsorbed on the clay-humus colloids. From there they are taken by plant root contact exchanging hydrogen, a non-nutrient cation, for them. Such is our vision of how calcium, magnesium, potassium, sodium and other positively charged nutrient elements are not soluble in the soil but yet available to, and taken by, plant roots for crop nourishment. This understanding is built on the simpler facts of inorganic chemistry, the first step in our learning that science.

But our vision of how negatively charged nutrient elements, like phosphorus, sulfur and nitrate-nitrogen, are mobilized into the crop from insoluble forms within the soil still resides in the simple belief, that, by some miraculous dynamics, encouraged by soil microbes struggling for energy from the soil organic matter, these negatively charged matters (anions) enter the plant as nutrition for the crop.

Our vision of the mobilization of anions is not one for efficient management of the soil when our application of even the ammonia (a cation), which changes to nitrate (an anion) in the soil, does well to get one-third of the nitrogen into the crop while two-thirds are lost. Likewise we apply phosphate forms and recover less than one-tenth in the immediate year, and diminishing portions during succeeding years. We know that of all the soluble phosphates applied along the eastern coast, since fertilizing by them began, two-thirds of them have not been recovered in the crops when they are still in the soils as tests have shown.

Yet Nature was growing crops requiring phosphorus from the soil before man arrived on the scene. She must also have been growing crops requiring nitrogen, and certainly without such large losses of it from the soil at two-thirds. Here we come face to face with the conviction that Nature must have managed these nutrients by way of her return to the soil annually of the organic matter near the place of its growth. That suggests itself as a basic requisite when sulfur, nitrogen and phosphorus are so much more efficient when associated with the use of barnyard manure as the empericism of farm use reports.

Nature's dynamics of soil as plant nutrition certainly were not limited to those of inorganic chemistry alone, as seems often the belief of agricultural students who barely arrive at organic chemistry. Nature's creative biochemistry was not divided into those two separate phases, as we did in the beginning study of that science. She operated her biochemistry of creation on molecular dimensions far beyond and contrary to the belief that plants could not take from the soil large organic molecules of living processes in a living soil enabling crops to catch the sunshine's energy in synthesizing compounds of still unknown complexity. While we have progressed commendably in our knowledge of the inorganic phase of plant nutrition, much of that is still unknown while we have not associated it with the concept that plants may possibly be nourished also — or more effectively so — by organic compounds, and by those delivering many of the inorganic ones. There is a tremendous area of unvisioned facts hidden by the dimness in our comprehension of soil as nutrition by means of its organic matter content, so little yet considered.

Soil, Microbes, Plants . . . Life's Supporting Triplet

Doubtless, the first forms of life on the earth were single-celled ones, or the microbes. They were created in the sea and were moved out on the land later. Our vision of that historic biological event recognizes already then an interdependency of at least two — possibly three — of them, namely, the filamentous fungi and the chlorophyl-bearing — if not nitrogen-fixing — algae. We can scarcely picture the absence of bacteria from that combination in its setting. Accordingly we see the algae catching the sun's energy and supplying carbohydrates to the other two; the bacteria, so supplied, could be the digesting agencies to nourish algae and could be fixing atmospheric nitrogen for synthesis of proteins; and the fungi, with their power to scale off rock particles, were probably the source of mineral nutrients for all three of these single-celled progenitors.

But in the development of our sciences to date, we selected from bacteria that crowd of three microbes, and took up war on the bacteria as "germs" causing "diseases." We neglected the understanding of their healthful nutrition as basic, while emphasizing our chemical synthesis of poisons to destroy them. Microbial nutrition is still a new science. The algae brought study of, and emphasis on, green plants and their chlorophyl as source of energy foods in all our agricultural crops. But the fungi were forgotten until the late advent of their complex, highly poisonous compounds, i.e. the antibiotics, so commercially lucrative in the medical practices. The functions of those highly poisonous cyclic-carbon compounds in the survival of those microbes were not considered when they serve, apparently, as means of eliminating bacterial competitors with the fungi for "Lebensraum" in a soil of such low fertility that it represents a desperate struggle for survival by even the fungi feeding on the lowest grade of soil organic matter.

A Naturalist Observes . . . Symbiotic Fungi and Legumes Via Soil Organic Matter

The last decade has seen others, besides the industrialist Titans, turning to the study of soil fungi, the first of the wrecking crews to attack the coarse, woody parts of crop residues. We now know, according to research studies in Great Britain,[3] that wood-destroying fungi are able to decompose its lignaceous matter. They do that by splitting the six-carbon ring compound, long considered chemically impregnable, but now shattered by fungi in connection with some of its particular side chain structures.* This occasion here is the result of fungi studies of more than a decade searching out these forms, not only destructive of organic matter but also constructive, thereby, in serving symbiotically with even non-legume plants for their improved nutrition via that combustible fraction of the soil.

The research during nearly fifteen years of retirement from the U.S.D.A., by the naturalist-scientist, Mr. S.C. Hood of both Tampa, Florida and Pizgah Forest, North Carolina kindled into flame the smothered spark of interest at Brookside Research Laboratories in that same area of study. With four-score and five years behind him, Mr. Hood's accidental contact with the Brookside Research Laboratories led him to find a kindred mindedness where he believed his research thinking on soil organic matter as well as his laboratory equipment and manuscript records would continue their growth into recognized natural facts and organized principles undergirding soil productivity along with more complete soil conservation in supporting our increasing human species.

Mr. Hood's offer of his mental and material matters organized into facts of Nature about soil organic matter prompting a symbiosis between soil fungi and non-legume plants — much as we know it for soil bacteria

---

[3] *Miora E. K. Anderson. Journal of General Microbiology. 26: 149–154, and 155 ff. 1961.*

* *Since the preparation of this manuscript, we have learned that detergent pollution can be remedied through short, successive amputations of the saturated hydrocarbon chain by certain fungi.*

and legumes — were presented to Mr. E.R. Kuck, the Founder of Brookside Research Laboratories. They encouraged him to match Mr. Hood's contribution to this cause of agriculture with similar and other matters necessary to establish research studies at Brookside Laboratories of the microbial dynamics of soil fertility centered about soil organic matter - the most neglected factor in soil productivity.

Some Visions . . . of the Future

Our view of soil microbes seems to parallel what Shakespeare reported about our view of other humans, when he said: "The evil that men do lives after them, while the good is oft interred with their bones." *We are prone to* see only evil, not good, in any microbe. That was long the persistent view of Rhizobia bacteria, *those in the nodules on the roots of legume plants* making the *millions of pounds of gaseous nitrogen* over every acre marriageable with carbon and hydrogen coming from the plants' carbohydrates to give proteins, or living tissues. It required many years of research before the vision of that natural possibility was revealed by Nature in chemical and quantitative values considered proof of the fact, once no more than only a vision.

The biochemical dynamics bringing about that symbiosis naturally between microbe and plant when we are prone to believe those two species usually in deadly combat, are still unknowns. And that ignorance of Nature's abilities prevails when in the U.S., and her near surroundings, more than a hundred industrial plants are synthesizing atmospheric nitrogen even into urea, the same as the excretory residue carrying nitrogen combined with carbon from our body's digestion and metabolism of the protein we take as food.

When the legume plants of higher physiological complexity demanding more inorganic fertility also require that latter in accurate balance before they will join with Rhizobia bacteria for mutually more rapid growth through nitrogen fixation, shall we not envision at lower levels of fertility that the non-legume plants and the fungi might also strike up a symbiotic partnership whereby each would be getting more nitrogen from the soil organic matter, predigested — as it were — by the fungi, provided the soil organic matter represents a high level or amply suited supply? Can this not be another one of those interdependencies by which Nature exercises conservation of mass and energy which we are slow to recognize as the first law of thermodynamics?

Shall we suddenly accept soil fungi entwined on plant roots as friends, when to so many plant pathologists they have been considered foes, attacking and destroying plant tissues while fruiting there as rusts, wilts and other decided damages? But from Mr. Hood's studies we learn that the finer roots of innumerable plants, on natural soils well-stocked with organic matter, are compactly enshrouded by networks of fungi. Some of their mycelia go into and come out of, the root cells with seeming improved growth of both root and top of the plant.

His more critical studies usually revealed three different fungi of increasing fineness of their filamentous parts of mycelia. The coarser two, namely, Gliocladium and *Trichoderma viride* are readily seen under the microscope. But the third one, namely, Fusarium, with the finest mycelia, requires root sectioning, staining and highest magnification for careful examination. These latter are the same fungi said to migrate up from the soil through the plant's fibro-vascular system to interrupt its conduction of water and to wilt the top of the plant. It is said to be the fungus causing "Fusarium Wilt." No fungicide or destructive treatment for the "foe" is yet known.

Mr. Hood also reports that these three fungi disappear as seeming friends of the healthy plant roots in the above order of their decreasing diameters of mycelia. *Likewise, they disappear with the declining supply of organic matter, particularly under its higher rate with more use of commercial salt-fertilizers.* Shall we not envision these fungal associates as friends of the plant roots only as long as both are nourished on soil organic compounds? Then would it be illogical to believe that the Gliocladium and *Trichoderma viride* of less intimate root contact become extinct early with depletion of the soil organic matter? Then too, might we not view the Fusarium as a mere movement of that seemingly friendly fungus, or symbiont, on the root in highly organic soil up through the plant to become foe and parasite and cause of Fusarium wilt when the soil organic matter fails to nourish both the fungus and the host simultaneously?

Vision and Workers are at Hand

Does such a stretch of the imagination exceed its elasticity, in the light of the reports by Mr. Hood after his decade of careful study of fields and forests? Perhaps these few unleashings of a restless imagination are enough from reading Mr. Hood's reports to let us appreciate his contributions to kindred minds and souls. They are enough as ample stimulators of staff members of Brookside Research Laboratories who, with the new facilities at their disposal, will add to their past visions and search out their possible revelations as truths of Nature. As fast as Nature gives her revelations, this research institution will be equal to their challenges, and, in the light of its past service to agriculture, will do much to understand the microbial dynamics of soil organic matter for better plant nutrition. Surely that unexploited half of Nature's soil fertility management will do much for agriculture when we learn to use and to conserve soil fertility as she did before we took over the pseudo-controls of crop production.

CHAPTER 2

Our Soils — Under Construction

WHILE SOIL IS a temporary reststop by rocks on their way to the sea, their journey is made roughly in two stages in relation to the soil. The first is construction of soil into the particular soil body and its possibilities of crop production. The second is the destruction, not so much of the soil body as of its potentialities in growing crops of high values.

As long as rocks remain in the large, unbroken bodies of mineral mass, they offer little possibility by which any plants can be grown. But as soon as they begin to disintegrate and when but the slightest crevice forms, even that suggestion of a disintegrative process is a chance for the forces of soil construction to fill the crevice and offer a root-hold to some plant form. With such a major part of the mass as rock and such a minor part as soil, there is, nevertheless, the beginning of the soils in the process of their construction. During the process the ratio of rock to soil with its clay as residues of rock weathering becomes smaller. The minerals are breaking down, the clay is increasing and taking over for plant nourishment many of the elements originating in mineral decomposition. These are the processes of Nature in weathering the rock and in building the soil. By these slow means she is filling her pantry. She is increasing the possibilities for feeding the myriads, of life forms dependent on the soil.

The Soil's Function in Feeding Us is More Interesting than its Beauty of Body

Since a soil initially is made up mainly of finely powdered rocks intermingled with some organic matter in various stages of decay, one may naturally ask, how does that composite develop into the successive and different layers that we see in the horizons of the humid soil profile or vertical cut? One is prone to ask, how does that development enhance or jeopardize our chances for getting from that soil the foods we need for growing bodies and supplying energy that keeps them active? Though the interest prompting such questions may apparently be selfish, would you be concerned about the soil if it were not so basic to our living as is this provider of our food?

Surely there is nothing beautiful or attractive about the body of the soil at first sight or thought. Of much more interest for anyone are its functions, particularly those in feeding us. Like the steam shovel, it is not a thing of beauty to gaze upon. But have you ever seen a steam shovel in action without a crowd watching it closely? As with this machine so it is with the soil, it is not the body form but the function that interests us. We are concerned about building the soil in order to build our foods and our own bodies.

Natural Forces Grind the Rocks to Form the Soil Materials

Rocks are broken down into powdered forms for soils by many natural agencies. Heating, for example, with its consequent expansion; cooling and its resulting contraction; wind with its pressures and its driving of dust and fine rock particles to chisel more rocks away; plant roots acting as chemical solvents and pressure forces; burrowing insects and animals grinding the fragments over each other; all are some of the means by which soil is built up as a new body distinct from the original magmatic, rocky surface of the globe.

Imagine, then, the original hot, molten masses cooled into crystalline rocks and later disintegrated into gravel, sand, and the much smaller particles we call still. In these we have the skeleton of the soil body over which the clay as the chemically changed rock residue is draped to give what is soil. But with water as the ever-present meteorological agent and universal solvent, the breaking down of the rock is not left to physical forces alone. Water dissolves carbon dioxide from the atmosphere to become carbonic acid. This is Nature's main and almost universal chemical reagent. It is the seemingly quiet but powerful force that is dissolving and changing the rocks while moving them in suspension and in solution on their way to the sea. Rocks can disintegrate without much water but undergo both disintegration and decomposition when more water is present.

Water is a powerful physical force as it soaks into the rocks, much as it is powerful when it soaks into wood to make it expand. Its pressure amounts to tons per square inch when it freezes. But far more powerful are its forces when it serves in the chemical change known as hydration, or its chemical union with the molecules of the rock rather than when it infiltrates into the crevices and spaces among the mineral crystals. Rock crystals behave much like the blue copper sulfate that loses water on heating to become white and of less weight and volume, but then returns to the initial blue color and greater volume again as it takes on water. Water as a force causing chemical changes also brings significant physical changes with them.

Some chemical changes by water create two compounds or multiply them instead of only modifying one. Here again changes in volume, weight, density, and hardness occur also, just as compounds are built larger by water additions or smaller by water loss.

CHAPTER 3

Potassium in the Soil Colloid Complex & Plant Nutrition

CARBOHYDRATE FORMATION is the particular role commonly assigned to potassium. This does not deny possible precursor service in the production of proteins, when these bear close structural resemblance to carbohydrates. The specific performances of potassium, however, are still enshrouded in mystery. With fuller understanding of the behavior of nutrient elements in the soil there is hope of elucidating potassium performances in both soil and plant. It was through the use of colloidal clay as a growth medium, that the concepts reported in this paper regarding potassium were formulated.

Relation of Soil Development to Potassium of Colloid

Potassium makes up a part of the crystal structure of colloidal clay. It is also adsorbed on the clay surface in a mobile form. In the beidellitic clay of Putnam silt loam, more particularly the fraction consisting of electrodialyzed particles with maximum dimensions of 0.2 μ, the potassium within the crystal comprises less than 1 percent,[1] whereas that in the adsorbed form may be as much as 2.535 percent of the weight of the clay, of which the exchange capacity is 65 m.e. per 100 gm. As this clay occurs naturally in the soil, however, only a small portion of the exchange capacity is taken by potassium. The maximum is usually 0.1 percent of the weight of the clay, or less than 5 percent of its capacity.

[1] *See analyses by Marshall and by Ferguson.*

Magnesium stands next to potassium in amount within this colloid crystal. It is also low in the exchangeable form.[2] Within the crystal, calcium is less than one fifth of the potassium. In their exchangeable forms, however, the calcium may be 10 times as great as the potassium.

These relations vary within different soils under different degrees of development. It is because of the resulting changes in the clay crystal, in the adsorbed nutrient cations, and in the accompanying amounts of the adsorbed nonnutrient hydrogen, that the soil may control both the kind and the amount of vegetation.

Potassium behavior on the colloidal clay, even when this is isolated from the other separates of the soil, is complicated by the fact that the clay varies in its crystal composition and in its exchange capacities and components, as a consequence of the climatic and other factors that produced it. The parent material of the clay is apparently not a significant determinant.

Analyses by Brown and Byers of eight colloids from the B_1 horizons of eight different soils of granitic origin in the humid region under variable temperature on the eastern slope of the Appalachians showed that K_2O ranged from 0.14 to 1.58 percent, CaO from 0.04 to 0.75 percent, and MgO from 0.07 to 1.36 percent. In only one case was the amount of potassium less than that of calcium. Similar studies of nine colloids in B_1 horizons from limestone valleys in eastern United States by Alexander *et al.* showed that K_2O ranged from 0.15 to 2.30 percent, CaO from 0.10 to 0.77 percent, and MgO from 0.49 to 2.18 percent. In each case the potassium content was higher than the calcium. In a tenth case all three constituents were high, and the calcium was higher than the calcium. In a tenth case all three constituents were high, and the calcium was higher than the potassium. These two studies point to dominance of potassium over calcium in the colloids in well-developed soils, whether of granitic or limestone origin.

In some so-called "very young" soils in the Hawaiian Islands, Hough *et al.* report eight of nine colloids higher in calcium than in potassium. In so-called "older" soils from similar parent materials, three of five had more potassium than calcium in their colloids. This suggests, in agreement with the other analyses, that weathering under higher rainfall gives colloids of higher potassium than calcium content, whereas under lower rainfalls calcium may dominate over potassium in the "younger" colloids.

---

[2] *Unpublished data of E. O. McLean and W. J. Pettijohn.*

The potassium content in the crystal of the colloid may, ther be mainly a matter of climatic origin.

In a recent study of the clay fraction of the loessial soils of central United States so selected as to maintain all other factors in soil development constant while rainfall and temperature increased, it was clearly demonstrated that potassium behavior must be viewed in relation to several variables affecting both the colloidal clay and the plant nutrients derived from it. This is illustrated by the data in Table 1 for four loessial profiles of silt loam in different locations extending through rainfall increase from 27 to 55 inches. The temperature increase in these four locations was from 8.72 to 17.66°C (48 to 64°F).

With increasing rainfall and temperature, the nature of the clay changed markedly as its silica-sesquioxide ratio narrowed from 5.06 to 2.56, and its exchange capacity decreased from 73 to 44 m.e. per 100 gm. of clay in the B horizon. At the same time potassium, in general, occupied an increasingly smaller percentage of the exchange capacity. Since at Sioux City, Iowa, the potassium saturation was only about 2.5 percent, its reduction to less than 1.5 percent at Wickliffe, Kentucky, with an increase in rainfall of 21 inches means decidedly reduced supplies of available potassium for plants. These facts indicate that there is cause for concern about potassium for crops when the exchangeable supply is no larger than 100 pounds per 2,000,000 of soil, as in these more highly weathered soils. The weathering forces are reflected in the composition of the clay they produce.

Relation of Potassium to Other Cations on the Soil Colloid

Although the soils under study showed decreasing amounts of both exchangeable potassium and calcium with increase in weathering, the decrease in calcium was at a much greater rate. This is shown in Table 1 by the calcium-potassium ratio. For each of the three horizons in the solum, this became smaller as the location of the sample moved southward into higher temperature and rainfall.

These facts suggest that differences in total exchangeable potassium alone would be a less reliable index of soil productivity than the relation of potassium to other nutrients. Such a relation would appear to be a potent factor in determining the kind of vegetation a soil will support.

Magnesium in its relation to potassium, in Table 1, is also of interest. In their exchangeable amounts, these two cations decline at similar rates with

Table 1

Some Ratios of Exchangeable Cations and Other Properties of Colloids In Soils Developed from Similar Parent Materials Under Different Climates

Location	Annual Rainfall	Horizon*	Exchange Capacity†	SiO_2/R_2O_3	Ca‡/K	Mg‡/K	Ca‡/Mg
	inches		*m.e./100 gm.*				
Sioux City, Iowa	27	A			64.3	7.7	8.2
		B	73	5.06	132.8	16.5	8.0
		C			177.2	29.4	5.9
		D			205.6	39.3	5.2
McBaine, Missouri	40	A			37.2	14.0	2.6
		B	66	4.03	33.0	13.4	2.4
		C			61.7	22.4	2.7
		D			51.9	23.0	2.2
Wickliffe, Kentucky	48	A			29.0	18.3	1.6
		B	50	3.24	24.2	24.7	0.95
		C			33.3	27.2	1.6
		D			121.1	84.6	1.4
Vicksburg, Mississippi	55	A			24.5	12.0	1.0
		B	44	2.56	15.8	14.0	1.1
		C			18.7	20.6	0.91
		D			186.1	96.4	1.9

**A = 0–7 inches, B = 12–20 inches, C = 36–48 inches, D = 15–20 feet.*

†This determination was made on the B horizon only.

‡Calculated on basis of milligram equivalents, rather than weight equivalents.

increasing intensity of climate, since the ratios for the corresponding horizons of the solum are not significantly different in the locations other than Sioux City. This suggests that magnesium and potassium are weathered out as exchangeable forms at about the same rate. It suggests further, that the ratio of calcium to magnesium on the colloid, like that of calcium to potassium, might be used as an index of soil development and productivity. The data for the former ratio (Table 1) are of small range, however, and therefore not so revealing of differences as the values for the latter.

Influence of Potassium-Calcium Ratio of Colloid on Plant Composition

The behavior of potassium in the clay colloid, as revealed by chemical analyses and treatments, must be reconciled with its behavior in the plant. Potassium is lower than calcium in exchangeable form on the soil colloid, yet the former makes up 1.68 percent in plants in contrast to 0.62 percent for calcium as averages.

In view of the shifting ratios of these two exchangeable nutrients on the colloid with increasing degree of soil development, the question arises whether vegetation reflects corresponding differences in composition. As a test, chemical analyses of different crops were assembled. The different crops were allocated according to dominance on (a) slightly developed, (b) moderately developed, and (c) highly developed soils. Though the numbers of cases are not extensive enough to warrant unqualified conclusions, they are suggestive, as presented in Table 2.

The data show that the increasing degree of soil development, which gives decreasing calcium in relation to potassium on the colloid clay, gives correspondingly increasing potassium over calcium in the plant composition. Plants are lower in percentages of both potassium and calcium as the soil is more highly developed, but the potassium content drops to about one half while the calcium drops to about one seventh in going from slightly developed to highly developed soils. At the same time, the combined percentages of potassium, calcium, and phosphorus drop to two fifths. The ratio of phosphorus to potassium in the vegetation was constant.

If these are the facts in general for the assay of the soil by means of vegetation, it would seem that, among the plant nutrients on the colloid, potassium moves most actively into vegetation as the soil is more highly developed.

Table 2

Composition of Plants According to the Degree of Soil Development.

	Plants Growing Naturally on Soil Developed		
	Slightly, 38 cases	**Moderately, 31 cases**	**Highly, 21 cases**
Dry matter contents as			
K_2O...............*percent*	2.44	2.08	1.27
CaO..............*percent*	1.92	1.17	0.28
P_2O_5.............*percent*	0.78	0.69	0.42
Combined.......*percent*	5.14	3.94	1.97
Amounts relative to highly developed soil			
K_2O..........................	1.9	1.6	1.0
CaO..........................	6.8	4.1	1.0
P_2O_5..........................	1.9	1.6	1.0
Ratios			
K_2O:CaO...................	1.2	1.8	4.5
K_2O:P_2O_5...................	3.0	3.0	3.0
CaO:P_2O_5..................	2.4	1.6	0.66

In previous experiments soybeans were grown on colloidal clay supplied with exchangeable calcium and potassium in different ratios, but with constant supplies of calcium, nitrogen, and phosphorus, to determine whether the varying ratios influence plant composition. The results demonstrated that the increase of potassium relative to calcium increased the vegetative yield; reduced both the percentages and the totals of nitrogen, of phosphorus, and of calcium in the vegetation; and increased both the percentage and the total of potassium according to the variable supply offered. All these characteristics suggest a crop of more proteinaceous nature containing higher concentrations of calcium and phosphorus when calcium dominates on the colloid, and of a more carbonaceous nature when potassium is high relative to calcium.

As a further test of the hypothesis, soybeans were grown similarly but for three successive crops in order to exhaust the soil fertility. The carbonaceous phases of the plants were separated into sugars, starch, and hemicellulose. In the first crop, nodule bacteria were withheld and the soybeans were grown as a nonlegume. The second and third crops were nodulated and behaved as legumes.

The results showed that in the first, or nonlegume, crop the total sugars were low and decreased in concentration while the vegetative yield was increasing with the increasing ratio of potassium to calcium. More noticeable, however, was the behavior of the starch, the concentration of which almost doubled and the total almost trebled with increasing potassium. When the same kind of plants behaved as legumes, their sugar concentrations were much higher and again suggested decrease with extra potassium. The starch concentrations were lower than those for the nonlegume, but increased for increments of potassium initially put on the colloid. The greater exhaustion of nutrients from the colloid by the third crop indicated that lowered soil fertility, like excessive potassium in relation to calcium, gave dominance to the carbonaceous character of the crop, as shown by the higher sugar and starch contents in the latter of the two leguminous crops.

The hypothesis that relative calcium reduction in the soil tends to reduce the proteinaceous nature of the vegetation is further supported by the decreasing protein content of wheat in going from west to east in Kansas, as reported for 1940. Between western Kansas, with an annual rainfall of 17 inches, and eastern Kansas, with 37 inches, the protein in the wheat dropped from 18 to 11 percent. This traverse represents a distinct change in the original grass vegetation and a reduction in the amount of calcium in the soil, the calcium carbonate being at greater depths in the profile.

Still further support of the hypothesis is given by the recent studies of Allen[3] with percolating nutrient solutions for soybeans, and of Converse *et al.*,[4] with colloidal nutrient media for corn. Both show the association of the calcium-potassium ratio with protein content, whether the crop was legume or nonlegume.

Although calcium and potassium are seemingly reciprocals in plant composition, calcium supporting the proteinaceous and potassium the carbonaceous properties, there is a question whether the high level of phosphorus associated with the former and its low level with the latter are

---

[3] *Allen, D. I. Differential growth response of certain varieties of soybeans to varied mineral nutrient conditions. Doctoral thesis, University of Missouri, Columbia, 1942.*

[4] *Converse, J. D., Gammon, N., and Sayre, J. D. The use of ion exchange materials in studies on corn nutrition.*

not involved. Apparently the phosphorus level deserves attention in connection with this ratio.

Movement of Cations Between Soil and Plant

If, on well-developed soils, potassium dominates the activities within the vegetation — for any form of which carbonaceous skeletal structure is requisite — then the universal presence in soils of this nutrient in active form must be demonstrated. Chemical breakdown of the clay to deliver potassium is of no significance in providing active potassium. It must, therefore, be either the adsorbed potassium, or that provided by the breakdown of the mineral silt and sand separates of the soil, that serves. Plant growth may return potassium to the soil in temporarily mobile form, since this nutrient may go not only from the colloid clay to the plant, but also in the reverse direction during plant growth. Phosphorus and nitrogen have been found to return similarly. To date, calcium has been found to go only from the clay to the plant. Magnesium behaves much like calcium. The facts that potassium may be leached back to the soil by rain from the above-ground parts of more mature plants, that it goes back via roots, and that it dominates all cations in plant composition, emphasize its nomadic nature, which hinders our understanding of its performances.

Recent studies suggest that vegetative growth tends to maintain an equilibrium level of potassium in the clay. Data are given in Table 3 which show that the soil originally without exchangeable potassium acquired this nutrient during the growth of soybeans while other nutrients were being exhausted to the extent that nitrogen fixation was prevented. In spite of this exhaustion, the plants still produced appreciable yields of dry matter and were higher in carbohydrates relative to protein than is common for this legume.

Nutrient shortage in the soil apparently may reduce protein manufacture in the plant severely but allow carbohydrate production at a liberal rate, even when losses of potassium from the plant to the soil are sufficient to lower the crop content below that in the planted seed. The trials indicated that this returning potassium became temporarily nonexchangeable. The amount of the potassium initially active (seed and supplied) that became "fixed" was relatively constant (5.23-7.35 m.e.). This "fixation" is a function, apparently, of the amount of potassium rather than the amount

Table 3

Increases in Potassium-Saturation of Colloid at Low Levels and Decrease at High Levels During Growth of Soybean Forage

Culture Number	Nutrients Supplied*			Yields† Three Crops	Remnant Potassium in Culture			Percentage of Potassium "Fixed"		Saturation Equivalent of Remnant	
	Ca	K	Seed K		Total‡	Ex-changeable	"Fixed"	Initial	Remnant	"Fixed"	Ex-changeable
	m.e.	m.e.	m.e.	gm.	m.e.	m.e.	m.e.			percent	percent
1	10	0	13.84	37.122	5.23	0.99	4.24	30.6	81.0	14.1	3.3
2	10	5	13.84	42.057	5.41	1.49	3.92	20.8	72.5	13.0	4.6
3	10	10	13.84	48.390	6.23	1.50	4.73	19.8	75.9	15.7	5.0
4	10	15	13.84	46.247	7.35	1.90	5.45	18.8	74.2	18.1	6.3

* Other nutrients were adsorbed as constant amounts.

†Separate crop yields are given elsewhere.

‡Calculated from potassium supplied and removed in crops. No leaching loss was possible.

of the clay, as shown by the saturation equivalent of the remnant which increased in both the fixed and the exchangeable forms. For the three cultures to which potassium was supplied in addition to that in the seed, the ratio between these two parts of the remnant remained fairly constant as they both increased. It is this mobility and these differences in exchangeability that must be understood before chemical tests of potassium in the soil can be interpreted in terms of crop results.

Other aspects of potassium must eventually be given consideration. The interaction between the hydrogen colloid of the soil and the potassium-bearing minerals in the coarse soil separates serves to buffer the colloid with respect to potassium saturation. The universal occurrence of potash minerals in silts and sands, from which the exhausted colloid may obtain exchangeable or "fixed" potassium, as Graham has demonstrated for calcium, complicates the matter. Then, too, the degree of hydrogen-ion saturation that is a helpful factor in mobilizing calcium, magnesium, and some other cations into plants is apparently not so effective on potassium. It is possible that potassium may be adsorbed on the colloid with so much less force than some other nutrients that the presence or absence of hydrogen does not significantly alter its relative place in the lyotropic series. This would leave potassium undisturbed by the degree of soil acidity and would help to explain why potassium nutrition in plants does not fit into the concepts for other nutrients centered about soil acidity.

Another aspect warranting attention is the apparent association of potassium and silica in plants on certain soils. Although silica is the reciprocal of calcium, silica and potassium seemingly rise and fall together to a degree that is somewhat modified by amounts of potassium, phosphorus, and acidity in the soil. The degree of soil development and the kind of vegetation associated with it are apparently reflected in this potassium-silica partnership, much as in the calcium-potassium ratio.

Although the calcium-potassium ratio has been emphasized as a reflection, via the plant, of these nutrients on the colloid complex and in the soil mineral reserve, one must not deduce physiological functions to the extent of exclusion of one by the other. Before any plant can grow, it must have both calcium and potassium. At starvation levels and even at more nearly balanced concentrations, calcium and potassium are directly associated, and either one may be instrumental in moving the other into the crop.

In considering these many phases of potassium independently, one must be cautious about interpreting plant growth on the basis of any single-factor behavior. Interactions of factors are usually quite different from the sums of their individual effects. Plant growth is the result of numerous factors, the possible interactions of which may be legion. The interpretation of these interactions calls for more delicate tests than are commonly used. There is some hope that animal assays of the crop may demonstrate that potassium is a soil factor that modifies the feeding value of forages.

The agricultural use of potassium may receive more attention in the future, not so much because the supply in the soil has declined suddenly, but because the supplies of calcium and phosphorus have suddenly risen through their stimulated applications as soil-conserving measures. Potassium may become more widely appreciated as a hidden deficiency by contrast through legumes producing heavily under calcium and phosphorus stimulation. This deficiency may not express itself immediately in the form of decreased tonnages of non-legume crops, but may be reflected in nutritional disasters through consumption of cereals and nonlegumes grown in exaggerated legume-soil-building programs. Calcium and phosphorus are necessary to guarantee the nutritious, body-building values of leguminous forages, but the question arises whether this fertilizer combination will make cereals equally as valuable as energy suppliers in animal nutrition. This question must be answered in the negative, if the calcium-potassium hypothesis in the ecological picture has good foundation. For cereals in the agricultural program, including graminae, and all their uses in general, the potassium supply may well be liberal in relation to calcium, whereas for legumes the reverse seems to be demanded. Concern about potassium may well arise while legumes and nitrogen fixation are carrying enthusiasm for calcium and phosphorus as soil treatments to unusual heights.

Summary

Degree of soil development is reflected not only in the amounts of potassium in the colloid crystal and in the adsorbed form, but also in its ratios to other adsorbed plant nutrients. For some nutrients the ratios are inverse, and for others direct. These ratios are reflected in plant composition, and the calcium-potassium ratio is suggested as a basis for ecological plant array. Differences in soil development apparently determine whether the vegetation will be chiefly proteinaceous or carbonaceous. Because of the prevalence of its minerals in the lithosphere, of its readily soluble nature, of its readiness to become insoluble and inexchangeable from the colloid, of its movement from vegetation to the soil through leaching from the tops or exchange from the roots, and of its reserve in the silt and sand minerals to buffer the clay, potassium is so nomadic that its performances in any particular situation are difficult to interpret. Apparently potassium is almost uninfluenced by the hydrogen ion that mobilizes other cations into plants. Its adsorbed form becomes "fixed" to a significant extent even during short periods of plant growth. It manifests many and varied chemical aspects in connection with the soil colloid. There is the hope, nevertheless, that when more of the possibilities for potassium outgo from and income to the colloid have been quantitatively evaluated, its behavior on the colloid complex and its service in plant nutrition may be better understood.

CHAPTER 4

Saturation Degree of Soil & Nutrient Delivery to the Crop

WITH THE BETTER understanding of the physico-chemical aspects of the clay fraction of the soil, the mysteries of the migration by the nutrient ions from the soil into the plant are rapidly submitting to solution. In fact, we now know that the reverse movement is possible, so that in fertility-depleted soils the nutrients may be going back to the soil to reduce the cation stock in the plant originally contributed by the seed. The colloidal phenomenon of exchange of cations is helping us to understand soil fertility more clearly. With more research attention to the anions, even these may let their behavior come within the pale of understanding. If the colloidal system in the plant root is opposed to the colloidal clay system with the not wholly invulnerable root membrane interposed, we may look to equilibrium of forces within and without as a helpful explanation. Should we reason on this simple physico-chemical basis, then the questions naturally arise whether soil fertility applications should be an attempt to provide but that needed for most economic service to the plant, or that for modification of the soil. It becomes a question whether applied nutrients should be used to saturate highly limited soil areas in the immediate root zone or to give low degree of saturation of the soil throughout the plowed layer of the common 2 million pounds.

This viewpoint prompted an experimental study of the degree of saturation of the soil by calcium as cation and by phosphate as anion as a factor in plant growth and in the movement of these ions from the soil into the crop as nutrient harvest.

Plan of Experiment

An extensive series of 2-gallon pots of surface soil of the Putnam silt loam was arranged to include treatments of one-fourth of the soil with calcium in amounts equivalent to that needed to saturate it completely; and but one-half that quantity. These same amounts of the calcium were also distributed through the entire soil. Additions of phosphate representing 100 pounds and 200 pounds of 38% phosphate per 2 million pounds of soil were applied in similar manner.

Thus, in the case of calcium, there were jars in which the upper fourth of the soils was completely saturated; some in which the deficit in calcium in this layer was remedied by but one-half; some in which only a light application was given to the entire soil body; and another in which it was given a heavier application. These latter two treatments amounted to roughly 600 and 1,200 pounds per 2 million pounds for a soil that had an initial pH of 5.6 and was originally only about half saturated with calcium. This soil was also low in soluble phosphorus and responds readily to such application by better crop yield. It gives, however, the best responses to lime alone, and to phosphates used in conjunction with lime. For purpose of convenience these treatments will be spoken of in the case of the limestone treatments as (a) partial saturation and (b) complete saturation; and in the case of phosphate treatments as (c) light dosage and heavy dosage in either case of treatment through the larger or the smaller soil volumes.

In mineral nature, this surface soil of the Putnam silt loam contains few, if any, "other than quartz" minerals which carry calcium. The subsoil is an impervious clay containing a high percentage of the beidellite clay colloid with an exchange capacity of more than 65 m.e. per 100 grams of clay. The surface soil used carried approximately 15% clay of which the exchange capacity combined with that of the organic matter gave it a total capacity of about 18 m.e. per 100 grams of surface soil.

Four crops were used in quintuplicate for each treatment. These included two grasses, bluegrass and redtop, and two legumes, sweet clover and Korean lespedeza. These selections were made in accordance with the generally accepted fertility demands by these crops, ranking those for bluegrass and sweet clover above those for redtop and Korean lespedeza.

The growths were harvested as forages at regular intervals to give five harvests of quintuplicate pots as carefully weighed amounts on constant moisture basis. Analyses were made for their contents of calcium and phosphorus to determine the fertility harvest for these nutrients applied in contrast to such from the untreated soil.

Experimental Results

Forage Harvests

The single outstanding result throughout the experiment is the much larger yields of forage and fertility harvest that resulted when the treatments were applied to only the smaller portion of the soil to give it the higher degree of saturation by the ion of the treatment. The increases in forage yields as percentage over the untreated soil are assembled in Table 1. Comparison of the second column of figures with the first under each separate crop shows the much larger percentage increases where the treatment was put into the smaller soil volume.

In the case of limestone this increase held for the nonlegumes as well as for the legumes. In fact the figures for the former were generally larger than those for Korean lespedeza, though not as large as those for sweet clover. The yields show clearly that, as measured by forage increases, the higher degree of saturation by calcium in a limited soil area was more effective than a moderate or less degree of saturation in a larger soil area. This raises the question, and answers it forcefully, whether the economical

Table 1

Increases (Percentage) in Forage Harvests from Limestone and Phosphate Distributed Through Large and Small Soil Volumes

Soil treatment		Grasses				Legumes			
		Redtop		Bluegrass		Lespedeza		Sweet clover	
Kind	Magnitude	Large soil vol.	Small soil vol.	Large soil vol.	Small soil vol.	Large soil vol.	Small soil vol.	Large soil vol.	Small soil vol.
Limestone	Partial saturation	15.5	15.5	-3.8	9.7	4.8	13.7	25.1	50.1
	Complete saturation	1.0	36.0	0.0	33.0	2.5	28.0	23.2	89.1
Phosphate	Light dose	8.8	4.3	9.0	34.4	20.0	23.0	22.8	51.0
	Heavy dose	14.3	12.3	15.7	18.0	21.4	22.4	27.2	70.8

use of lime is not one of feeding the plant calcium more than one of neutralizing the entire soil area of the root zone.

Phosphate, like the calcium carbonate, also showed more influence on the crop yield when the treatment was concentrated into a part of the soil, though this illustration was not as pronounced, in general, as that of the effects by the limestone. In the case of sweet clover, the effects by phosphates were almost equivalent to those by limestone in terms of percentage yield increase. For both the single soil treatments of calcium and phosphate additions in general, the crop yield increases were larger as the treatment was used to give a higher degree of soil saturation.

Fertility Harvest of Calcium

Analyses of the crops for calcium when lime was applied show that the crop content of this plant nutrient as totals per acre responded with larger differences in the increases than was the case for the forage yields. The higher degree of soil saturation by the application of the calcium into a limited soil area gave increases as much as 2½ times as large as where this same amount was distributed through more soil. This is demonstrated clearly in Table 2. Again, the nonlegumes demonstrated increases in calcium harvested from the soil which were even greater than the increases taken by the legumes. Redtop was superior in this respect to Korean lespedeza, and bluegrass to sweet clover. It suggests that because these crops manage to produce vegetation on soils low in lime, we have perhaps not been giving sufficient attention to the capacity of the grasses to take lime for their possible improved feeding value.

Fertility Harvest of Phosphorus

The total phosphorus harvested in the crops where the soils were given phosphates shows greater increases when the treatment was concentrated into the lesser amounts of soil for all but two of the eight cases as given in Table 2. Redtop and Korean lespedeza with the lower phosphate applications failed to give greater increases where the phosphate was applied in the surface soil only. In the other cases the differences were very significant and larger than any others in the case of sweet clover. In terms of forage, of calcium harvest, and of phosphorus harvest through the crop, this last crop showed the outstanding response to both calcium and lime applications into the limited soil area.

Table 2

Increases (Percentages) in Calcium and Phosphorus Harvests from Limestone and Phosphate Distributed Through Large and Small Soil Volumes

Soil treatment		Grasses				Legumes			
		Redtop		Bluegrass		Lespedeza		Sweet clover	
Kind	Magnitude	Large soil vol.	Small soil vol.	Large soil vol.	Small soil vol.	Large soil vol.	Small soil vol.	Large soil vol.	Small soil vol.
Calcium Harvest									
Limestone	Partial saturation	19.5	45.0	16.2	58.6	12.6	27.7	34.2	59.5
	Complete saturation	37.7	87.5	48.7	129.0	21.0	43.9	46.0	94.0
Phosphorus Harvest									
Phosphate	Light dose	31.0	6.0	27.3	70.0	41.3	41.3	28.0	94.0
	Heavy dose	16.0	23.4	43.6	34.4	39.1	46.7	29.6	130.0

The crop responses rank these crops in the order as they are commonly arranged in fertility requirements. The bluegrass and the sweet clover showed greater response to the soil treatments than was true for the other two. They also removed larger amounts of calcium and phosphorus from the soil.

Fertility Harvest of Nitrogen

Since both nonlegumes and legumes were included, the significance of concentrating the calcium and phosphates into less soil as these influence nitrogen fixation by legumes and nitrogen removal from the soil can be measured. The data assembled into Table 3 are in agreement, in principle, with those previously given. The increases in nitrogen harvested were much greater again where these soil treatments were used so as to provide them at higher degrees of soil saturation. Even for nonlegumes the higher concentration within the soil of the same application of limestone was much more effective in delivery of nitrogen from the supply in the soil to the crop. Small dosages or lower degree of saturation gave negative increases or amounts in the crop below that in crops on unlimed soil. This suggests

Table 3

Increases (Percentages) in Nitrogen Harvests from Limestone and Phosphate Distributed Through Large and Small Soil Volumes

Soil treatment		Grasses				Legumes			
		Redtop		Bluegrass		Lespedeza		Sweet clover	
Kind	Magnitude	Large soil vol.	Small soil vol.	Large soil vol.	Small soil vol.	Large soil vol.	Small soil vol.	Large soil vol.	Small soil vol.
Limestone	Partial saturation	-26.4	15.0	-18.5	14.3	20.0	30.6	39.8	67.3
	Complete saturation	-13.0	23.1	-4.5	40.8	13.0	52.4	35.4	113.7
Phosphate	Light dose	-12.8	-6.2	-15.5	25.0	47.3	54.0	25.9	65.1
	Heavy dose	-10.0	-10.0	-5.8	0	50.5	41.8	34.1	80.8

that the introduction of limestone encouraged microbiological competition sufficient to utilize the effect by the calcium to the detriment of the crop competing for the supply of nutrients even other than calcium. Similar situations were provoked by the addition of the phosphatic fertilizers for the nonlegumes.

In the case of the legumes, the treatments all increased crop yields. The Korean lespedeza, however, was not correspondingly responsive to the higher applications of phosphate into the smaller soil volume. The sweet clover gives distinct evidence of the influence by both the calcium and the phosphate on the nitrogen increase by this crop, but especially of the effects when these treatments are concentrated into small soil volumes to give them higher degrees of nutrient ion saturation. Thus in this crop the higher nitrogen harvest, probably much through nitrogen fixation, agrees with the higher fertility delivery as calcium and phosphorus by the soil to the plant.

Discussion and Summary

The data all emphasize the fact that more nutrients were delivered by the crops because of the higher degree of the soil saturation even of only a limited part of the soil. This area of soil was seemingly large enough to prohibit injury through excessive salt concentrations. These increased movements of the nutrients into the crops were roughly paralleled by increases in forage yields, though not directly so. Thus, there has resulted in most cases increased concentration of nutrients within the crops to give them higher forage feed value. Thus, the efficiency of the treated soils in terms of tonnage yield per unit of nutrient delivered is lower than the efficiency of the untreated soils, but it may be far more efficient in producing an animal feed of higher calcium, phosphorus, and protein concentrations. The increased use of nitrogen by the crop points to the significance of calcium and phosphorus in making this phase of plant metabolism operate effectively in case of the nonlegumes as well as for legumes.

Since calcium and phosphorus are the two most significant soil needs in the corn belt, as shown by past agronomic experience, by soil development, and by crops in their ecological array, we may well look forward to their wider use. For more effectiveness in practice, however, limestone and phosphate should be applied in more limited soil areas rather than distributed through the soil zone. Possibly not only the concentration within limited soil zones should deserve consideration, but also some efforts toward retardation of their rate of adsorption for reaction with the soil. Effectiveness of granular forms of such soil treatments may be premised on the greater efficiency of the nutrients when in areas of higher degrees of saturation. Efforts to improve applications for such effectiveness should give results in terms of crop increases.

Since the very acid clay is active even to the point of removing calcium from the mineral lattice[1] and since a calcium clay is not so active in the removal of bases from plant roots,[2] perhaps the higher degree of calcium saturation in limited soil areas lessens the activity by the soil in adsorbing the anion phosphorus. If this is the case, then the applied phosphorus remains longer in the soil without reacting with it and may explain in part,

[1] *Graham, Ellis R. Primary minerals of the silt fractions as contributors to the exchangeable base level of acid soils. Soil Science (In press).*

[2] *Jenny, Hans, and Overstreet, R. Cation interchange between plant roots and soil colloids. Soil Sci., 47:257–272. 1939.*

the greater efficiency of phosphates when used on limed soils[3] or those liberally stocked with calcium.

These results suggest most forcefully that in liming and fertilizing the soil, attention must go to the degree of saturation of the soil. The use of such soil treatments will be more effective when applied in limited soil areas to feed the plant than when applied through greater areas to modify the soil condition.

---

[3] *Albrecht, Wm. A. and Klemme, A. W. Limestone mobilizes phosphates into Korean lespedeza. Jour. Amer. Soc. Agron., 31:284–286. 1939.*

CHAPTER 5

Adsorbed Ions on the Colloidal Complex & Plant Nutrition

ADSORPTION OF IONS and their exchange by colloids have done much to provide a clearer concept of the mechanism of those soil and plant root interactions, commonly spoken of as plant nutrition. There has always been a wide gap between the behavior of soil in the test tube by which its stocks of plant nutrients are measured, and its behavior under test against the plant root as computed in terms of crop yield and crop composition. Reasoning from the chemical behavior of the soil in the laboratory to the crop behavior in the field has corresponded to a jump across a tremendous abyss into which most reasoners eventually have found themselves plunged. With the clearer concept of the chemical behavior of the colloidal clay fraction of the soil as it may take, or may give, nutrient cations and anions, it is now possible to bring the clay composition and the plant growth together, and to observe with laboratory accuracy their chemical interactions. We are narrowing the abyss, not only by pushing the chemistry of the soil closer to the plant behavior, but are also using the plant metabolism as a biological reagent — possibly more delicate than chemical regents — to give suggestions regarding the chemical nature and behavior of the colloidal clay fraction of the soil. Such suggestions are already numerous enough to warrant presentation of some at this time for critical examination and further experimental verification.

Colloidal Clay Versus Aqueous Solutions as Growth Medium

The soil solution has long been found inadequate as explanation for the relatively generous delivery of nutrients by the soil to the plant, particularly of the element phosphorus. Even the aqueous nutrient cultures may soon be discarded as media simulating plant behavior in the soil. Such solutions demand carefully controlled concentrations, osmotic relations, and other physico-chemical conditions that are quickly upset with only partial removal of the ions by the plant. The nutrient delivery per unit of solution volume is very low, and even then there is the danger of nutrient excess. Only the more experienced plant physiologist with continually renewed dilute solutions seems successful with this research tool. On the contrary, the colloidal clay as a nutrient medium is the haven of safety within which the most embryonic plant physiologist may sail about naively yet successfully. The colloidal clay offers its ease of suspension but yet a low solubility; its large supply — even to excess — of adsorbed nutrient ions but nearly constant physico-chemical conditions; and its capacity to remove from solution those injurious items bringing about what is commonly known by that cause-concealing term of "toxicity." It permits a wide range in kind and amount of nutrient offerings to plants under experiment while other conditions so disconcerting by their fluctuations in nutrient solutions remain almost constant. At a pH of 5.0 in an aqueous solution, for example, the presence of 0.01 mg hydrogen per liter is an approach to the danger point, while in a 2% colloidal clay suspension at the same pH there would be 650 times as much hydrogen with no great danger. When the chemistry of the behavior of anions on colloidal clay is understood as well as that of the cations, then the colloidal clay medium will permit research in plant nutrition in the laboratory for interpretation in terms of field results with a satisfaction to which aqueous nutrient cultures can be no equal.

Simplified Concept of Nutrient Absorption by Plants

The ordinary equation of a chemical reaction at equilibrium may be helpful in formulating a concept of plant root and colloidal clay interactions. Suppose we consider it as a case of colloidal clay suspension with possibly some ions in solution as the left side, and the plant cell protoplasm, or a colloid, plus its aqueous accompaniment as the right side of the equation. Then in place of, or rather along with, the arrows between and pointing in opposite directions, we must interpose a membrane or the wall of the root hair. This may be represented as follows:

Colloid clay with its exchangeable ions	+ Solution	Membrane or Cell Wall ⇄	Colloidal cell contents of plant	+ Solution

Imagine, further, the removal of the water to varying degrees or to the point of eliminating the solution phase on each side of the equation. Then we can write it as a case of soil colloid and plant colloid on opposite sides of the cell wall of the root hair. This brings us to the concept of two colloids in contact. We can believe them at equilibrium or as exchanging ions in either direction as regular chemical laws dictate, except for the modifications caused by the nature of the membrane and its changes in relation to the colloidal interactions or the plant metabolism products.

Unfortunately, we know very little about the chemical properties of the plant colloid *in vivo*. Chemical behavior of the plant cell contents, like the goose that laid the golden eggs, does not submit readily to internal observation. Thus, the conditions prevailing on the right side are not well known. In addition, the time factor, as a kind of fourth dimension, must be introduced. Displacement of equilibrium by the plant is a matter of a growing season of, say, 100 days and not an instantaneous performance. Thus, we can measure the accumulated displacement result on the right side of the equation, only after that interval of plant growth at which we choose to make analysis of the plants.

More fortunately, the colloidal clay and its properties, its behavior, and possible changes are known definitely enough to serve more nearly as the known side of the equation for solving the plant unknown side. The beidellite type of clay isolated from the claypan layer in the subsoil of the Putnam silt loam has been subjected to enough physical, chemical, mineralogical and other studies to establish its relative constancy in behavior as an anion, and its capacity for wide variation in kind of, and degrees of, saturation, by nutrient cations and anions. Thus, the relative concentrations of exchangeable ions are controlled by their degree of saturation on the clay. The total amount of ions is controlled by this character coupled with the amount of clay offered the plant. This simulates then the degree of ionization and the concentration of ions in the ordinary solutions.

By means of this simplified approach with considerable knowledge of the properties of the clay and its changes on the left side of the equation, we may observe, or measure, the plant growth behaviors, the incidence of plant disease, and the seed and plant compositions with their indications of the movements of both cations and anions from the colloidal clay to the plant, or in the reverse direction, or any other plant manifestations and clay changes, all as helps to interpret what has happened chemically on the right side. From such we may learn whether plant nutrition may not finally conform to the more commonly accepted laws of chemical behavior.

Calcium the Most Important of the Adsorbed Nutrients

Because several nutrient cations are required for plants, some preliminary trials were conducted in order to ascertain their relative importance. The choice of a legume as the plant for experimental service eliminated one nutrient, namely nitrogen, from the medium, because of its introduction into the plant from the atmosphere. The use of the soybean plant with a large seed of selected size and constant composition removed the necessity of providing on the clay medium those ions used in very small amounts but amply supplied through the seed for the early life period at least. Farmer experience of the common failures of legumes without limestone treatment pointed to calcium as the first nutrient warranting consideration as the limiting factor on the clay, particularly that from claypan soils.

Aqueous nutrient solutions served to demonstrate calcium as the first requisite for growth of soybeans (Fig. 1). Much better growth occurred when potassium and magnesium were not supplied than when calcium was absent (Fig. 2). Incidence of disease with low calcium, and conversely

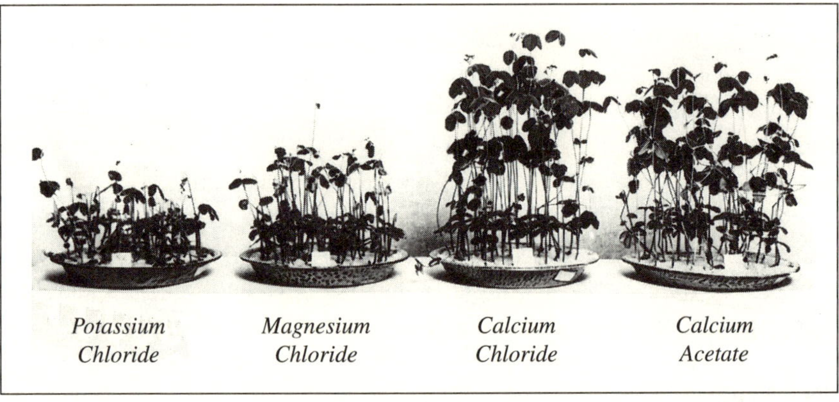

Fig. 1. — Calcium is the first requisite among cations required by plants. Its absence encouraged incidence of diseased plants.

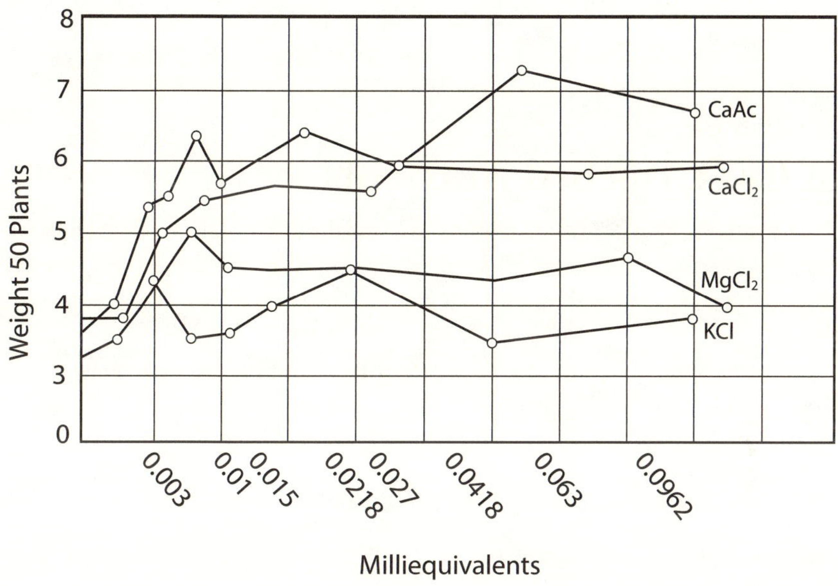

Fig. 2. — Magnesium and potassium failed to give growth equal to that by calcium.

healthy plants with high calcium, showed calcium requisite for growth (Fig. 3). Clay on which only calcium was adsorbed produced growth that improved with increased clay (Fig. 4). It was superior in giving growth over a wider range of calcium offered the plant than was possible by aqueous solutions (Fig. 5). These results suggested that calcium occupying so large a portion of the adsorbed and exchangeable store of cations on the clay becomes plant nutrient number one in importance, and even for the soybeans, a supposedly "acid-tolerant" legume.

Irregularities in the growth response by legume crops to limestone treatments threw doubt on the belief that the hydrogen ion concentration of the soil, or its pH, is the causal factor in legume crop failure. Some acid soils, failing to grow clover, were given limestone and showed no measurable change in pH after a year but yet produced clover successfully. This beneficial effect by the added calcium, when there was no change in pH, pointed to calcium deficiency in the soil rather than to an injury by the excessive hydrogen ion concentration as the problem of so-called "acid" soils. Electrodia-

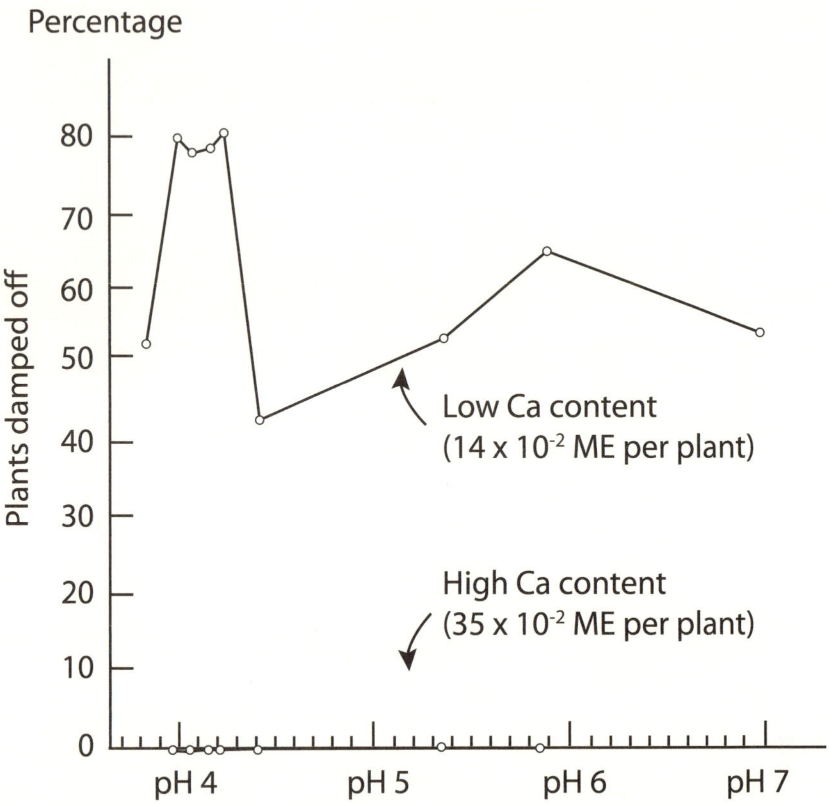
Percentage
Plants damped off
80
70
60
50
40
30
20
10
0
Low Ca content
(14 x 10-2 ME per plant)
High Ca content
(35 x 10-2 ME per plant)
pH 4
pH 5
pH 6
pH 7

Fig. 3. — Plant disease shows relation to the calcium level rather than to pH.

H-Ca-clay pH 4.4

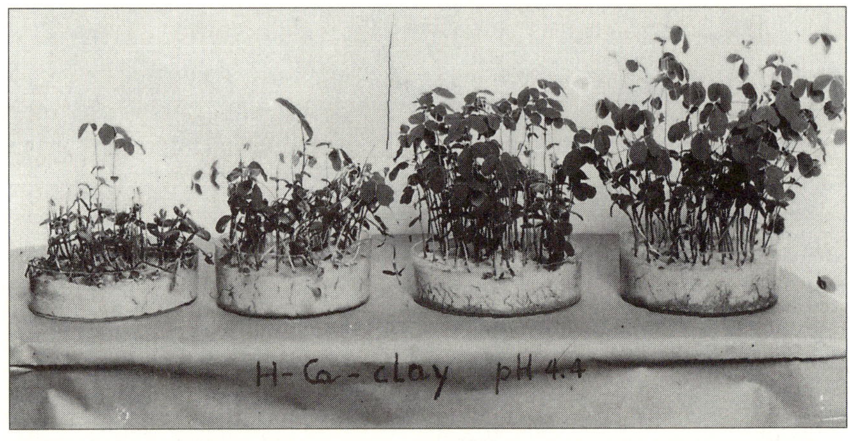

Fig. 4. — Increasing the clay to deliver more calcium at pH 4.4 (left to right) gives better growth.

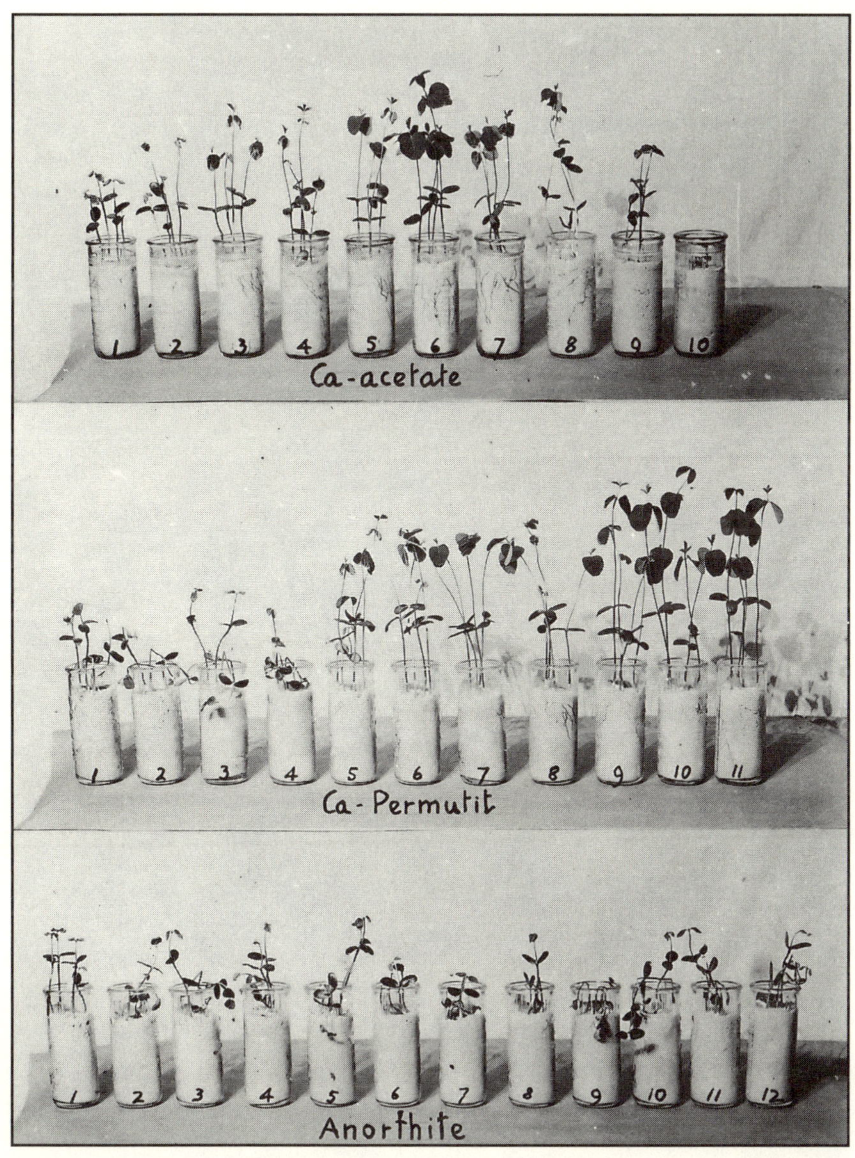

Fig. 5. — Adsorbed calcium on Permutit is as effective as ionic calcium. (Increasing calcium, left to right).

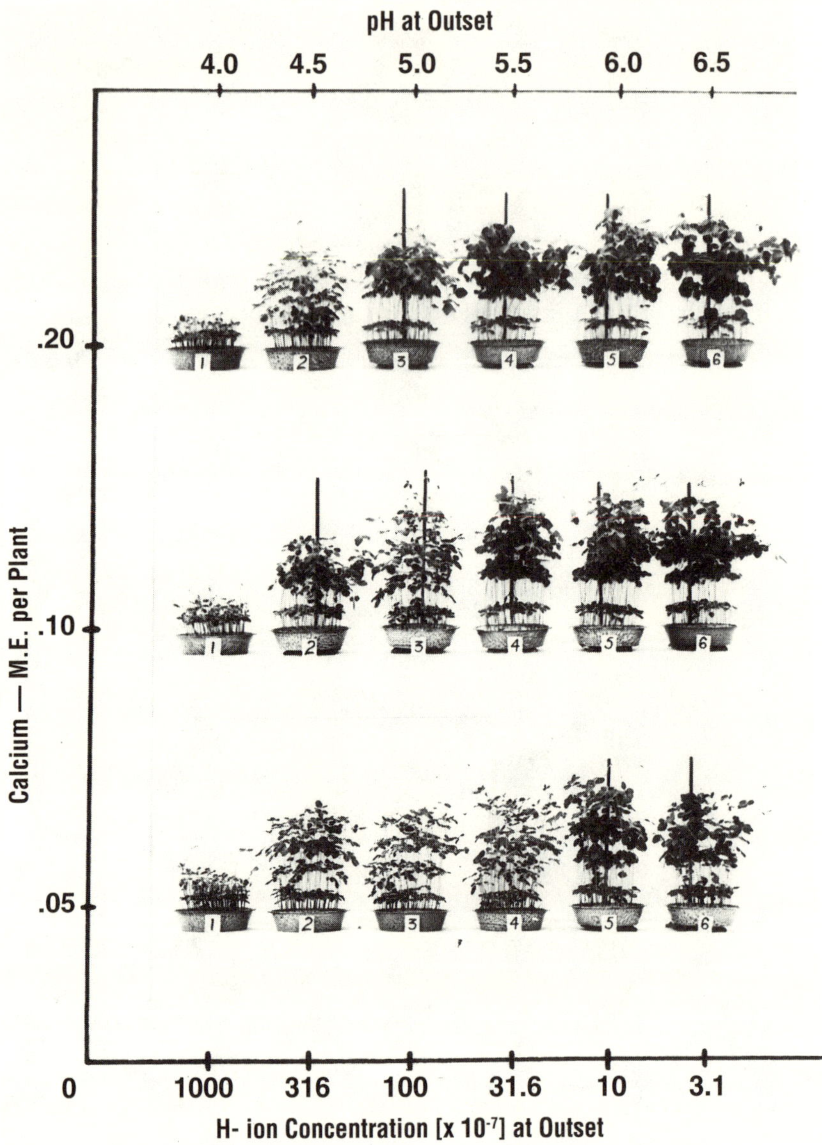

Fig. 6. — Soybean growth according to different calcium levels at different degrees of acidity of colloidal clay.

lyzed hydrogen clay on which the exchangeable hydrogen was neutralized by calcium hydroxide to varying degrees to give soils of different pH values, provided means of separating the effects by the hydrogen ion concentration from those by the amount of calcium. Controllable and variable amounts of calcium could be offered to the plant at any pH by varying the amount of the clay that had been titrated to any particular pH. Plant growth on such a series of clays in sands varied according to the degree of acidity, or pH, but was influenced far more by the amount of calcium offered to the plants (Fig. 6). Thus, in trying to relate plant growth to the pH of the soil, the facts indicated that it is related in reality to the approximate reciprocal of the hydrogen saturation and ionization, namely the calcium saturation.

Nutrient Cations May Move from Plant to Soil

Changes in the pH of the colloidal clay medium as the result of the plant growth pointed to a displaced equilibrium, but a displacement toward both the right and the left. By using the analyses for calcium of the seed and clay at the outset and again of the final plants as a means of determining the di-

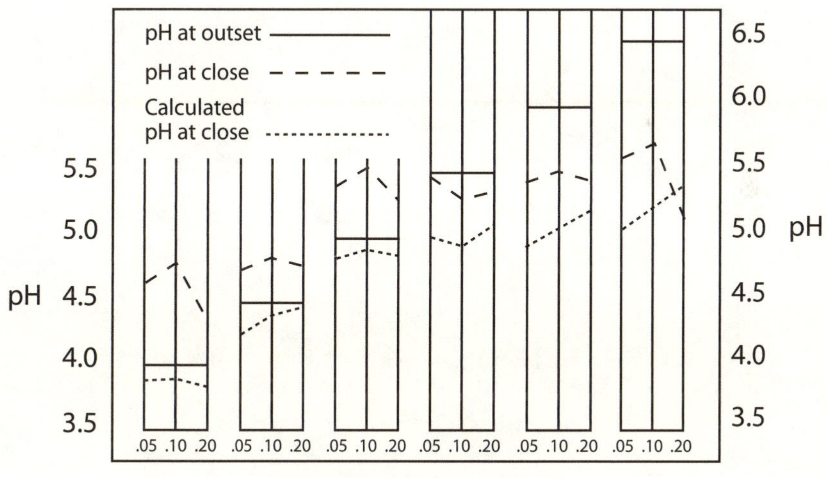

Fig. 7. — Changes in pH of clay in consequence of soybean growth.

rection of movement of the calcium, and then by calculating its amount left in the clay and the corresponding pH at the close of the growth of the series, it was discovered that the pH figures for the clay by determination were higher than those by calculation (Fig. 7). In other words, the clay was less acid than it should have been by the calculations based on the calcium removal and its assumed substitution by hydrogen. Increase in calcium in the crop over that in the seed established movement of calcium from the clay soil to the seed in every case, with growth parallel to the amount of calcium delivery. The fact that the pH was not lowered as calculated pointed to a return to the clay from the plant of some elements other than calcium, serving as bases or cations to raise the pH of the clay. Whether anions of plant origin were also moving to add to the confusion may well be considered.

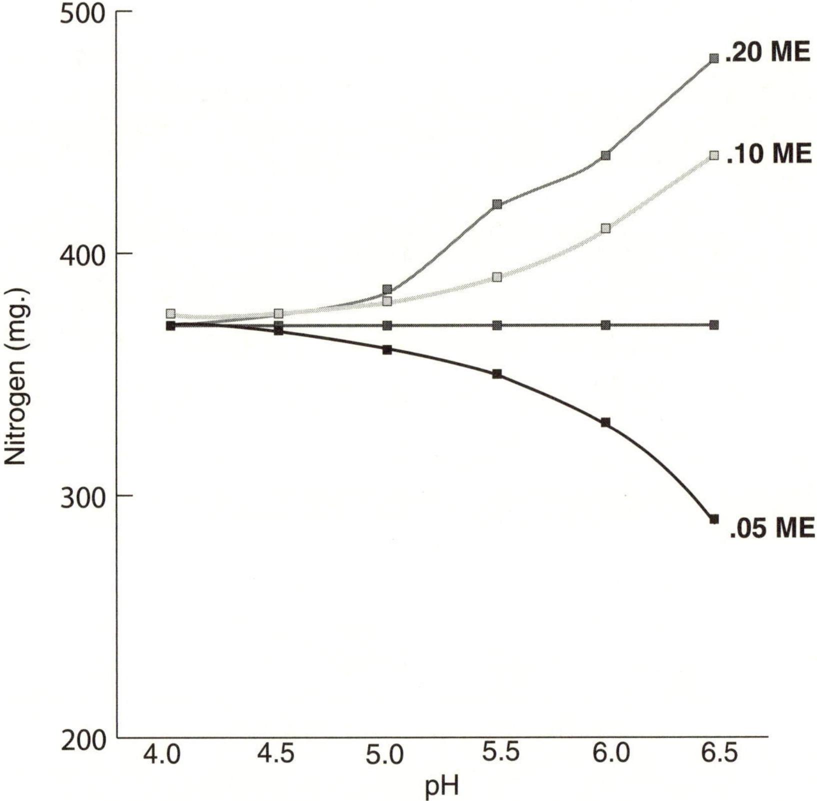

Fig. 8. — Nitrogen fixation as correlated with calcium levels rather than with the degree of acidity. (Horizontal line represents nitrogen content of seed.)

Here was the first indication that exchange cations — possibly nutrients — may move from the plant to the soil as well as from the soil to the plant. Certainly, as shown by analysis, the element calcium did not go from seed back to the soil. Instead it moved into the plants. Its equilibrium was displaced by movement to the right. At the same time, some displacement toward the left occurred because of movement of other cations in that direction.

In the clays with pH figures below 5.5, the reduction in pH by calcium removal and hydrogen substitution (dotted lines in figure) corresponded to approximately 0.12 pH as average. In clays with pH values above 5.5, the change in pH through calcium removal was greater with increasing values of the initial clay, namely 0.45, 0.90, and 1.25 pH for clays at pH 5.5, 6.0, and 6.5, respectively. Equilibrium displacement by calcium removal from the clay was greater as the clay was more nearly saturated by calcium or as its pH figure was higher.

In spite of the calcium removal from the clay, a reaction which should have lowered the pH, measurements of this property of the clay reported the pH varying from those obtained by calculations by some rather consistent differences. These differences were not related to the pH level of the clay growing the crop. They were seemingly related inversely to the total calcium offered to the crop. Offerings of 0.05 m.e. of calcium resulted in differences which averaged 0.55 pH. For calcium offerings of 0.10 m.e., the change was but little less and for 0.20 m.e. of calcium allotted it was a shift toward alkalinity by only 0.25 pH.

Nitrogen determinations of the seed and crop showed losses of this element at the pH figures below 5.5. Here may have been a cation that was going back to the clay in the form of ammonia to make it more alkaline. But since an increase in nitrogen in the system occurred at pH 5.5 and above for the offerings of 0.10 and 0.20 m.e. of calcium per plant (Fig. 8), there was nitrogen fixation or use of atmospheric nitrogen. This raises the question whether nitrogen fixation may be going on while losses of it to the soil are occurring at the same time. Since the pH shifts were so consistent for the calcium offerings at all six pH levels used, it seems doubtful if the plant losses of ammonium ion to affect this change could be so consistent when coming from such widely varying sources as seed only in some cases and from seed and atmospheric fixation in other cases. Doubtless this shift toward higher pH by cation movement from seed to the soil must be ascribed to cations other than the ammonium of seed origin, in this case using a calcium-hydrogen clay delivering only calcium to the plant.

Fig. 9. — Increasing saturation degree (left to right) by calcium is without effect on growth (lower row) when calcium is accompanied by the organic ion methylene blue in contrast to effects when accompanied by hydrogen with its varying acidity (upper row) or potassium with neutrality (center row).

Calcium Movement Related to Degree of Calcium Saturation of Clay

In order to list more accurately the significance of the degree of calcium saturation in the delivery of this element to the plant, clays were prepared with different degrees of calcium saturation, ranging from forty

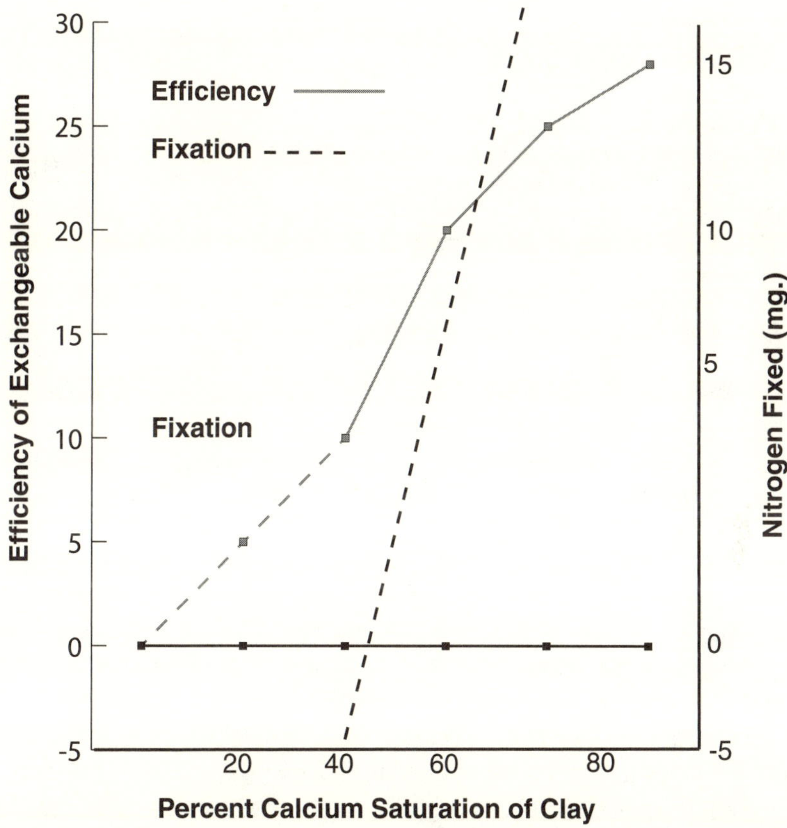

Fig. 10. — Efficiency of exchangeable calcium as related to the degree of calcium saturation and the nitrogen fixation by soybeans.

percent to complete saturation. The balance of the exchange capacity of the clay was taken individually by hydrogen, giving variable acidity, by barium, magnesium, and potassium all giving complete neutrality in the form of readily exchangeable ions; and finally by methylene blue, a non-exchangeable ion of a large and an organic mass. Such quantities of clay were added to sand as would supply equal amounts of calcium per plant.

Plant growth followed the degree of clay saturation by the calcium, whether it was accompanied by hydrogen or by the other inorganic cations. In all of the trials in this test, as well as in the others, growth was insignificant unless the seed content of calcium was doubled within the growth period, which was five weeks. Increased degrees of saturation delivered an increased percentage of the exchangeable calcium into the crop.

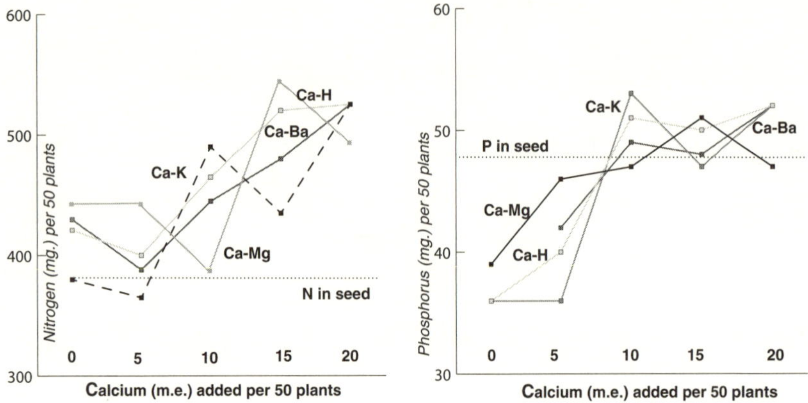

Fig. 11. — Phosphorus and nitrogen contents of the soybean crop in relation to calcium levels. (Seed nitrogen = 385 mg., seed phosphorus = 47 mg.)

These percentage figures representing the efficiency of the exchangeable calcium varied from 6 to 25 of the constant, exchangeable supply (Fig. 10). When a large complex organic ion, like methylene blue, accompanied the calcium, the variable degree of saturation was without effect and the growth followed the constant amount of exchangeable calcium (Fig. 9).

This situation is not easily explained on chemical bases, though it certainly excludes any effect by soil acidity. Seemingly as more calcium is placed on the clay molecule, those ions added at the more nearly complete saturation stage are more active in entrance into the plant, or they may be less forcibly held to the clay molecule. Much less of the same total calcium moves into the plant with the low degree of saturation on many clay molecules than with the higher degree of saturation on less clay molecules. Seemingly chemical equilibrium pressure is changed, particularly increased when less clay surface for root contact is the case in the higher saturation degree.

Such effects suggest that we should place the calcium into limited soil areas for more complete clay saturation rather than placing it throughout the root zone for only partial saturation, if the calcium is to have the most pronounced effects, and the application used most efficiently. In agricultural practice this would suggest drilling the limestone in the manner used for fertilizers.

Movements of Nutrients from Plant to Soil Under Calcium Deficiency

More complete chemical inventory of seed and clay at the outset was undertaken in order to determine the behavior of other nutrient ions beside calcium and nitrogen. The latter had been found seemingly moving from plant to soil, the former had always been going from soil to the plant when growth occurred. Trials were undertaken to determine the behavior of phosphorus in connection with different calcium levels and different amounts offered the plants. The element phosphorus, though not a cation, suggested its classification with nitrogen in this movement from plant to the soil. Unless larger offerings of calcium were given the plant, it failed to contain all the phosphorus originally in the seed (Fig. 11).

Phosphorus and nitrogen, both constituents of protein, apparently are moved into the plant from its seed, rather than being lost from the seed back to the soil, only at high levels of delivery of calcium by the soil to the plant. Whatever the nutritional role of the calcium in the plants may be, it certainly raises the question whether it is not instrumental in metabolizing the nitrogen and phosphorus within the plant into insoluble protein to keep equilibrium displaced to the right, or whether it may not play some role in

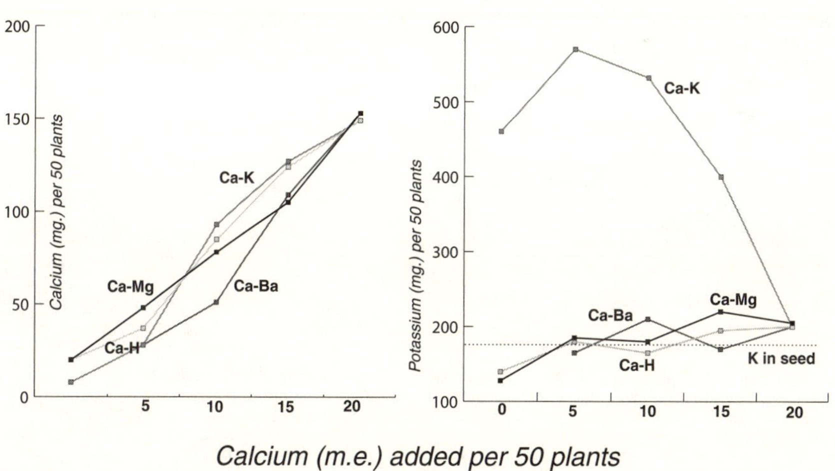

Fig. 12. — Movement of seed potassium (lower graph) into the crop with increased calcium taken by the plants (upper graph). (Seed potassium = 171 mg.)

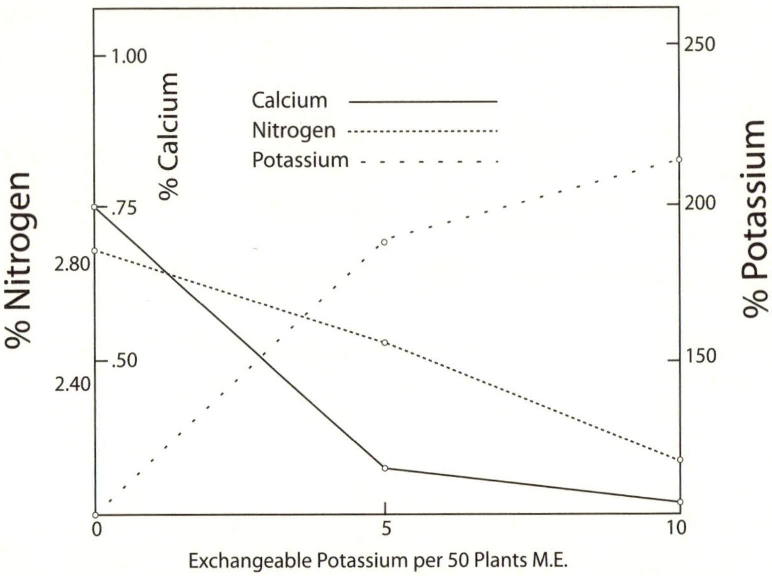

Fig. 13. — Reciprocal relations of calcium and potassium concentrations associated with declining nitrogen concentrations.

determining the nature and activity of the plant membrane interposed. The latter may seem such a function, according to the work of the late Professor True of Pennsylvania though the former can scarcely be denied when calcium, nitrogen and phosphorus run so closely parallel in the plants growing near the lowest possible levels in these different trials. If calcium plays this role in membrane function, its significance in the early life of a plant is greater than that of merely adding calcium to the content of the seeds.

In other tests it was revealed that potassium moves from the plant back to the soil (Fig. 12). Since this element appears in the seed in quantities larger than those of calcium or of phosphorus by roughly 15 and 3 times by weight, respectively, it is interesting to note that the magnitude of potassium movement to the left in our type equation has been as high as 50% of the seed content in some later experiments. It might be easy to imagine a "sour" soil serving as an acid extracting agent for taking potassium out of the plant, but the potassium was moving back to the soils when they were neutral, moderately saturated with calcium and containing no potassium.

One crop which exhausted only part of the applied potassium brought potassium return to the soil when the second crop followed. This brings our viewpoint nearer to the equilibrium concept again and the belief that potassium must occur liberally on the clay, with calcium accompanying it if the potassium content of the crop is to increase over that in the seed.

The replacement of calcium in no small measure by potassium at certain calcium levels (Fig. 13) serves to bring up the calcium-potassium ratio and the significance of these two nutrients in determining the type of vegetation that dominates on the soil.

The full significance of calcium in these cases where nitrogen, phosphorus, and potassium have gone from the plant back to the soil unless calcium was liberally supplied is not yet explainable. It may not be as significant as first indications show, but it is significant that in no case has growth been possible unless calcium moved into the plant in its early life, while losses from the plant to the soil have occurred for nitrogen, phosphorus, and potassium. The quantities of these in the seeds may have some significance when we note calcium present in soybeans in a very small amount. The calcium, magnesium, phosphorus, potassium, and nitrogen occur in the seeds in the approximate ratio of 1 : 1 : 2 : 7 : 42 as molecular equivalents, respectively. Those in larger quantities may be more readily lost from the plant to the soil and yet permit plant growth. The shortage of calcium in the seed may be related to the need for delivery of it by the soil in the early plant life for plant growth.

When magnesium is considered in relation to its influences on soybean growth and nitrogen fixation, it comes into importance quickly, but seemingly not directly. Improved plant manifestations, including nitrogen fixation, were not related to the amounts of magnesium taken by the plant but rather to the increased effectiveness by larger amounts of calcium from a constant source which went into the crop as the exchangeable magnesium on the colloidal clay was increased. Magnesium is apparently instrumental in bringing about greater effectiveness in the calcium use by plants in a manner much as calcium is apparently needed to make nitrogen, and phosphate more effective in the plant functions.

Another interesting relation of the calcium is that to manganese. Recent studies of the so-called "minor" element in plant nutrition point out that as more calcium carbonate is mixed throughout the soil, there is a reduction in the amount of manganese taken by such crops as bluegrass, redtop, lespedeza, and sweetclover. But when these same amounts of limestone are put into only the surface part of the soil to "feed" larger amounts of calcium into the plants, then the plants take more manganese from the soil. Here calcium carbonate seems to be playing a detrimental role to manganese delivery to the crop by its neutralizing effect throughout the soil, and a beneficial role to the same when it provides the plant with calcium as a nutrient in only a limited zone of the soil. Here are two distinct effects by calcium if this visualization of its role is correct.

Studies so far have seemingly emphasized the role of calcium as an adsorbed ion. Such emphasis has been one of dominating facts and overwhelming evidence. The calcium factor stands out clearly in soil development when the degree of this process is measured mainly in terms of calcium accumulation and calcium depletion. Vegetation in its ecological array also fits into the calcium picture. The plant composition with its requisite calcium for nitrogenous vegetation and the calcium depletion and potassium dominance for carbonaceous vegetation add importance to calcium for our understanding of the possibilities on our different soils. Then, too, the close linkage of phosphorus to calcium in its behavior must not be omitted. Phosphorus shows different chemical behavior when adsorbed on a calcium saturated beidellite clay than when on such carrying no exchangeable calcium. Microbial behaviors in colloidal clay medium suggest phosphorus-to-calcium linkage as these are adsorbed. Plant behavior suggests plant use of them in such combination and certainly in animal physiology, at least of the vertebrate class — these two elements cannot be separated very widely. These are some of the aspects of calcium that have given it emphasis, not because of its importance per se but because of its seemingly significance in relation to the behavior of the other ions and the entire physico-chemical structure of plants and soils.

To date the behavior of all the plant nutrient ions adsorbed on the colloidal clay complex can by no means be catalogued completely. However, a beginning has been made which has called attention first to calcium. One nutrient after the other can be brought into the picture in relation to calcium and then the different nutrients in relation to each other. The colloidal clay concept and its behavior as if in equilibrium with the plant colloid on the other side of a cell wall as membrane has opened fields of study in plant physiology and soil fertility that are bringing the soil and plants closer together with every research effort using this tool. These studies may point to a fuller significance when we learn of their reflections from plant to animal and human nutritional behaviors. Perhaps in time, even the mystical matters of plant growth will reveal that in the last analyses they can be catalogued as results of combinations of the more commonly accepted laws of simple chemical behavior.

CHAPTER 6

Surface Relationships of Roots & Colloidal Clay in Plant Nutrition

THE RECENT INCREASE in national concern in regard to the losses of soil by erosion may well lead us to appreciated the fact that the land has gone nude because cover growth is prohibited by man's management and because of the declining store of fertility in the soil. This fertility consists of the chemical elements which the soil contributes to the plants. This contribution to any single crop is small. For many plants it represents but five percent of the total dry matter in the plants, or even less. Air and water worked up into chemical combination by the energy of the sun constitute the bulk of most plants. This process of carbohydrate synthesis — the dominant one of all plant growth activities — can be carried out, or even initiated, only as the soil contributes from its store of essential plant nutrients. The declining supply of soil fertility must of necessity shift the plant population more and more to those kinds whose final composition represents less from the soil and more from the air and water. That is, considering rather broadly the functions of the nutrient elements within the plant, the crops must shift toward those with less of protein and mineral content and more of materials with mere fuel significance. Naturally, lessened possibilities for proper animal and human nutrition must accompany these changes. In the light of these considerations, the contributions by the soil to plant contents, the mechanisms through which such contributions are made, and the relative supplies within the soil become of much concern to all of us.

More recent concepts of mechanisms of nutrient delivery by the soil. With the increased knowledge of the colloidal behavior of the clay separate of the soil and of the exchange of adsorbed ions between colloids through their contact, it is no longer necessary to consider the supply of nutrients in the soil as limited to those in the displaceable soil solution. The immediate stock is not only that which is in true solution or that which would leach out, but also that which is exchangeable by other ions, more particularly those of similar electric charge. This exchangeable stock is of far larger magnitude than that of the simple solution. For better understanding of plant nutrition we must understand this cationic exchange behavior in which the soil gives up its adsorbed nutrient elements of positive charge for hydrogen, which is a cation contributed in exchange by the plant. Whether anionic behavior is similar is a question that is awaiting specific information, though it is not unreasonable to anticipate some likeness.

Plant nutrition may be mainly a surface phenomenon. If the cations of nutritional value are given up by the soil through this exchange in which the hydrogen, coming from the plant's liberation of carbon dioxide, displaces them from the clay in direct contact with the root, then the extent of the performance resolves itself into one of surface nature and areas. The rate of reaction, as well as the total of cations taken from a given soil by the plant roots, is then a question of magnitudes of root and clay surfaces in contact, and of the kinds and concentrations of adsorbed ions on the clay.

Should all other factors be removed from consideration, it will be of theoretical interest, at least, to view plant nutrition as largely a surface phenomenon determined by the surfaces of the plant root, and the surfaces of the soil or colloidal clay on which the exchange activities are possible. The following discussion uses some recent root surface data and some clay surface values in an attempt to elucidate plant nutrition hypothetically as an exchange phenomenon.

Some root surface values for plants. The studies by Dittmer give values for the root and root hair surfaces for soybeans, oats, rye and bluegrass in a specific soil. Since, in the last three of this group, more than 90 percent of the surface of the root system is that of the root hairs, the values for the entire root system will be used, even though adsorptive activities are commonly attributed to the root hairs only. The values for the total surface of the roots are given in Table 1 with figures ranging from 1.0 to 25.6 square centimeters per cubic centimeter of soil.

Some surface values for colloidal clay. As for the surface offered by the soil for contact with the roots, this can be determined from the size of the particles of the colloidal clay. Numerous studies of this fraction of the Putnam silt loam subsoil have been made. If we disregard the sand and silt fractions of this well weathered soil for their exchange activities, and if we accept the general fact that this clay constitutes one-sixth of the

Table 1

Total Root Surfaces of Different Crops in Given Soil Volumes

Crops	Square inches per 42 cu. in. of soil	Square inches per Cu in. of soil[a]	Sq. cm. per cc. of soil[a]
Soybeans	106.1	2.5	1.0
Oats	583.4	13.9	5.9
Rye (winter)	1,267.9	30.0	11.8
Bluegrass (Kentucky)........	2,779.9	66.1	25.6

[a] *Values are calculations from those by Dittmer.*

surface soil of the Putnam profile, then the clay content will amount to .222 gm. per cubic centimeter of soil which weighs 1.33 gms. By placing the approximate general size of the clay particle at one-tenth micron, or .00001 cm. (10^{-5} cm.), as the effective diameter, the value will be that into which about 35 percent of the clay falls. The shape of the particles is of disc nature, but for the purpose of simpler concept, we may visualize the shape as cubical with faces of the above effective diametric dimensions, *viz.*, 10^{-5} cm.

Small portion of soil's clay content is in root contact. Should we visualize that these colloidal clay cubes are carrying their adsorbed nutrients on their surfaces and are in contact with the root with one face of the cube against it, then each particle would present a contact area of 10^{-10} sq. cm. According to the root areas given in Table 1, the numbers of clay particles which would be required to cover the entire root area in a cubic centimeter of soil are those given in Table 2 (Column 1). With a specific gravity of 2.5 and a particle volume of $(10^{-5}$ cm.$)^3$, the weight of the clay in root contact for the root surface per cubic centimeter of soil volume would be that given in the same table (Column 2). Since there is but .222 gm. clay in this soil volume, then the clay in contact with the roots represents but a small percentage of the soil's total clay, or those fractions of percent given also in Table 2 (Column 3).

Adsorbed nutrients represented by contact exchange. As a means of determining the amount of nutrients delivered by the clay surface in root contact, we may use the total exchange capacity of the clay, *viz.*, .65 m.e. per gm., or .65 pound equivalents per thousand pounds of clay, as has been reported from many determinations. In a cubic foot of soil weighing 83.2

pounds (1.33, volume weight, × 62.4 pounds per cubic foot of water), of which one-sixth, 13.85 pounds, is clay, the exchange equivalents would be but .009 pounds (13.85 × .65/1,000). When considered per acre six inches deep, this would be but 196.02 pound equivalents (.009/2 × 43,560 sq. ft. acre area). Should this clay be saturated completely with calcium, then the clay per acre six inches deep would contain twenty times the equivalent, or 3,920 pounds of exchangeable calcium. If the percentage of surface in contact as given in Table 2 is applied to this calcium value and if the calcium on the clay surface in contact is completely taken by the plants, then the amount of calcium so obtained by the different crops would be those in Table 3 (Column 1).

That removal to completion, or 100 percent, by exchange is not easily conceivable as common occurrence was shown in the work by Ferguson and Albrecht, where only 85 percent of the exchangeable calcium was taken by three successive crops, but not without significant irregularities in plant growth. A single crop took but 40 percent. If we should assume as usable only 85 percent of the adsorbed calcium on the clay faces in root contact, the amounts taken per acre would then be those in Table 3 (Column 2). If only a single crop had been grown with 40 percent of the exchangeable calcium taken, then only those amounts as given in the table (Column 3) would be taken per acre six inches deep.

Table 2

Clay in Contact with Plant Roots Expressed as Numbers and Weights of Clay Particles and Percent of Clay in the Soil

Crops	Clay in root contact per cubic centimeter of soil expressed as		
	Number of clay particles[a]	Weight,[b] gms.	Percent of total clay[c]
Soybeans	1.0×10^{10}	$.25 \times 10^{-4}$	.011
Oats	5.9×10^{10}	1.47×10^{-4}	.066
Rye (winter)	11.8×10^{10}	2.95×10^{-4}	.133
Bluegrass (Kentucky).........	25.6×10^{10}	6.40×10^{-4}	.289
	(Column 1)	(Column 2)	(Column 3)

[a] *Root area in sq. cm. divided by area of face of particles (10^{-10} sq. cm.).*

[b] *Number of clay particles × $(10^{-5})^3$ × 2.5.*

[c] *Weight of clay particles × 100/.222.*

Normal calcium use by crops is greater than the delivery by direct contact only. When one considers the acre yields of these crops and the calcium contents of their above-ground parts as found by chemical analyses, then the fact is immediately evident that the soil delivers to this crop portion and particularly to the entire plants, roots and tops, more calcium than would be provided if only that adsorbed on the clay surface in immediate root contact were taken. In Table 3 (Column 4) are given the amounts of calcium commonly found in these crops as harvested from conservative acre yields.

Movement between clay particles by adsorbed ions is suggested. If these figures represent the facts, they suggest that there must be adjustments in concentration of the adsorbed ions, particularly nutrient ions, even on the colloidal clay surfaces of the individual particles and between the different clay particles. Calcium removal, according to these calculations for the commonly harvested parts of the crop, suggests adsorbed ion movement toward the roots through more than a few layers of clay particles, especially for the soybeans. When the entire plants are considered, the evidence is more convincing. Still further, the movement of ions cannot be wholly from clay in a silt loam of which only one-sixth is clay. Some of the root area is in contact with silt. From the mineral faces of the silt it would seem that the source would be the face in contact only. With

Table 3

Calcium Available by Root Contact (Pounds per Acre 6 Inches Deep) and Contained in Normal Crops

Crops	With contact exhaustion of surface calcium at			Content of normal crops
	100%	85%	50%	Pounds
Soybeans	.43	.36	.17	5.4 per ton forage
Oats	2.58	2.19	1.03	4.1 per 25 bu. grain and 1,200 lbs. straw
Rye (winter)	5.21	4.43	2.08	2.8 per 15 bu. grain and 1,000 lbs. straw
Bluegrass (Kentucky)....	11.33	9.62	4.53	10.0 per ton forage
	(Column 1)	(Column 2)	(Column 3)	(Column 4)

the silt so little active, the clay must be all the more active in the movement of adsorbed ions over the particle, and through several layers of particles.

Movement of cations between clay particles demonstrated. That such movements of ions from one clay area to another are possible has been demonstrated. By bringing a sand-clay mixture, the clay of which was saturated by calcium, into contact with a similar one saturated by hydrogen, the migration of these cations from one location to the other within a period of thirty days was demonstrated. Calcium had moved more than two inches into the hydrogen clay area, and the hydrogen had similarly moved into the calcium clay area. These migrations took place when all the calcium was adsorbed, and when no significant solution activity can be considered as playing a role in this exchange.

Cationic movement of adsorbed nutrients is a possibility, then, along the faces of the clay particles, if such activity may be visualized as occurring in the exchange atmosphere or in the adsorption layer on the face of the clay crystal, and if these plant and soil behaviors may be considered as evidence.

Movement of ions from mineral crystal into colloidal adsorption atmosphere. Since three successive crops may reduce the supply of exchangeable nutrients of the clay to 85 percent of exhaustion, we are immediately confronted with the fact that continuous cropping on many experimental fields has gone forward for more than half a century without even approaching such a high degree of depletion of the exchangeable nutrients in the soil. How then is the supply on the exchange atmosphere of the clay maintained? Graham, in his use of the colloidal hydrogen-clay in contact with pure minerals of silt size, has demonstrated that the adsorbed hydrogen on the clay is active in exchanging itself for the cations of the mineral. This exchange serves to nourish plants. The silt fraction with its mineral store is then the supply from which that of the clay is replenished after depletion by plant growth.

Ion movement from silt particles directly to plant is possible but small. That ions can be taken in some measure by the plants directly from mineral particles of silt size without the intervention of the clay has also been demonstrated by Graham. Plants failed, however, to grow as well under such conditions as on the silt in the presence of other colloids less active than clay, and decidedly not as well as on the silt mixed with the colloidal clay. It was only when an acid clay was mixed with the minerals of silt size that the growth of the plants was most effective. Plants can then use the minerals directly and the silt size separates may serve, but their contribution is small.

This may be a case of limitation strictly to surface contact area, since ionic movement from crystal to crystal does not seem so probable.

Exchange concept clarifies relation of soil development to crop production. Only in those soils, in which the mineral reserve is ample both as to the kinds and the amounts of necessary elements, will production be maintained for more than a three-year period of continuous cropping. Mineralogical studies of the silt fraction of the soil with its classification as dominantly quartz or "other-than-quartz" will contribute much to better understanding of the continued productivity of some of our lands. By knowing the extent to which the clay is exhausted of its nutrient cations, or the reciprocal, namely, the extent to which the clay has become saturated with hydrogen, and by knowing, in addition, the extent to which the reserve of mineral crystal nutrients in the silt fraction is exhausted, we can make some estimate of the degree of soil development and of the possibilities of crop production as to kind and quality. Such understanding of the soil in its practical significance is more easily obtained by aid of the concept of exchange between the colloidal clay and the root surface.

In the inorganic portion of the soil, then, the immediate supply of nutrients for plants would seem to be on the colloidal clay in the adsorbed form. The "other-than-quartz" minerals of silt size would then seem to be the reserve supply for either direct or indirect use in the future, if not for part of the immediate growing season. The colloidal clay, then, aids through two steps in nourishing plants. In the first, through its root contact, it serves to deliver nutrients by cation exchange. In the second, it serves in connection with the mineral breakdown of the silt fraction of the soil. By means of this view of the soil and root behaviors mainly as contact and surface phenomena, we may visualize more clearly and interpret more simply the processes of plant nutrition, of depletion of soil fertility and others connected with crop production and soil maintenance.

Summary

By means of some data giving the root surface per unit volume of soil and some giving the surface areas of colloidal clay, the calcium delivery to the crop through exchange phenomena was calculated. The calculations suggested that a crop gets more calcium than is present on only that clay surface in immediate root contact. The data suggested that exchangeable ions move from one clay particle to the next clay particle through several such layers.

Hydrogen movement from hydrogen clay into calcium clay and the reverse movement of calcium were demonstrated. Hydrogen clay contact with mineral crystals demonstrated similar exchange from the crystal to the clay colloid. Ionic movement from the mineral crystal to the root by direct contact failed to nourish the plants amply, yet the crystal in contact with the clay served effectively.

Thus in terms of these surface phenomena of the colloidal clay and the root, we may get a clearer concept of how the adsorbed nutrient supply of the clay is replenished from the mineral crystals of the soil. By means of this concept we can visualize more clearly the mechanism involved in plant nutrition, soil fertility depletion, and various aspects of crop production and soil maintenance.

CHAPTER 7

The Use of Mulches

IN CONSIDERING THE USE of mulches in gardening, it is necessary — at the outset — to define the word "mulch." Let us agree that a mulch is a particular arrangement of, or addition to, the surface of the soil to stimulate, or to provide, a cover.

According to this definition, then, a mulch may be made, either by Nature or by man from the upper or surface portion of the soil itself. It may also be the result of applying on the soil some cover consisting usually of organic materials, particularly plant residues.

When a soil has been watered generously by rain and when the drying of its surface starts, it is by that rapid surface drying that Nature herself makes a soil mulch. In some cases, this is a soil crust of one or two inches of depth. In others it is a granular, non-crusting cover. Both of these dried soil layers are mulches to help to reduce evaporative loss of water up through them.

While the crust mulch functions to cut down water loss by evaporation, it fails in the second function of the mulch-soil-water relations: namely, it does not facilitate ready entrance of the rain water into the soil. Aiding infiltration of the rain is the really significant function of the mulch or the soil cover in relation to water. For this function alone, the breaking of the soil crust and the mechanical maintenance of the granular mulch are well considered practices.

The use of a straw, leaves, sawdust, and other organic materials as mulch is a well-known and good gardening practice. The use of these mulch materials assumes that the soil under them has been brought up in its fertility level to the point of discounting any possible disastrous effects by microbial competition with the crops for the nutrients in the soil's supply.

It is around this simple principle, that the wisdom of the use of the mulch turns for failure or success.

More recently there have become available mineral materials, of very little weight per unit volume which serve as mulches, particularly in potted plantings. The most prominent of these, known by various commercial names, are the expanded micaceous materials. Almost completely inert chemically, as they are — save for possibly the contribution of some potassium — they are long-lasting and bring about an open structure when incorporated into the soil. This effect is particularly advantageous on soil of more clayey nature. Such soils are benefited highly by the mulches in preventing crusting and cracking and then still more by the successive incorporations of these flakey mineral materials into the body of the soil itself. This repeated incorporation brings on the improved granular condition for self-mulching, so much desired.

That the mulch might be a by-product of the crop itself or that extra fertility might be added to the soil for growing one crop that is to be the mulch for another, is a newer concept in the use of mulches.

Nature's Suggestions

While the soils in the Midwestern United States form a granular mulch naturally under sparse grass vegetation, nature has been applying an organic matter mulch in the form of either heavy prairie grasses or forest leaves and litter on the more humid soils in the Eastern United States.

Here is Nature's suggestion that the degree of development of the soil, according to the differing degrees of weathering under the climatic forces with the resulting different levels of soil fertility, points out the mulching procedure that would be wise. If the soils of the Eastern United States are to be self-mulching by their own granulation in place of requiring applied mulches, then they must be brought up in their fertility to the level duplicating that of the soils in the Midwestern States.

Self-mulching

Only by building up the organic matter and the fertility contents in the more highly weathered humid soils will they become granular and mulch themselves effectively. With the naturally more granular Midwestern soils, the high fertility and the organic matter contents make each unit of rainfall more effective.

Mulching artificially seems to have come into vogue because the soils were less fertile. But the emphasis went to the water rather than to the creative power of the soil. If such is the case then, by reasoning conversely and building up of the soil fertility to enable the soil to grow into itself more organic matter, the need for extra mulching should be less or the extra mulching should be so much more effective.

Better Use

Nature's climatic patterns of the soil are giving their suggestions by which we can make better use of mulches. Our soil will find itself undergoing conservation much more extensively and will be used more efficiently when we see nature's pattern of natural mulching with its benefits according to the levels of soil fertility concerned.

Mulching alone, as a mechanical ministration, cannot offset completely the shortage of fertility in the soil. Conversely, however, building up the fertility can be all the more reason for mulching also, a combination with doubled benefits because of the more efficient use of both the soil and the mulch that covers it.

CHAPTER 8

Physiology of Root Nodule Bacteria in Relation to Fertility Levels of the Soil

THE PHYSIOLOGY OF NODULE bacteria, like the physiology of crops for example, demands the application of physiological methods to their vital phenomena if we are to determine the optimum conditions and the limiting factors for their growth, their nodulation, and their nitrogen fixation. It is the nitrogen fixation in particular which shall be considered as the real function of root nodule bacteria. Conditions can be classified as optimum and factors as limiting according to the criterion of extensive or limited nitrogen fixation. Nodulation of the host plant can also be included as a part of the proper functioning of the root nodule bacteria.

Control of Separate Factors Difficult. Observation of the vital phenomena of nitrogen-fixing bacteria becomes a problem about as difficult as that of learning the physiology of the goose laying the golden eggs as cited in fabled literature. The life processes of the bacteria are hidden within the plant and modified by the soil. Thus, we are confronted with conglomerate problems of bacteria, plant, and soil. This triad lends itself with difficulty to scientific control for investigation of its complicated performance. The bacteria are subject to wide variation when successive generations follow so rapidly on each other. The soil and the plant are each not a single factor but again a composite of several. It is, thus, almost impossible to hold any two of these three factors at a constant performance while the third is varied in experimental way to determine such effect on the process of nitrogen fixation, or the physiology of the nodule bacteria.

Study of Isolated Factors Insufficient. These factors cannot perform truly independently of each other. The complete and supposedly normal physiology of the nodule bacteria in the process of nitrogen fixation cannot be learned by their isolation from the nodule into artificial media.

There they either refuse to fix nitrogen, or if they do, its amounts are insufficient to serve as indicators of variable conditions or limiting factors. Within the soil and in the absence of the plant, the nodule bacteria are again beyond control and even careful observation. Chemical measures of their performance are impossible. When active within a plant that is growing in an aqueous cultural medium, accurate measures and careful observations are possible. These conditions are, however, still far removed from those obtaining in the soil. The influence on the plant and, thus, possibly on the nodule bacteria, Rhizobia, by ionic nutrients in high concentrations may easily be expected to be far different from the low ionic concentration and the adsorbed condition of nutrients found in the soil.

Studies up to the present time by these various approaches have not been entirely complete, because of their failure to control the soil, but they have contributed much to our knowledge of the physiology of Rhizobia. The literature is voluminous as has been shown by the monograph of Fred et al. Any phase of these approaches is too extensive for review here. Such studies have, however, made it possible to produce pure laboratory cultures of known inoculating ability and quality. Aqueous growth media for legume plants have elucidated the importance of the nutrients required in much larger amounts by these than by non-leguminous plants. They have pointed to the influences of many factors operating and to the complexity of the entire process. Little has been possible, however, in controlling the soil accurately enough so as to venture the study of nitrogen fixation with the soil as one of the three items under chemical control.

Soil Factors under Control by Use of Colloidal Clay. Agronomists may not be interested in the legume bacterial physiology, per se, but certainly they are interested in nitrogen fixation by legume plants for increased production of these crops as better livestock feed and for soil enrichment in organic matter and in nitrogen. In this respect the soil factor becomes very essential. It must be brought under careful and accurate control if we are to learn legume bacterial physiology with controlled bacteria, controlled plants and controlled soil — all of the factors involved in the process of nitrogen fixation.

The sand and silt fractions of the soil are of such particle magnitude, of such insignificant surface, and of such insoluble nature, that their rate of chemical reaction is too slow to be significant in a period as short as a growing season. The clay fraction, however, is quite the opposite and constitutes, in the main, the physico-chemically active portion of the soil. For experimental purposes we can then eliminate the sand and silt of the soil, purify and standardize the clay fraction, and then add it to a known sand to approach chemically controlled conditions. By the use of electrodialyzed clay; of a single kind and variety of legume plant in the form of the Virginia soybean; and of pure laboratory cultures of Rhizobia; maximum control of all conditions was attempted in the experiments which serve as the basis for discussing the physiology of the root nodule bacteria particularly in relation to the fertility of the soil.

Calcium, Phosphorus, Potassium, and Magnesium for Nitrogen Fixation

The soil serves as the supply of a composite lot of plant nutrients. The list of these is too extensive for each nutrient to have been assigned its proper physiological role, as yet, by means of its control through colloidal clay use, with the legume plants and their bacteria all under careful control. Attention has been given to those more commonly considered in soil fertility. The discussion, herewith, will consequently be confined to the possible physiological importance to nodule bacteria of calcium, phosphorus, potassium, and magnesium.

Calcium

Importance as a Nutrient. The importance of lime for legumes has been appreciated for centuries, but the relation of the calcium to the physiology of root nodule bacteria has not been so commonly recognized. The application of calcium as a carbonate has led to confusion in our thinking because this compound plays a dual role by reducing acidity at the same time that it fertilizes the soil by supplying calcium. Emphasis has been given to liming because it removes a supposedly harmful agent, soil acidity, rather than because it adds a beneficial one, the nutrient calcium. In order to separate these two effects, it was only necessary to treat a soil with calcium acetate or with calcium chloride. These compounds which do not reduce the hydrogen concentration were equally as beneficial as the carbonate or hydroxide in giving improved growth in soybeans, as shown in Figure 1. These results point to a possibly significant role of the calcium in the plant and bacterial physiology. The plant growths were larger, greener, and of higher nitrogen content because of the calcium treatment accompanied by no change in soil reaction.

Fig. 1. — Calcium compounds serve effectively for legume crop improvement without neutralizing soil acidity. (Right to left, calcium nitrate, calcium chloride, and calcium hydroxide in remaining strips.)

Calcium Effective Through the Plant. In order to learn about the effects by calcium through the plant as separate from those on the bacteria within the soil, sterile seeds grown for ten days in sterile sand, part with and part without calcium carbonate, were transplanted into an acid soil already stocked with nodule bacteria. At intervals of ten days, fifty complete plants were harvested, weighed and analyzed for nitrogen. The data are presented in Table 1.

It is evident that the calcium taken into the plant tissue during the first ten days of the plant's existence was of decided significance. In the first place, after only the first ten days in the soil, and even before nodules developed, the limed plants made larger growth and contained more nitrogen. Since nodules were absent — they could scarcely develop in this short period — it would seem reasonable to believe the limed plants more effective in feeding on the nitrogen of the soil. If this is a safe conclusion for nitrogen, it may not be far amiss to consider that potassium, phosphorus, and other soil nutrients are absorbed more effectively from the soil in the early life of the limed plant. Further, the roots of the limed

Table 1

Nitrogen Content of Soybeans as Influenced by Calcium in the Seedlings

Age of Plants	Previous Treatment	Average Height (cm.)	Percent Increase Over No Lime	Oven-Dry Weight 50 Plants	Percent Increase Over No Lime	Nodule Numbers Per Plant	Percent Nitrogen	Nitrogen Content 50 Plants (gms.)	Increase Over No Lime	
									mg.	%
Seedlings	None	7.0	71	4.77		0	6.57	.3134		
10 days	Lime	12.0		4.77		0	6.51	.3105		
Soil	None	13.5		6.64		0	5.58	.3703		
10 days	Lime	20.0	49	10.03	50.1	0	4.33	.4387	684	18.4
Soil	None	21.6		10.90		1.09	4.82	.5247		
20 days	Lime	31.8	47	17.87	63.9	9.06	3.44	.6147	900	17.1
Soil	None	30.4		23.9		6.04	3.40	.7799		
30 days	Lime	35.6	17	29.7	24.2	16.30	2.85	.8467	668	8.5
Soil	None	31.0		24.8		13.81	2.92	.7243		
40 days	Lime	39.0	25	38.4	54.4	17.51	2.46	.9472	2229	30.7
Soil	None	31.0		35.2		17.30	3.13	1.1020		
50 days	Lime	41.0	32	41.0	16.4	17.02	3.00	1.2340	1320	11.9

plants were effectively entered by the nodule bacteria at an earlier date and in larger numbers because the plants carried calcium. Then too, their nitrogen content was regularly higher and the plants taller and heavier throughout the remainder of the test. All of these effects point out that calcium within the plant plays a significant role in helping the process of nitrogen fixation and should be considered as important in the physiology of the nodule bacteria.

Adsorbed Calcium vs. Crystal Calcium in the Soil. Calcium in the ionic form is readily taken by the plants but it is well to note that this element within the mineral crystal, as anorthite for example, will not serve. However, when it is weathered out of the crystal and adsorbed on the colloidal complex it is readily taken by the plants. In addition, concentrations large enough to be injurious in ionic form are not injurious in the adsorbed form, as shown in Fig. 2. This adsorbed form offers possibilities of supplying calcium to the plant in quantities much larger and without injury than by any other method. With clay as the carrier of calcium, the use of simply more clay in a clay-sand mixture serves to increase and improve the growth of soybeans by providing the plants with larger amounts of adsorbed, or exchangeable calcium. We may well look to this form as the source of the nutrient for those plants in which the nodule bacteria are to be effective nitrogen fixers.

Calcium Effect Separated from pH Effect. The detrimental effect of high degrees of soil acidity on legume crop growth is no longer disputed. Soils can be too seriously sour for effective nutrition, but defective nutrition on sour soils need not be due wholly to the presence of excessive hydrogen-ion concentration. It is more likely due to the deficiency of basic nutrients, cations, among which calcium is the foremost. By using acid clays saturated to increasing degrees with calcium, (carrying reciprocally decreasing amounts of hydrogen), and, therefore, lowering hydrogen-ion concentration, it was possible to provide plants with equal amounts of calcium at varying degrees of acidity. Increased amounts of clay in the sand increased the amounts of calcium offered the plants. Crop differences, as given in Fig. 3, show not only differences according to the varying acidity but much greater differences according to the quantity of calcium supplied. The nodule numbers given in Table 2 differed more in response to the amounts of calcium than to the degree of acidity. They trebled and quadrupled for doubled quantities of calcium when such increases were not the rule with a decrease in acidity by ten times. The weights of the tops

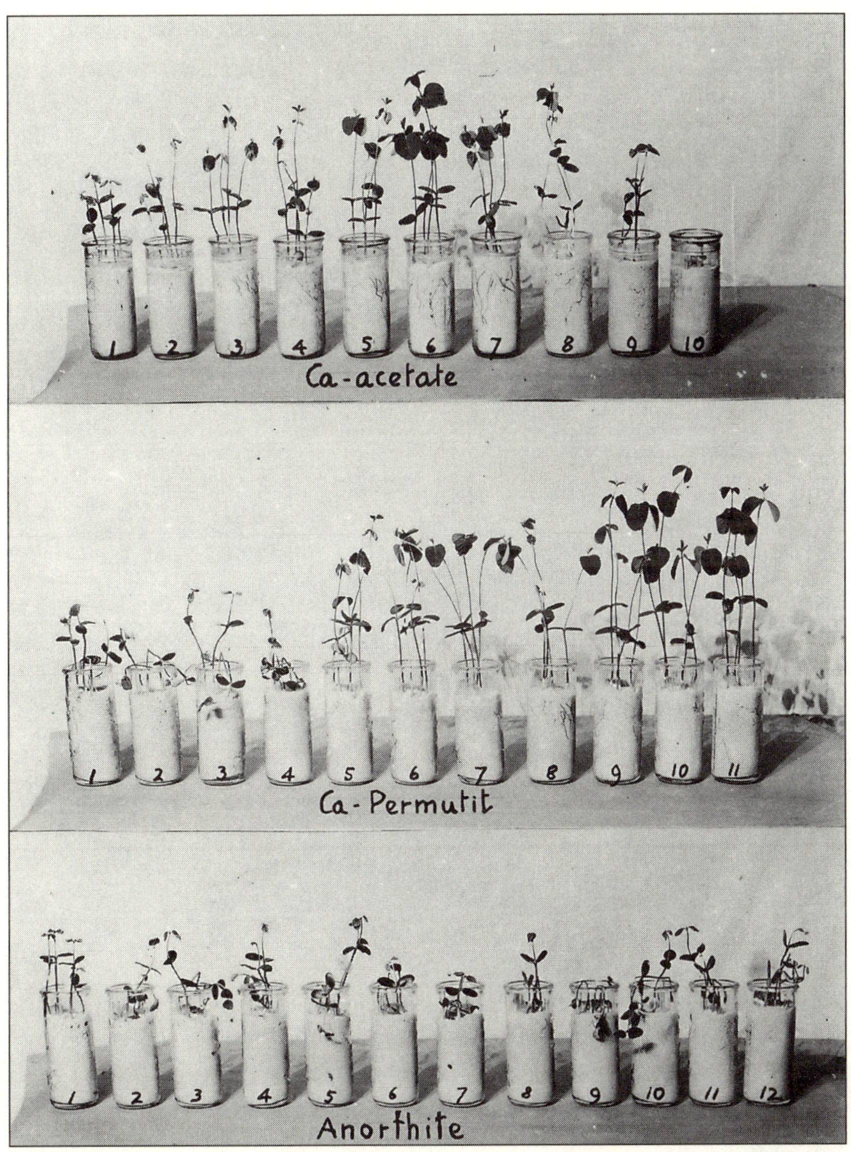

Fig. 2. — Calcium adsorbed on colloidal permutit serves more effectively at high concentrations than does ionic calcium acetate. Crystal calcium as anorthite fails to serve. (Increasing calcium from left to right.)

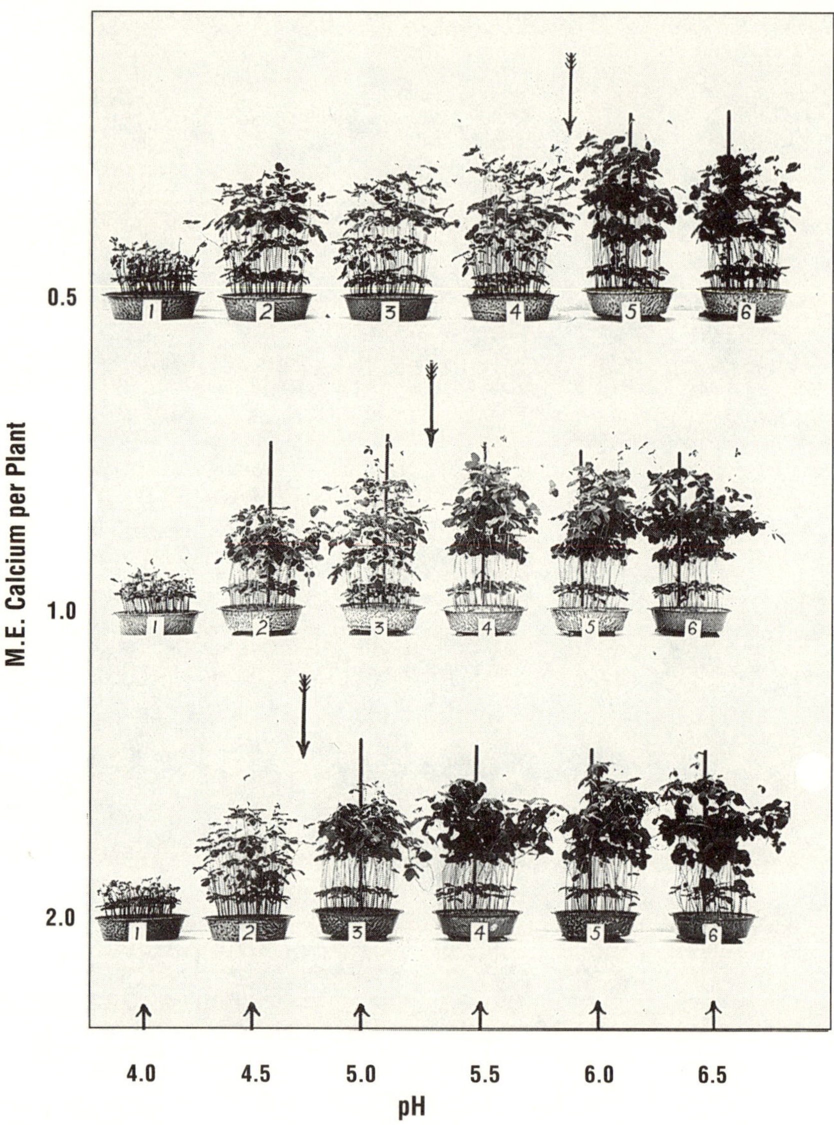

Fig. 3. — Higher levels of calcium counteract the influence of higher degrees of acidity.

also, were more responsive to the differences in calcium than to the differences in acidity. The effects by calcium were roughly two and one-half times as large as those by the hydrogen-ion concentration so far as crop appearances are concerned.

Table 2

Nodulation and Growth of Soybeans as Influenced by the Calcium and by the pH of Calcium-Clay Soils

Plant Characters		Calcium Per Plant m.e.*	pH at Outset					
			4.0	4.5	5.0	5.5	6.0	6.5
Nodules (50 Plants)		.05	0.0	0.0	0.0	0.0	7.0	14.0
		.10	0.0	0.0	0.0	8.0	28.0	40.0
		.20	0.0	0.0	0.0	60.0	69.0	127
Height cm.		.05	11.0	26.0	28.0	31.0	36.0	36.0
		.10	9.5	27.0	34.0	42.0	44.0	45.0
		.20	8.0	25.0	40.0	45.0	48.0	52.0
Weight (50 Plants) Grams	Tops	.05	4.8	6.3	6.8	7.0	7.9	7.6
		.10	4.2	6.3	7.3	8.9	9.5	8.7
		.20	4.6	6.0	8.7	9.2	9.4	9.9
	Roots	.05	1.5	2.5	2.0	2.0	4.0	3.6
		.10	1.7	2.2	2.1	4.3	4.3	4.2
		.20	1.0	1.7	2.5			

** Milliequivalents per plant.*

The nitrogen fixation improved with the lessening degree of soil acidity when ample calcium was supplied. Unless calcium was liberally provided there was no nitrogen fixation in the clay as nearly neutral as a pH of 6.5, as shown in Fig. 4. This encourages the belief that the presence of high hydrogen-ion concentration is not so injurious. Rather, it is the absence of the calcium which is a disturbed physiological condition that prohibits the root-nodule bacteria from exercising their normal function of fixing nitrogen.

The changes in the reaction of the clay brought about by the growth of the soybeans is interestingly correlated with the differences in nodulation, in growth, and in other properties previously cited. The crop growth moved the reaction of the more acid clays toward the neutral point. The clays which were more nearly neutral at the outset were made more acid. These changes suggest calcium removal through hydrogen exchange in the more nearly neutral clays and the loss of bases by the seeds and plants to the more acid clays. The maximum extent of the base removal or the degree of acidity to which plant growth could change the clay was a pH

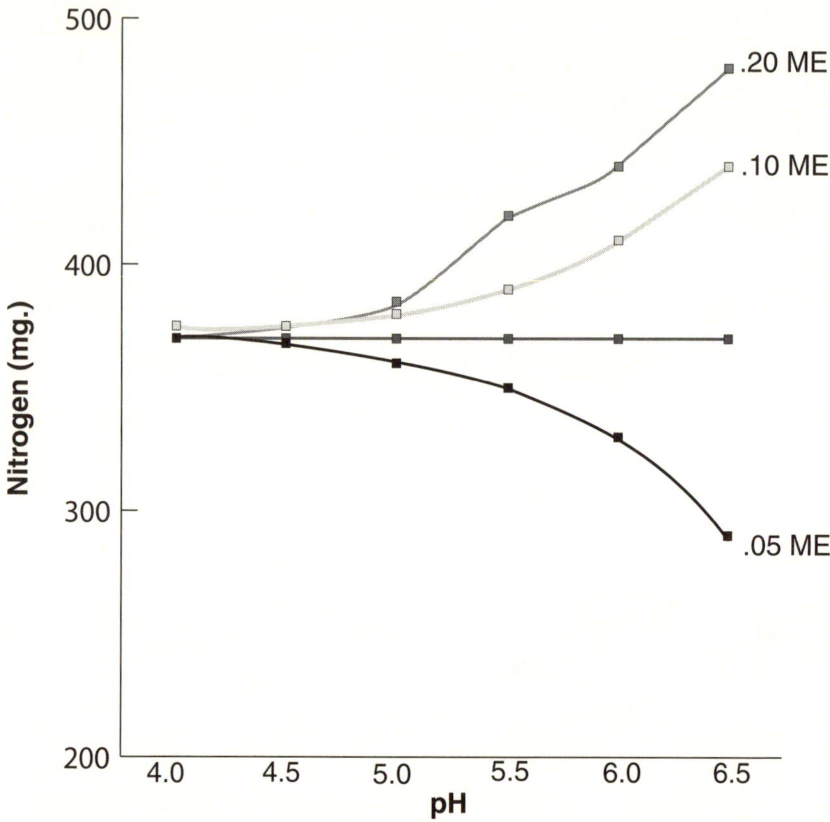

Fig. 4. — Nitrogen fixation at different calcium levels with varying degrees of soil acidity. (The horizontal line represents seed nitrogen.)

of about 5.5. Below this pH figure the plant mechanism seemed to have broken down, and the plants lost bases to the soil. Nodulation and nitrogen fixation were effective only when the plant was taking bases from the soil. The figure, pH 5.5, may be considered as the equilibrium point. When the reaction was above this with liberal allowances of calcium provided, active nitrogen fixation was the evidence of a more nearly normal physiological condition for the nodule bacteria.

On these very acid soils, the soybean crop of fair appearance contained less bases after six weeks of growth than were contained in the seed at the outset. As a livestock feed, the crop is poorer in minerals than the original seed. The crop has fertilized the soil through its contribution of a small amount of bases rather than through its activity as a nitrogen fixer. Under such soil condition the physiology of the nodule bacteria may be classed as abnormal. It is necessary to add calcium carbonate to such soils for the sake of both of its possible effects, namely neutralizing acidity and supplying calcium before these microorganisms can be expected to function normally.

Degree of Calcium Saturation Influences Nitrogen Fixation. As the degree of calcium saturation of a clay increased, the growth of soybeans improved, even though equal quantities of calcium were provided. Such is true whether the reciprocal ion is hydrogen that invokes acidity, or barium which keeps the clay neutral. If growth follows the degree of calcium saturation of the clay whether variable hydrogen is present or absent, the detrimental effect by hydrogen must be given less importance and the presence of the calcium greater significance.

Data on the crop properties and its content of calcium and nitrogen given in Fig. 5 show the close relation of these to the degree of calcium saturation. Nodule numbers run parallel with the calcium intake by the crop. The same close correlation existed for the nitrogen fixation shown in Fig. 6 whether the accompanying cation was hydrogen or barium, and whether the soil was acid or neutral respectively. It is significant to note that unless the degree of calcium saturation was greater than 40 percent no nitrogen fixation occurred even though the crop was of fair appearance.

Organic Matter Possibly Effects Calcium Availability. When the variable degree of calcium saturation of the clay had an organic complex like methylene blue as its reciprocal or was brought to neutral reaction by adsorption of this large organic cation as a supplement to the calcium, the plant growth responded to the total amount of calcium rather than to its percentage saturation of the clay as demonstrated in Fig. 7. Perhaps the large amount of energy involved in the adsorption of the organic molecule prohibits its removal from the clay in response to the plant root activity. The latter is then wholly effective on taking only the calcium and obtains this according to the amount present rather than according to the degree of saturation. Perhaps "humus" molecules of the soil behave as does the organic, methylene blue. In this phenomenon may lie some suggestion for the underlying facts of the farmer's observation when he said, "soil acidity isn't so dangerous to clovers on the more fertile soils or on those that are rich in humus."

Nitrogen fixation as a normal function by nodule bacteria demands liberal quantities of calcium within the plant. Unless such is the case the microorganism fail to enter — as judged by absence of nodules — and fail to exercise their nitrogen-fixing functions. The physiology of the nodule

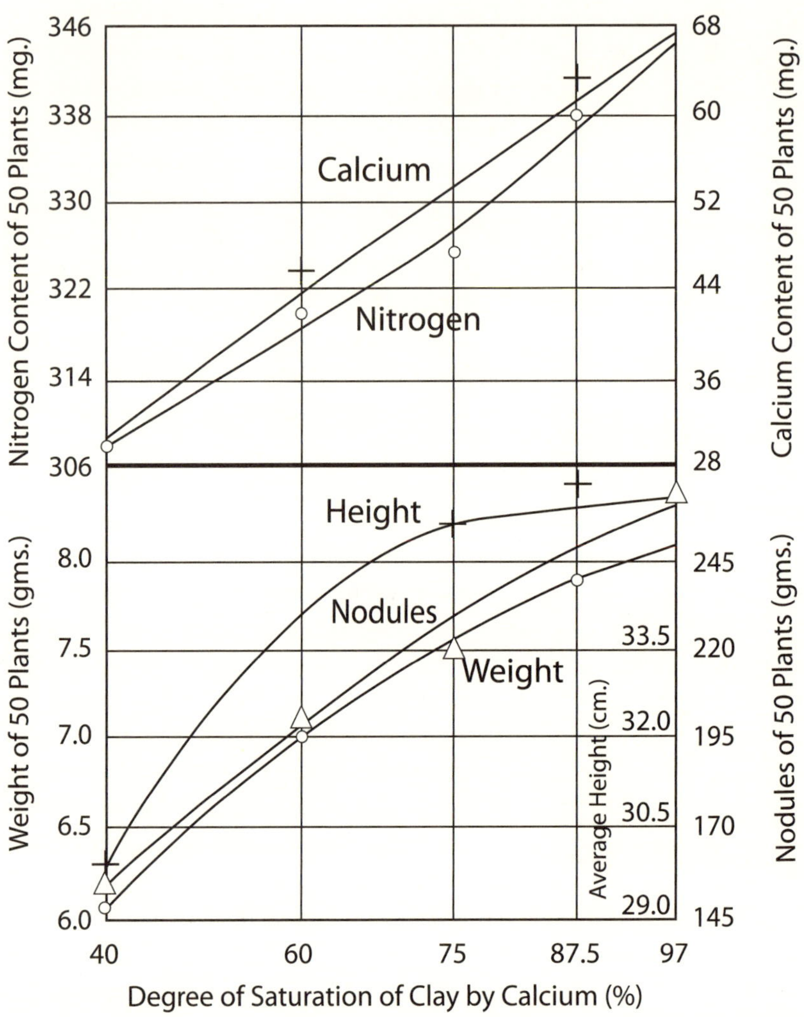

Figure 5. — Calcium and nitrogen contents and other crop properties as related to the degree of calcium saturation of the clay.

bacteria is tuned to high levels of calcium, and is abnormal or ineffective in legumes unless these plants can obtain this nutrient in large amounts. Perhaps non-legume crops would inoculate by nodule bacteria if their calcium and other base content could be raised to the corresponding level at which nodule bacteria function within the legume.

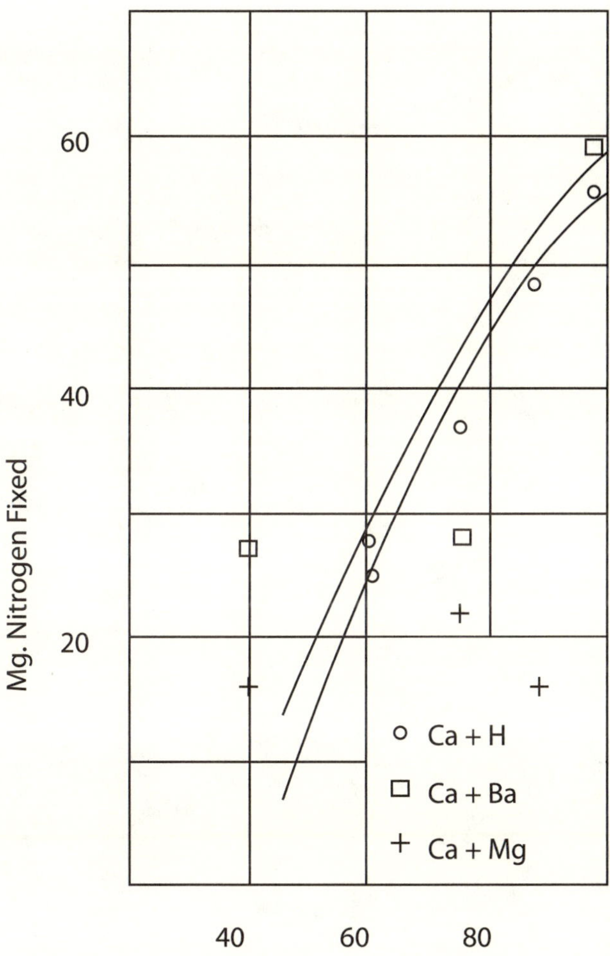

Figure 6. — Nitrogen fixation by soybeans as related to the degree of calcium saturation of the clay.

Phosphorus

Effects by Phosphorus Related to Calcium Levels. Attempts to disturb the nitrogen fixation by soybeans through variation in phosphorus levels failed to indicate phosphorus of the importance in the early life of the plant as one might anticipate. The relation of the phosphorus behavior to the level of calcium was more significant. When no phosphorus was added, the appearance of the original seed phosphorus in the plant was dependent

Figure 7. — Soybean growth as related to the degree of calcium saturation when the accompanying cations are hydrogen and potassium and to the total calcium when methylene blue is the associate of calcium. (Increasing calcium saturation from left to right.)

on a liberal supply of calcium as shown in Fig. 8. Only when 10 m.e. of calcium were supplied per fifty plants and when the calcium content of the crop was .55 percent or greater, was the maximum amount of seed phosphorus present in the crop. Nitrogen fixation was insignificant below this phosphorus level in the crop, but was not restricted by it since larger amounts of calcium made the process more effective. This suggests that unless calcium is present in liberal amounts, the phosphorus in the young crop is not even equal to that in the seed at the outset.

The phosphorus of the seed then, as an anion, much like the bases or cations, is lost or given up to the soil by the seed and young plant unless liberal amounts of calcium are present. The degree of acidity cannot be considered as responsible for this reverse movement of nutrients. The phosphorus failed to be in the plant whether the variable calcium was accompanied by hydrogen, as variable acidity, or by variable barium, magnesium and potassium and therefore by neutrality. If the phosphorus deficiency is manifested so early in the plant's life, it seems evident that this effect would be magnified toward plant maturity when its demands on phosphorus would be much heavier for purposes of seed production. It was demonstrated for the seedling plants in Table 1, that calcium may be instrumental in helping the uninoculated plants to take nitrogen more effectively from the soil. There is a strong suggestion here that calcium functions in a similar manner toward the phosphorus in making it effective in plant metabolism and in the microbiological performance of nitrogen fixation. Calcium may be said to make the soil nitrogen and the soil phosphorus physiologically available.

Potassium

Effects by Potassium Possibly Associated with Calcium Levels. With the increase in adsorbed calcium offered the soybean plants, there was almost a direct increase in the calcium intake by the plants as illustrated

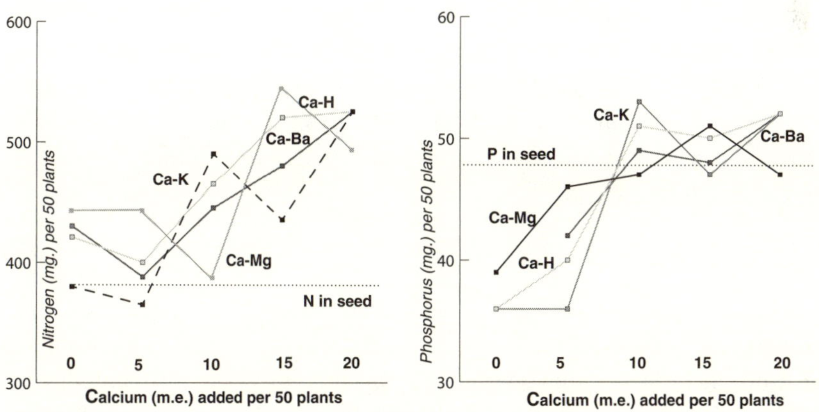

Figure 8. — Influence of calcium levels on nitrogen fixation and phosphorus utilization by soybeans.

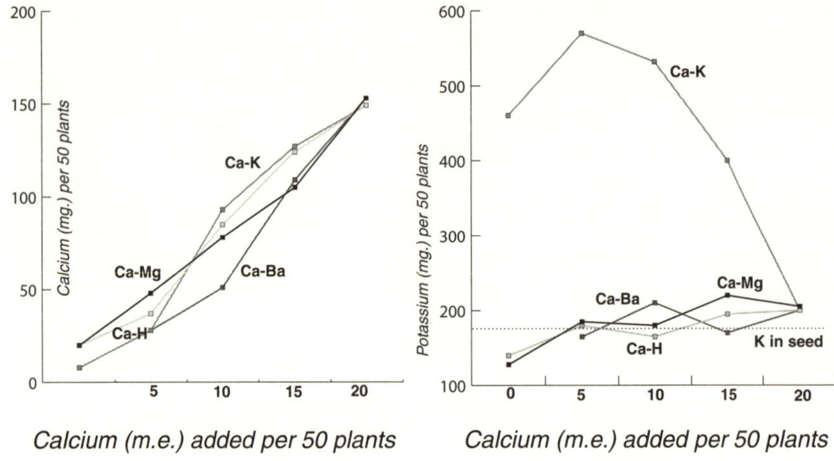

Figure 9. — Influence of varied calcium levels on the potassium utilization by soybeans.

in Fig. 9. Calcium controlled its own entrance into the plant irrespective of its cation association previously used. There is also a strong indication that the potassium intake goes up with higher calcium levels in the soil and higher calcium intake by the plants. If this is true, then potassium, like phosphorus and nitrogen, is metabolized more effectively with the plant's access to more calcium. If then there is increased nitrogen fixation accompanying the increases of calcium, phosphorus, and potassium with the plants, it may seem hazardous reasoning to ascribe causal significance to all three of these nutrients in the physiological activities of the nodule bacteria from this evidence. It will, however, be well to take cognizance of the strong possibility that potassium is also a significant item in the nitrogen fixation by legumes, and that its displacement from the colloid or its increased availability may be a factor in the generally beneficial effects to legumes from liming.

Magnesium

Magnesium Essential in Nitrogen Fixation. Variable supplies of magnesium accompanying liberal amounts of calcium exercised a pronounced effect on the growth of soybeans. That this effect extended to the nitrogen fixation is illustrated in Table 3. When no magnesium was added, fixation was insignificant unless extra calcium was available. As more magnesium was added, fixation increased. This was not greater, however, for the high magnesium levels than for lesser amounts, as shown in Fig. 10.

Synergetic Effect by Magnesium on Calcium Intake. The variable magnesium level had no significant influence on the composition of the crop as regards phosphorus and potassium according to the limited data shown in Fig. 11. It was, however, influential on the calcium content of the crop. This became larger with the increased magnesium even with constant calcium level. Magnesium made the total supply of calcium more effective. The percentages of the total available calcium taken by the crop were 31, 37, and 42 for the smaller increments of magnesium at the lower calcium levels, and 18, 21, and 27 for the larger increments and higher level, respectively. Thus, the calcium supply showed greater efficiency as the magnesium level was raised. Magnesium operating in conjunction with low levels of other nutrients does not stand out because of its benefits as does calcium similarly used. Yet when combined with calcium, the increased magnesium meant greater calcium intake by the crop.

The reciprocal effect, or a more efficient magnesium intake as the calcium increased, was not the case. The magnesium used was equivalent to 58 and 65 percent of the total magnesium offered with 10 m.e. of calcium present and 60 and 67 percent, respectively, when 20 m.e. of calcium were provided. Magnesium seems to aid the plant in using its calcium effectively more than the calcium improves plant efficiency in taking the magnesium, according to the nutrient levels here used.

If these are the facts, magnesium gets very little synergetic effect from calcium, while such effect by magnesium on calcium seems significant. It is possible then that with low calcium supplies in the soil, the presence of magnesium may make this low calcium supply more effective so far as plant intake is concerned. This increased calcium within the plant may be instrumental in bringing about better nitrogen fixation. Under this interpretation magnesium would aid physiological performances of nodule bacteria by delivering more of the much-needed calcium.

Nodule Bacteria Demand High Calcium Level in Artificial Culture. The preceding results point to the importance of a high level in the soil and within the plant of calcium, magnesium, and possibly potassium as cations, and of phosphorus as an anion for the proper functioning of nodule bacteria in nitrogen fixation. These microorganisms require a high calcium level also in artificial culture. Normal forms become abnormal in color and colony characters when the calcium supply is low. They can be restored

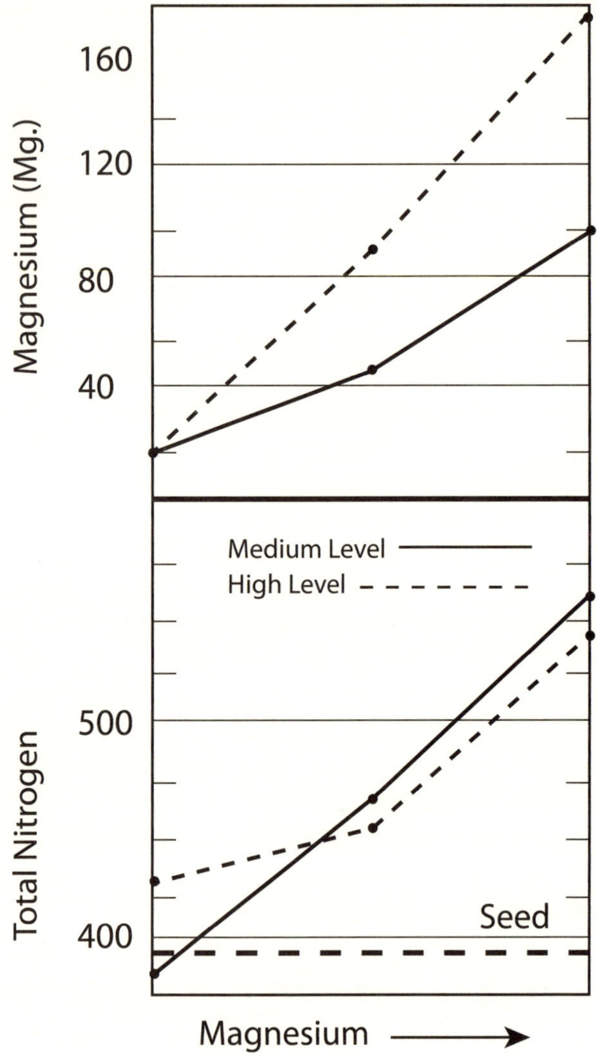

Figure 10. — Nitrogen fixation by soybeans and their contents of magnesium as influenced by variation in magnesium level supplied by colloidal clay. (Medium level = 0, 5, 10 m.e., high level = 0, 10, 20 m.e. magnesium per 50 plants.)

Table 3

Variation in Nitrogen Fixation and Crop Composition in Consequence of Variation in the Supply of Magnesium Adsorbed on the Clay

Pot Number	m.e. Offered 50 Plants			Crop Analyses — mg. per 50 Plants						
				Nitrogen						
	Calcium	Magnesium	Barium	Total	Fixed	Calcium	Magnesium	Phosphorus	Potassium	Barium
1	10	0	10	391	-3	66.2	20.2	35.1	172	25.9
2	10	5	5	465	71	79.5	48.3	36.2	185	13.2
3	10	10	0	558	164	89.8	100.0	33.1	162	0.0
4	20	0	20	432	38	76.8	19.5	39.2	147	52.0
5	20	10	10	455	61	87.6	92.2	41.9	203	5.4
6	20	20	0	541	147	114.1	178.1	35.5	185	0.0
Seed				394		12.2	16.7	39.4	171	0.0

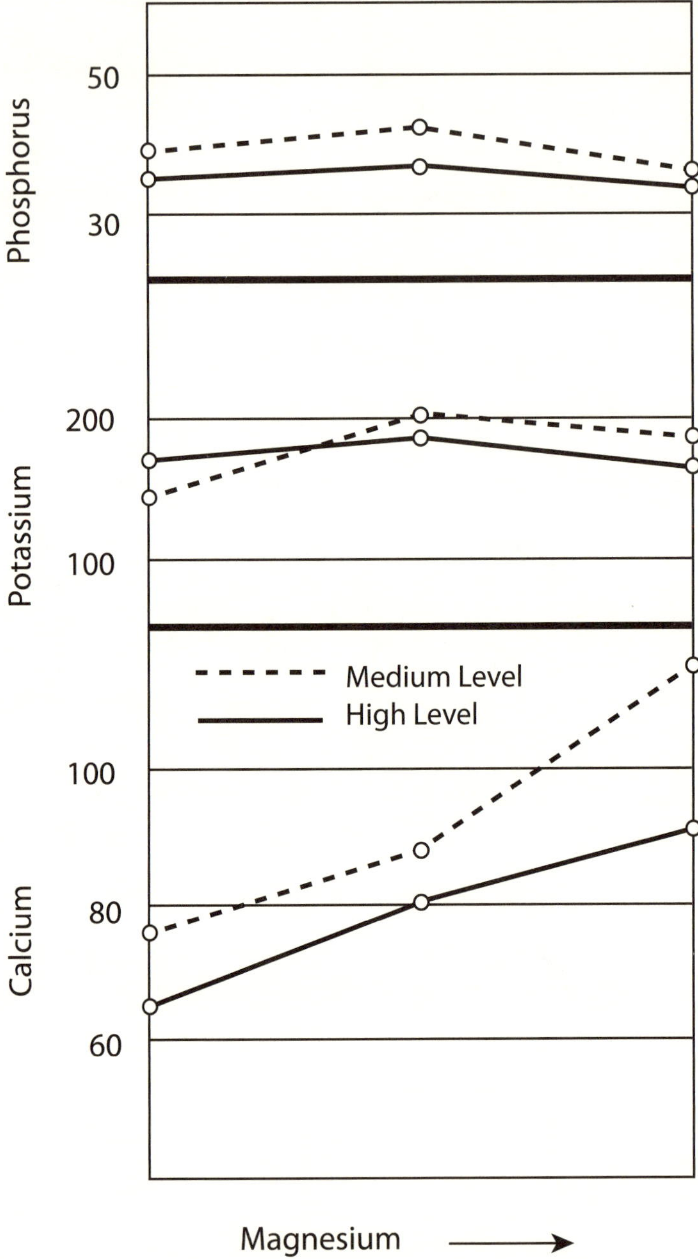

Figure 11. — Variation in composition of soybeans in consequence of a variable supply of magnesium adsorbed on clay. (Medium level = 0, 5, 10 m.e., high level = 0, 10, 20 m.e. magnesium per 50 plants.)

to normal again when ample calcium is supplied. Their growth rate is also accelerated with calcium increase. Both the bacteria grown independently of the plant and plant harboring the bacteria within are stimulated in their growth, nodulation and nitrogen-fixing activities when given higher levels of calcium.

Summary

The physiology of extensive growth of legume plants, their significant nodulation, and their effective nitrogen fixation centers around a liberal supply of adsorbed calcium in the soil. The phosphorus utilization becomes more efficient as the available calcium increases. This might raise the question whether phosphate fertilizer is of value in stimulating legumes in nitrogen fixation unless calcium is carried within, or applied with, the phosphorus fertilizer compound. Then also, potassium like the phosphorus may become more effective when the calcium levels are raised. Magnesium seems to play a physiological role somewhat different from that played by phosphorus and potassium. Instead of being prompted by calcium, its entrance into the crop is probably determined by its supply independently of influence by the other cations. However, it seems to have somewhat of a synergetic effect on the calcium of which the intake by the plant is improved as more magnesium is available. Calcium seems to help the metabolism of phosphorus and potassium, while magnesium in turn seems to aid the metabolism of the calcium.

In terms of pounds per acre, the amounts of these nutrients as found by calculation from values cited in the above tables, are so exceedingly small that it seems improper to speak of "liberal" supplies of calcium, magnesium, and others. The actual amounts taken by the soybeans are very small. The 10 m.e. of calcium on the basis of one bushel of soybean seed drilled per acre would demand only five pounds of pure limestone. These small amounts, however, must be delivered in such form that they are effective within the plant and deal only with six weeks of the plant's early life, or long before its seed-maturing activities begin. Other items, magnesium, phosphorus, and potassium are correspondingly small in amounts required. Studies carrying the plants to fuller maturity will contribute to our understanding of the needs in the later stages of growth and will doubtless push these requirements to much larger figures. Even then they should not be large when considered as field applications. The much better plant growth and nitrogen fixation under experimental condition in contrast to such of crops in the field emphasize the astoundingly low levels of nutrients that must prevail in some of the rundown soils which we are asking an occasional legume crop in a crop rotation to restore to productivity.

These results suggest that maximum soil improvement through nitrogen fixation by legumes may not be so much a matter of particular pedigreed bacteria, nor of supposedly acid-tolerant legumes, but rather a matter of supplying any legume plant with a high level of soil fertility in the form of calcium, magnesium, phosphorus, and possibly potassium and organic matter to provide the physiological conditions required for effective nitrogen fixation by nodule bacteria. These particularly helpful soil microorganisms are acclimated to plants that are high in their percentage content of calcium, magnesium, and other nutrients. When supplied liberally with these from the soil and through the actively growing plant, the nodule bacteria can give the plant its high percentage content of nitrogen by fixation from the atmosphere. Nodule bacteria are tuned to a high level of fertility, the decline of which may thus be considered as responsible for a disturbed physiology of the nodule bacteria and the resulting ineffective nitrogen fixation and even legume crop failures.

CHAPTER 9

Magnesium Depletion in Relation to Some Cropping Systems and Soil Treatments

THE CONCEPT THAT plant nutrition is an exchange process between adsorbed ions on the colloidal fraction of the soil and the hydrogen ions on the roots naturally directs attention to the cations on the list of the plant nutrients. Among these calcium and its singular activities have already had fruitful consideration. Studies have revealed the more or less baffling behavior of potassium that still is challenging attempts at explanation. Magnesium has been the subject of little research in the glacial soils, though it has had attention in soils more highly developed. Consideration may well be given to the magnesium supply and its exchange activities between the soil complex and the plant as these are related to the continued and sufficient delivery of this nutrient for utilization by the plant.

Now that calcium is becoming a common soil treatment, its companion cation, magnesium, deserves attention. This is particularly timely if we are to learn of its behavior in connection with the heavy lime applications given many soils. Then, too, the declining soil fertility manifested in greater magnesium-deficiency symptoms in plants, particularly the soybeans, must naturally demand early attention to magnesium in the soil. Because of these facts, magnesium was given exploratory attention in two soil studies. One consisted of a survey of the magnesium supplies in the soil as revealed by rapid tests in 600 soil samples collected in the State of Missouri during 2 years. Another study involved analytical attention to the soils of some of the plots from the research station at Bethany, Missouri, in cooperation with the Soil Conservation Service. In these, particular attention was given to certain cropping systems and soil treatments as they are related to the depletion of magnesium.

Magnesium in Missouri Soils

Of numerous samples received by the laboratory for tests, those which could be specifically classified as to soil type were used. In addition, samplings were made specifically for this study. Though about 100 soil types of Missouri were represented, the bulk of the samples were from approximately 12 of the most common types.

The tests of magnesium were made according to the rapid method of Baver and Bruner. The soil was leached with 0.3 N hydrochloric acid, and the magnesium was precipitated as a colloidal hydroxide colored with titian yellow. The values used by Baver and Bruner as standards ranged from 0.25 to 2.00 m.e. magnesium per 100 gm. of soil or from 60 to 480 pounds per acre 2 million. The medium figure was taken as 240 pounds per acre. Soils containing less were adjudged as "low" and those containing more were considered "high" in magnesium.

The results of this inventory are presented graphically in Fig. 1, which shows the soils as groups in the different geographic areas of the state. Two of the areas, namely, the southeastern part and the southwestern prairie were not represented by a sufficient number of samples. They are included, nevertheless, for their indicative values. The samples of the former of these two areas are all sandy loams. The remainder of the soils for the state were mainly silt loams.

The less leached soils contained the more magnesium. Those progressively more developed showed lower contents of this plant nutrient. The most significant revelation of this inventory is the fact that even the area of soils with the highest magnesium content did not reveal as much as 240 pounds per acre, considered as medium in amount. The mean for the 600 samples of the state was 168 pounds per 2 million. Thus, either all the soils of Missouri are significantly low in magnesium, in general, or the standards set for this test by Baver and Bruner are too high.

That the soils of Missouri may be generally low in magnesium is suggested by numerous cases of plant symptoms indicating magnesium deficiencies, particularly on soils with crops in close sequence under reduced amounts of plowing. Further suggestion comes from studies by Graham. When he used the separated silt fraction from an Iowa surface soil after it had been treated with acid clay, the magnesium content of the crop grown on it was no higher than that of the planted seed. These observations suggest that there may be insufficient exchangeable magnesium on the colloidal fraction of the soil, and insufficient active reserve of this element in the silt

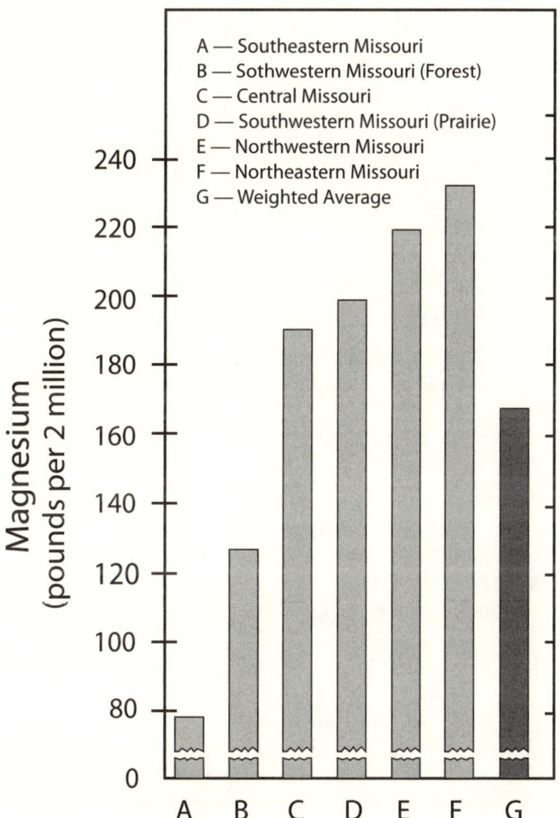

Fig. 1. — Exchangeable magnesium, as pounds per acre, in the soils in different areas of Missouri.

portion of even the recently glaciated soils. Such facts suggest attention to possible magnesium shortages for crops on Missouri soils of older glaciations and of more intensive development at higher temperatures.

Cropping Systems, Soil Treatments, and Possible Magnesium Depletion

In connection with the research work at the Soil Conservation Experiment Station on Shelby loam, a glacial drift soil, the exchangeable calcium and magnesium were determined in differently treated soils sampled to surface depths at three biennial intervals representing a total of 7 years

(1931–1937) in the history of the treatments. Similar determinations were made at the end of the fourth biennial period on successive 1-inch soil layers down to 13 inches in the permanent bluegrass sod in the plot series. Determinations were made, at the same time, of the nitrogen and of the organic matter by means of carbon. The soils sampled and studied for magnesium, included (a) three plots in a rotation of corn, wheat, clover-timothy, with no treatment, (b) similar plots with lime plus phosphate, (c) alfalfa with lime plus phosphate, (d) bluegrass with no treatment, (e) fallow treatment on a surface soil, and (f) similar treatment on an exposed subsoil. It was on only the permanent bluegrass sod that the samples were taken as 1-inch layers in 1939. The other samples were taken as the surface 7 inches in a single sampling, several samplings being composited in each case for the plot.

Table 1

Changes In Degrees of Saturation of the Soil Complex by Calcium and Magnesium and in the Organic Matter and Nitrogen Contents of the Soil from 1931 to 1937

Crop and Soil Treatment*	Saturation by		Percentage of	
	Calcium	Magnesium	Organic Matter	Nitrogen
Bluegrass — no treatment	Increase	Decrease?†	Increase	Increase
Alfalfa lime plus phosphate‡	Increase	Decrease	Increase	Increase
Rotation — lime plus phosphate	Increase	Decrease	Increase	Increase?
Rotation — no treatment	Decrease	Decrease?	Decrease	Decrease
Fallow surface — no treatment	Decrease	Increase	Decrease	Decrease
Fallow subsoil — no treatment	Decrease	Increase	Decrease	Decrease

** Complete data were reported by Whitt and Swanson (Table 3) for these treatments and crops.*

† Where the data are not entirely consistent in their trend for all of the four determinations, 1931, 1933, 1935, 1937, the general trend is given with a question mark.

‡ Phosphate and lime were applied in 1930, and phosphate at three-year intervals thereafter.

The changes in the amounts of exchangeable calcium and magnesium with time in these soils under different treatments direct particular attention to the magnesium. These trends along with those for the percentages of carbon and of nitrogen during the 7 years represented by four successive analyses are listed in Table 1.

Decrease in Magnesium Saturation Under Apparent Soil Improvement

It is particularly noteworthy that though the shifts in calcium saturation, in organic matter, and in nitrogen were generally in the same direction, the shifts in magnesium saturation seemed to be in the opposite direction. Under those crops and soil treatments which have commonly been considered as soil-building, *e.g.*, the use of lime and phosphate, the growing of alfalfa and bluegrass, or those that demonstrate trends toward increase in the organic matter, in the nitrogen, and in the degree of calcium saturation in the soil, there was a trend toward decrease in the degree of magnesium saturation of the soil. This was true for crops that allowed a minimum of erosion to bring soil from the lower into the upper layers through plowing. Then again, the rotation and the fallowing — all without soil treatment — which give a decrease in the organic matter, in the nitrogen, and in the calcium saturation, serve to give an increase in magnesium saturation. Here higher magnesium saturation in the subsoil layer plowed into the surface as a consequence of truncating the profile by erosion may be responsible. Thus, while soils were improving in calcium saturation and in nitrogen and organic matter content under little or no erosion, the magnesium saturation was decreasing. Contrariwise, while soil depletion with respect to calcium saturation, nitrogen, and organic matter was occurring along with possibly some erosion, the degree of magnesium saturation was increasing in this soil.

This suggests that the lower crop production and the fallowing, which allow exchangeable calcium to be lowered in concentration while some erosion is occurring, serve to increase the degree of saturation of magnesium. Bluegrass, however, without soil treatment has entirely the opposite effects. Its effects on the soil correspond with what happens when either a legume-containing rotation or continuous alfalfa is given lime and phosphate. Bluegrass is thus a soil-builder as shown by comparison of these soil properties.

That the bluegrass crop, without soil treatment, is singular in this respect among these limited numbers of cropping systems tested is further supported by the quantitative data from the 1-inch layers of the soil in the grass sod. This is indicated by the distinct differences between the upper seven 1-inch layers of surface soil and the lower six layers of subsurface soil. This was a profile that was not being truncated by crosion and was not given lime and phosphate, yet the surface soil bearing the bluegrass roots was decidedly low in magnesium saturation in contrast to the subsurface. The data are assembled in Table 2.

Here again the soil zone bearing the many bluegrass roots and experiencing the effects of the crop was higher than the subsurface with its few roots, in those respects that represented increase with time (Table 1); namely, organic matter, nitrogen, and calcium saturation, whereas it was much lower in magnesium saturation than the subsurface. Bluegrass apparently built up the soil in some respects while it was depleting the active magnesium supply in the absence of erosion.

Table 2

*Degree of Soil Saturation by Calcium and Magnesium, and Percentages of Organic Matter and Nitrogen in the Surface and Subsurface Layers of Permanent Bluegrass**

Bluegrass	Saturation by				Percentage by		C/N
	Calcium		Magnesium		Organic Matter	Nitrogen	
	%	*m.e.*	%	*m.e.*			
Surface seven 1-inch layers, mean..................	61.3	11.74	19.4	3.30	3.73	0.180	11.98
Subsurface six 1-inch layers, mean..................	56.9	15.52	30.4	8.28	2.06	0.106	11.22
Difference due to bluegrass roots..................	4.4		11.0		1.67	0.074	0.76
	Increase		Decrease		Increase	Increase	Increase

** This plot was seeded to bluegrass with timothy in 1930. It had been in cultivated crops previously. Complete data for the successive 1-inch layers were reported by Whitt and Swanson (Table 2).*

Table 3

*Increasing Organic Matter, Nitrogen, and Calcium Saturation and Decreasing Magnesium Saturation in a Treated Soil Growing Alfalfa**

Dates of Sampling†	Exchange Capacity	Saturation by				Percentage of	
		Calcium		Magnesium		Organic Matter	Nitrogen
	m.e.	*percent*	*m.e.*	*percent*	*m.e.*		
1931	18.95	58.10	11.01	21.16	4.01	3.79	.184
1933	19.17	64.79	12.42	17.06	3.27	3.91	.186
1935	20.02	87.71	17.56	17.33	3.47	4.05	.196
1937	19.72	77.33	15.25	16.84	3.32	4.02	.192

** These data were reported by Whitt and Swanson (Table 3).*
† Soil treated in 1930.

Alfalfa as a crop with the soil treatments of limestone and phosphate was similar to bluegrass under no treatment in giving increases in the organic matter, the nitrogen, and the degree of calcium saturation, while the degree of magnesium saturation was decreasing. This is shown by the data in Table 3.

Increase in Calcium Saturation and Decrease in Magnesium Saturation After Liming

Where the limestone was applied for alfalfa in 1930, as shown in Table 3, the calcium saturation, and with it the organic matter and nitrogen, mounted steadily until 1935. By 1937 the calcium saturation was declining, though it was still almost 20 percent above the value given by the determination in 1931. By that late date the contents of organic matter and of nitrogen were no higher than those of the sampling immediately previous. While these three factors were increasing, the degree of magnesium saturation was decreasing. According to these data, the alfalfa crop on the soil given lime and phosphate was reducing magnesium saturation more drastically than was the bluegrass on the same soil without treatment. The reduction was even more drastic under alfalfa than under rotation on the soil given limestone and phosphate. These reductions in magnesium under alfalfa were coincidental with an increase in the saturation of the soil by calcium.

Bluegrass without limestone applications was bringing about an increase in calcium saturation of the soil colloid similar to that under limed alfalfa. This movement of limestone, for 5 years, from the applied crystalline into the adsorbed form on the soil colloid and the resultant increasing saturation may be the explanation of the better legume crop growth with time after limestone applications. The increased calcium saturation under bluegrass without lime applications has been suggested by Whitt as an explanation for the periodic advent of white clover in bluegrass sods.

While the soils under cropping with no erosion (alfalfa and bluegrass) were undergoing reduction in magnesium saturation and increase in calcium saturation, those under fallow, with erosion, were showing the opposite effects. The cases under study were not numerous enough to warrant generalizations; nevertheless, they suggest that soil-conserving crops and soil treatments are associated with lowered magnesium saturation and that erosive crops are associated with increased magnesium saturation. Though the degree of magnesium saturation was reduced by bluegrass without soil treatment, it was reduced more by rotation with lime and phosphate treatments, and still more by alfalfa with these same soil treatments. Whereas bluegrass raised the percentage of calcium saturation by one fourth, it lowered the magnesium saturation by one twentieth. For the rotation with lime and phosphate, the saturation went upward as much as one third for the calcium and downward one fifth for the magnesium. Under fallow and erosion, the surface soil decreased in calcium saturation equivalent to about one twentieth but increased in magnesium saturation as much as one seventh. The desurfaced soil, or exposed subsoil, under fallow decreased in calcium saturation by about one twelfth but increased in magnesium as much as one third during the 6 years.

Truncation of Profile in Relation to Changes in Magnesium Saturation

Truncation of the profile by erosion on the 8 percent slope may offer an explanation of the increase in magnesium saturation in the fallow soils. What truncation was doing was shown by the successive 1-inch layers which were studied only under the bluegrass sod where no erosion took place. If we assume that the bluegrass crop was without disturbing effects at depths of 7 to 13 inches, and that the profiles of the bluegrass and of the fallow surface plots were the same at the outset, then if truncation from 1930 to 1937 were to increase the magnesium saturation of the fallow surface plot to the figure of 23.37 percent as a mean of the upper seven 1-inch layers, this would represent a shift downward in the profile to approach the mean magnesium figure of 22.63 percent under bluegrass for the seven 1-inch layers ranging from the depths 3 to 9 inches inclusive, or the mean figure 24.57 percent for the depths from 4 to 10 inches inclusive. This would demand truncation by erosion to the extent of 3 to 4 inches in 7 years, or the surface 7 inches in 14 years. Coincidently, the erosion data for these 7 years showed that this plot was losing soil at the rate of more than 86 tons per acre per annum. This would mean the loss of the surface 7 inches in about 12 years. Such a close agreement with the figure of 14 years, as calculated from differences in magnesium saturation, suggests that magnesium saturation was maintained by truncation of the profile through erosion.

In the fallow subsoil, the magnesium saturation was 29.75 percent in 1937. If this subsoil corresponds to the section in the bluegrass profile from 7 to 13 inches, then the mean magnesium saturation of these separate 1-inch layers would have been 28.69 percent, or if the collection were made as a 7-inch sample it would have been 30.36 percent. The fact that this subsoil was eroding at the rate of 7 inches in less than 17 years indicates an approach toward a relatively constant degree of magnesium saturation with increasing depth in the profile below the thirteenth 1-inch layer, the limit of the study.

That magnesium saturation is higher in the subsoil than in the surface soil in another glacial drift profile was demonstrated in some studies by Harris and Drew. Though erosion produced a soil with a clay content almost twice as great in their studies, the exchange capacity had become correspondingly larger. The exchangeable magnesium increased slightly more than the clay content, to show increasing magnesium saturation in going from the surface to the subsoil. Other soil properties, such as exchangeable calcium, exchangeable potassium, total nitrogen, and organic matter did not increase accordingly. In some of these there were decided decreases. The exchangeable hydrogen increased much more than the clay content, suggesting that the magnesium saturation was maintained in the presence of increasing hydrogen saturation and of decreasing saturation by some of the other cations.

In the deep, virgin loess as it is more highly weathered under more intense climatic forces near Vicksburg, Mississippi,[1] than under the Missouri

[1] *Reported by H. B. Vanderford in private communication.*

conditions concerned in this study, the exchangeable magnesium increases more than three-fold with depth in the solum. The calcium increases by only one eighth. At a depth of 20 feet the exchangeable calcium is tenfold and the magnesium over sixfold that in the surface horizon. Here again, truncation of the profile to the extent of 12 inches would mean little change in the calcium saturation but more than doubling in concentration of exchangeable magnesium.

Summary

The data presented in these studies, concerned with magnesium saturation of the soils under cropping with no erosion and in fallow soils with significant erosion, bring magnesium into the picture as a nutrient that is reduced significantly by cropping. They also suggest that erosion may have been serving in the past to hide what may be an impending serious deficiency in soil fertility. They point out further that the performances by bluegrass sod without soil treatment and by alfalfa and by rotation, both with lime and phosphate, ordinarily considered as soil-building effects, are decidedly depleting for magnesium, if decreasing degree of soil saturation of this nutrient may be taken as a criterion.

As our efforts in soil-building, particularly by liming, phosphating, cover cropping, and erosion prevention, serve with benefit to the active calcium and humus contents of the soil, they may be a detriment to the available magnesium supply. A liberal virgin store of magnesium in the more active form or a large stock in the mineral reserve may have been saving us from trouble in the past with respect to shortages of this nutrient. On some of the more highly developed soils of which the silt and sand fractions are very low in minerals other than quartz, and where such soils are now being maintained against erosion by conservation practices, it may not be long before the degree of magnesium saturation will be too low to guarantee good yields of crops. For some soils, as the Shelby silt loam used in this study, the practices in the past of using erosive systems of cropping, and of fallowing with its intensive erosion, may have prevented such troubles. Under intensive cropping with erosion prevention and the application of other fertilizer elements, however, the need for using magnesium as a soil treatment may soon become comparable to the present needs for calcium, potassium, and other fertilizer cations. The same fundamental principles underlying these in their plant and soil relationships will then help us to understand and manage the behavior of magnesium.

CHAPTER 10

Calcium in Relation to Phosphorus Utilization by Some Legumes & Nonlegumes

THE PLACE OF CALCIUM in soil treatment is no longer believed to be merely that of a cheap reducer of the hydrogen-ion concentration in the soil. Nor it is taking its position along with some 15, or more, essential elements as only a building block in plant construction. It has seemingly become more important as one of the essential nutrients by means of which other such elements may be moved into the crop plants. The very common association of phosphorus with calcium in nature, and the greater effectiveness of the former as a fertilizer in conjunction with liming, suggest some possible effects by calcium on the mobilization of the phosphorus into the crops. Previous studies have suggested such for lespedeza. The following is a partial test of such a hypothesis for some of the leguminous and the non-leguminous crops.

Plan of Study

Since previous investigations have pointed to the degree of saturation of the colloidal clay complex by calcium as a factor in the effectiveness by which a given amount of applied calcium is delivered to the crop, the amounts and placements of calcium carbonate used in this study were varied to represent different degrees of saturation of the soil. The soil used was a Putnam silt loam. Its capacity to absorb calcium was first determined. Then two rates of application, representing complete saturation and half saturation for one-fourth of the soil, were employed. These same amounts of lime were also mixed throughout the entire soil to give lower degrees of saturation corresponding to one-eight and one-fourth of the amounts needed to saturate it. The amount of phosphorus was double that commonly applied as fertilizer, and double this latter amount, representing 100 pounds and 200 (38%) pounds per two million of soil. Sodium phosphate and calcium phosphate were each used singly, and the latter in conjunction with the calcium treatments. Two-gallon earthenware pots were used.

The two phosphorus treatments were mixed into the surface one-fourth of the soil while the balance of it remained untreated. Korean lespedeza and sweet clover were used as the legume crops. Bluegrass and redtop served as the non-legumes. The growth period was long enough to permit five cuttings of each crop as forage. The data given are for composites of cuttings of 25 separate pots for each crop, except for lespedeza which is represented by 10 pots. The crop weights and compositions were taken on constant moisture bases. Chemical analyses, along with all other measurements, were made by the commonly accepted, more accurate methods.

Experimental Results

For simplicity sake, the data may well be assembled as harvests (a) of crop, (b) of phosphorus, (c) of calcium, and (d) of protein each as pounds per acre, and then as concentrations of phosphorus and of calcium in the crop, expressed as percentage in the dry matter. These are shown graphically in four of the above cases by two figures each. One figure represents the effects of variable calcium, or its combination with different amounts of calcium phosphate as soil treatments, while the other shows the effects by application of only the sodium and calcium phosphates to the soil.

Harvest of Crop

Perhaps the outstanding feature of the data is the improved yields of both legumes and nonlegumes on this soil by the use of lime, or calcium. A comparison of Figs. 1 and 2 shows clearly that the yield curves in the former, for soils given calcium, or its combination with phosphates, are higher on the scale for each crop than the curve for the corresponding crop in the second figure where phosphates were used without lime. An increase either in the calcium saturation or in the calcium amounts increased the yields almost as much for nonlegumes as for legumes. Doubling the phosphate application in conjunction with a lime application was about as effective for crop yield increase as was the doubling of the application of lime only. Increasing the lime in conjunction with constant phosphate was significant, and likewise the reciprocal, or the increasing of the phosphorus in conjunction

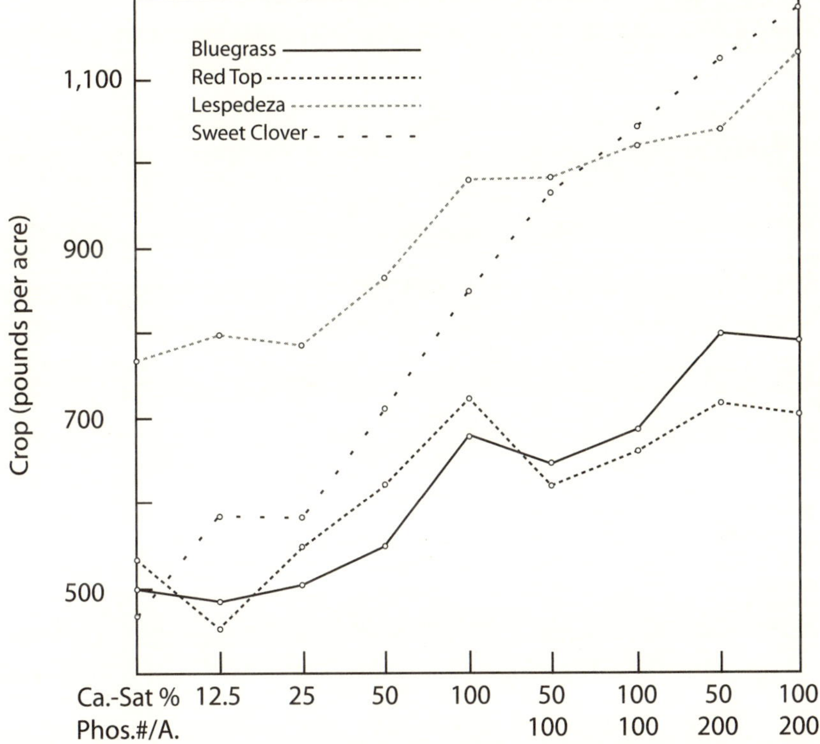

Fig. 1. — Harvests of crops as influenced by different degrees of calcium saturation of the soil or their combinations with phosphate.

with constant lime amounts. This is a distinct feature in that increments of either one serve to increase yields while the other is constant. Doubling the phosphate application in the absence of the lime, however, was not so effective as is shown in Fig. 2 where the phosphates improved the yields only slightly. The small amount of calcium supplied in the calcium phosphate, as compared with the effects by sodium phosphate was without significant effect, save for possibly the one case of sweet clover.

These yield data alone would suggest that the application of phosphate is more effective as a fertilizer on bluegrass, redtop, Korean lespedeza and sweet clover when used in conjunction with calcium, or lime, than when used alone. The limiting factor suggests itself as calcium for its service in nutrition of the plant rather than for its service in reduction of the hydrogen-ion concentration in the soil when the effects by different degrees of saturation are considered. Also, in place of the reduction in phosphorus consump-

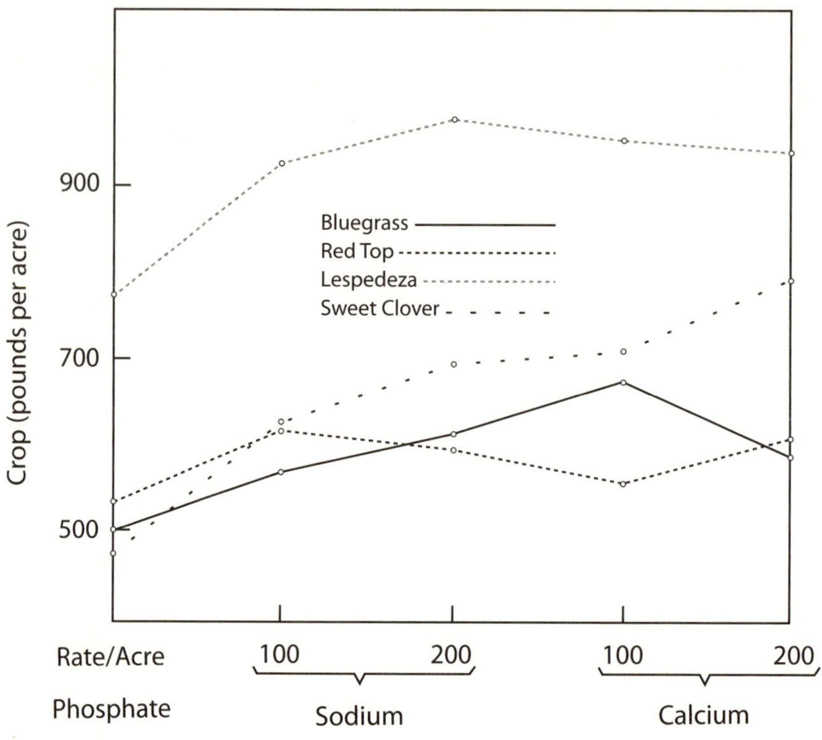

Fig. 2. — Harvests of crops as influenced by phosphates of sodium and calcium at different rates.

tion by the plants through reduced phosphorus solubility when the soil was given the maximum calcium saturation or complete neutrality in a portion of the soil, the very reverse was the case, or there was maximum consumption of phosphorus from the soil by the crop. This seemingly removes the phosphorus "availability" in the soil from the realm of control wholly by the degree of soil acidity. It suggests that as the soil was given more calcium, the phosphorus, existing in the calcium-deficient soil in combination with possibly iron or aluminum, became more usable by the plant.

Harvest of Phosphorus

The amount of phosphorus per acre removed by the crop increased as larger amounts of lime or calcium were added to the soil. It is significant, however, to note the importance of the degree of calcium saturation in this connection. When the calcium application was made to a portion only of

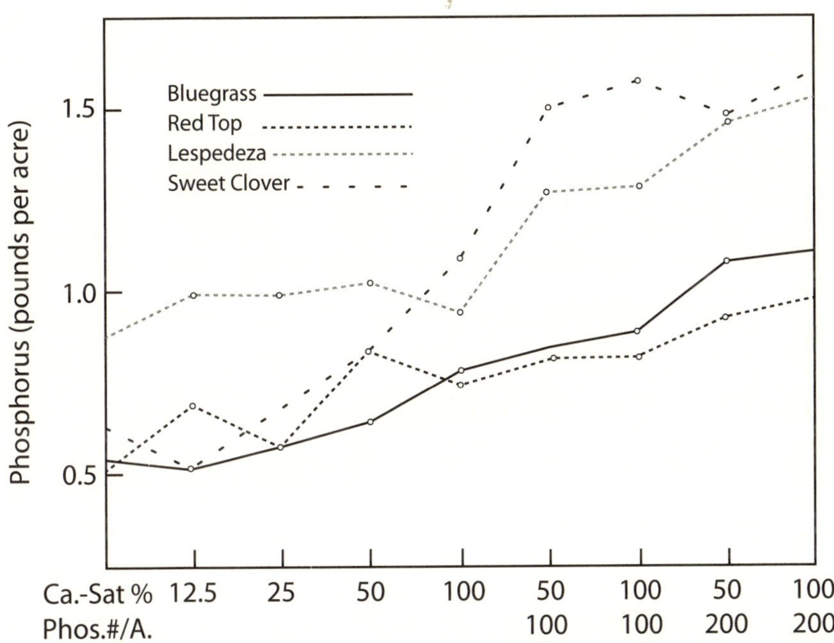

Fig. 3. — Harvests of phosphorus in the crops as influenced by different degrees of calcium saturation of the soil or their combinations with phosphate.

the soil so as to give a higher degree of saturation by this element, a greater mobilization of the phosphorus into the crop from the constant, original soil supply occurred. These facts are evident from the left hand portions of the graphs in Fig. 3.

As an average of the four crops, the removal of phosphorus by them was increased by less than 10% when the calcium deficiency in the entire body of the soil was lessened by either one-eighth, or by one-fourth. But when an amount of lime corresponding to the former reduction in the entire soil was applied to a smaller portion of the soil so as to lessen the calcium saturation deficiency there by one-half, then the phosphorus harvest increased 28%. When this same soil portion was completely saturated with calcium, then the phosphorus harvest was increased by 36%. Greater calcium saturation in a smaller portion of the soil by the smaller amount of lime was more effective in delivering larger phosphorus harvest from non-phosphated soil than was the lower saturation by larger amounts of lime in the larger body of soil.

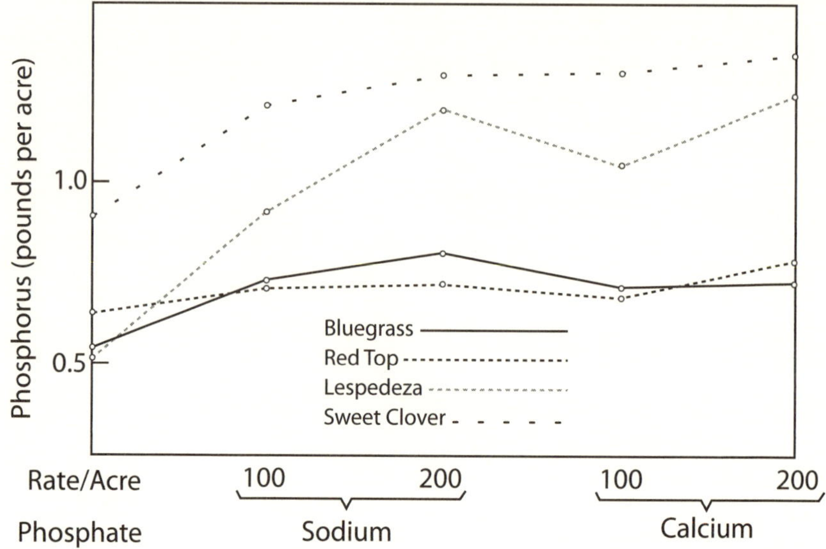

Fig. 4. — Harvests of phosphorus as influenced by phosphates of sodium and calcium at different rates.

When the two different amounts of phosphorus were each applied in conjunction with half calcium saturation and complete saturation, then the increasing amounts of calcium meant that more phosphorus was taken by the crop. This is shown by the right hand portions of the curves in the same figure. A comparison of these with those in Fig. 4 for the phosphorus harvest where phosphates alone were applied, shows that the phosphorus harvest by nonlegumes given these phosphate treatments only was even below that in these crops given only lime to complete saturation of a part of the soil in the absence of applied phosphates. Thus, in this soil, the addition of phosphorus is not as effective for increasing the phosphorus harvest in the crop as is the addition of only calcium. Also, effective recovery of applied phosphorus is premised on a liberal supply of calcium in the soil.

When the variations in a single treatment such as small limestone applications carrying no phosphorus can shift the so-called "phosphorus availability" for these different crops through a range from one quantity to double this amount, it would seem that any beliefs in the reliability of simple chemical tests for "phosphorus availability" in terms of plant consumption and yield, would be somewhat shaken.

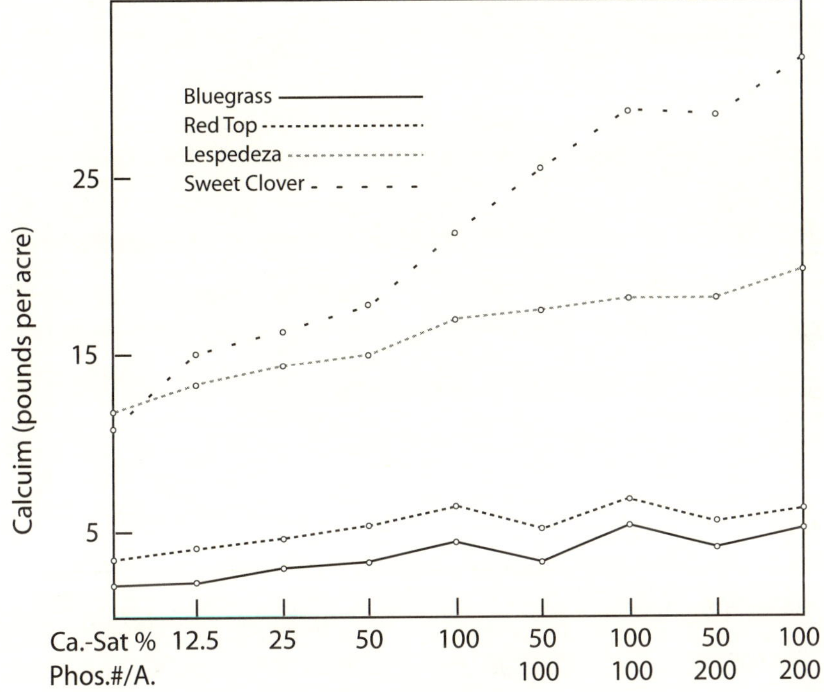

Fig. 5. — Harvests of calcium as influenced by different degrees of calcium saturation of the soil or their combination with phosphates.

The significance of the lime in connection with the nonlegumes on this soil is noteworthy. The increased phosphorus in this type of crop as a result of liming and of its combination with phosphates points to the need for soil treatment in case of even so common-place a grass as redtop. The legume crops responded with a far wider range of phosphorus removal from the soil. They indicate their greater possibilities in yield variations by which these crops might reflect lime, phosphate or other fertility deficiencies. As a consequence, fertility deficiencies have been more easily recognized in connection with legume failures than with grass crop failures.

Harvest of Calcium

In terms of the total calcium taken from the soil by the crops, it is interesting to note again the greater importance of the degree of saturation of the soil by calcium than of the total amount of limestone applied. This held true for both legumes and nonlegumes as shown in Fig. 5. It emphasizes

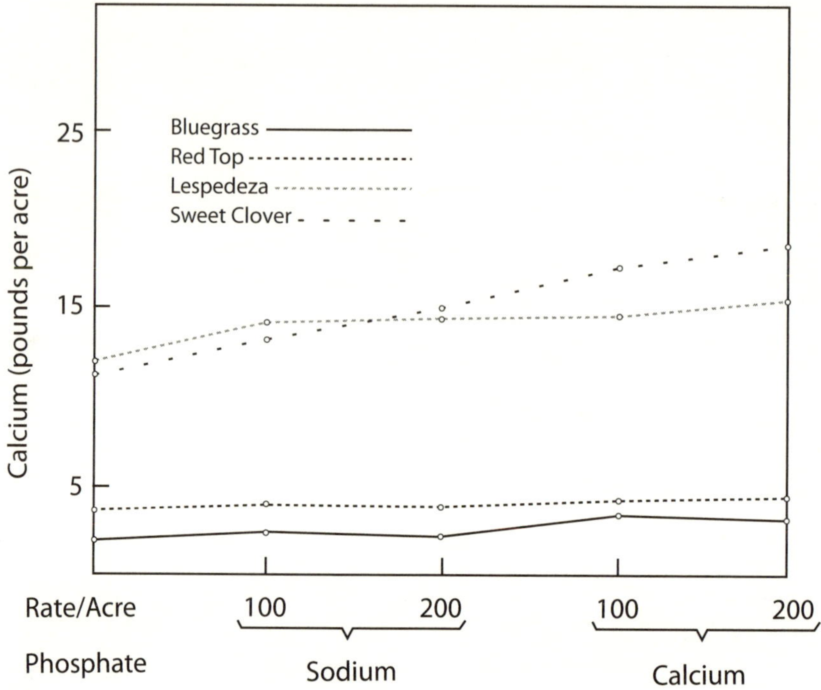

Fig. 6. — Harvests of calcium as influenced by phosphates of sodium and calcium at different rates.

the relative saturation of the soil as the factor determining the efficiency by which the calcium application to the soil is recovered in the crop. The recovery by the legumes is, of course, the higher. All curves show greater recovery for either of the two amounts of limestone mixed into the lesser quantity of soil.

Much as the phosphorus harvest was increased by the calcium application so there was a reciprocal effect by the phosphorus application on the calcium harvest. This calcium harvest was greater from a constant limestone application as more phosphorus was used with it. This is shown distinctly in the right hand parts of the curves in Fig. 5 for the two grasses and the sweet clover, but less so for the lespedeza.

This effect was seemingly impossible when phosphates were used in the absence of limestone, as is shown in Fig. 6. Heavier treatments of phosphates alone failed to get more calcium into the grass crops or lespedeza even when the form of phosphate used singly was the calcium phosphate. In case of the sweet clover, however, calcium phosphate alone was more

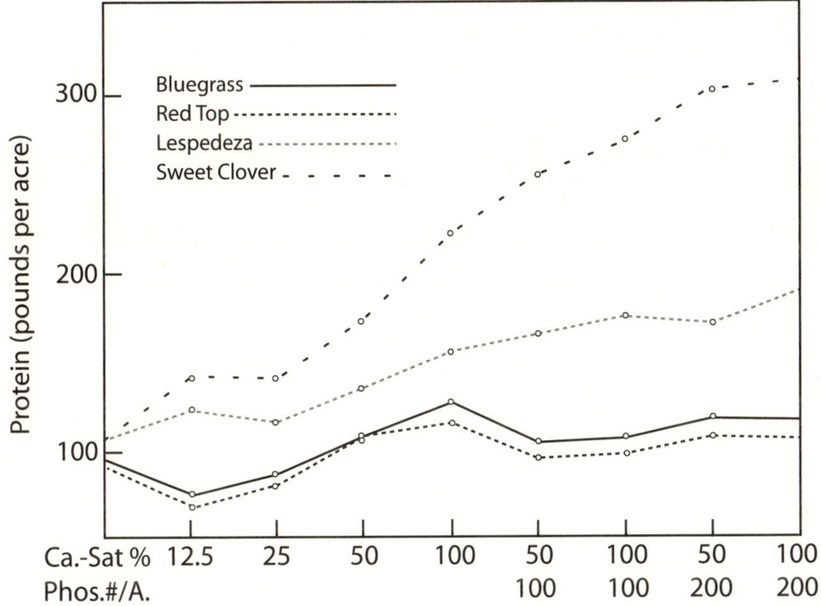

Fig. 7. — Harvests of protein as influenced by different degrees of calcium saturation of the soil or their combination with phosphate.

effective in delivering calcium harvest. This reciprocal effect on calcium by phosphate application does not appear on this soil when no limestone is applied to it. It suggests calcium as the foremost deficiency in this soil.

It seems, then from the studies of plant composition as well as of forage yield, that calcium was a limiting element holding down the plants' consumption of phosphorus, and likewise that phosphorus was a limiting element at the same time in reducing their consumption of calcium. Perhaps such an interaction in the plants' use of these two nutrient items has connected lime and phosphates more closely in the art of agriculture than we have up to the present connected calcium and phosphorus in its science. It remains difficult to understand how such mutual increased movement into the plant can be brought about.

Harvest of Protein

Should we hold to the belief that calcium is without direct effects on plant protein production, then with phosphorus as a protein constituent a study of the protein harvest might reveal indirect calcium effects on it

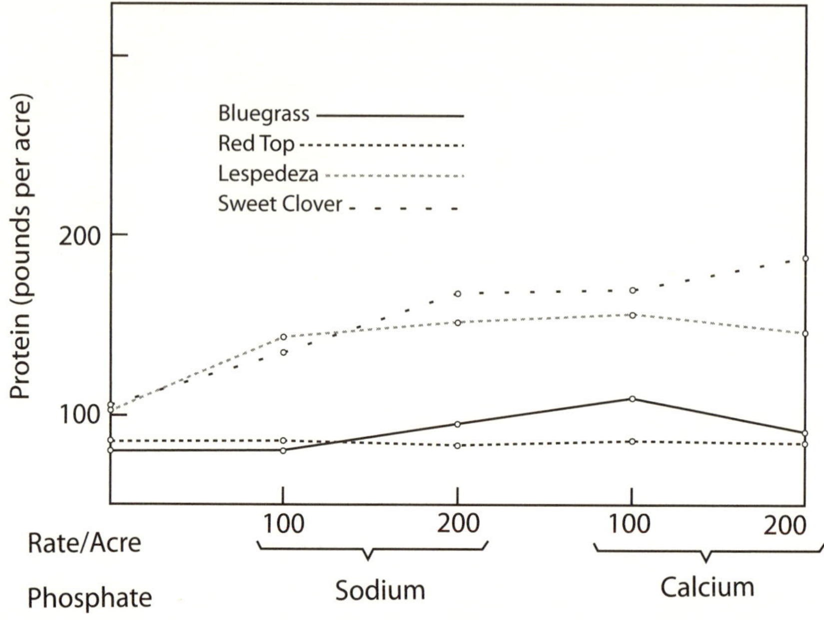

Fig. 8. — Harvests of protein as influenced by phosphates of sodium and calcium at different rates.

through influences on phosphorus. Comparison of Figs. 7 and 8 points immediately to the significance of the calcium in this plant activity by the higher level of the protein harvest where lime, or lime and phosphates were used, Fig. 7, in contrast to that by phosphates only, Fig. 8. Phosphates alone were more influential in the case of legumes than they were for the grasses.

The close agreement in protein production by redtop and bluegrass, Fig. 7, under lime only, or this treatment coupled with phosphate, is significant. Particular notice might well be taken of the lowered protein production, (below that of the check), by the lesser application of calcium or the lower degree of soil saturation by it, and the increased harvest with higher degree of its saturation of the soil. In contrast to these performances by the two grasses, all the lime treatments for legumes gave increases in protein production beyond that on the soil without treatment.

As to the possible cause for such response by the grass, one might consider the competition by the soil bacteria for the soil nitrogen because of their increased activity through lime additions. Such is not disturbing to the legumes which are able to draw on the atmospheric supply of nitrogen.

Heavier limiting may overcome this competition by speeding the period in the bacterial cycle when competition prevails. Perhaps similar competition is induced when the smaller phosphate application is added to the limestone. This combination is not so effective in giving protein harvest, as are either more of these two as soil treatments, or the higher degree of calcium saturation as is suggested in the second fall in the curves for the nonlegumes in Fig. 7.

The legumes give far larger response than the nonlegumes as protein harvest. Korean lespedeza responds to liming and gives additional protein from the phosphorus supplement. But this protein increment by phosphorus is by no means equal to that brought through lime. Thus, we might believe lime, or calcium, directly essential for protein production by lespedeza, if it is true that increasing protein harvest goes directly with increasing calcium harvest, Figs. 5 and 7, without the phosphorus harvest showing the corresponding increase, Fig. 3. In case of the sweet clover, the increments of lime as offered in terms of amounts or of higher degrees of saturation meant increased harvests of calcium, of phosphorus, and of protein. Such suggests a combined activity by calcium and phosphorus in producing protein. As a protein producer on this soil, the sweet clover is far superior to lespedeza. Both, however, respond with increased protein production from liming and seem more effective in this respect because the calcium enters the plant along with and in far larger amounts than does the phosphorus.

Concentration of Nutrients in Crop

As for the concentrations of the various nutrients within the crops, the variation by those given both lime and phosphate seemed insignificant as percentage figures. The average phosphorus contents of four crops in these cases ranged from but 0.134 to 0.139%. The calcium in these cases figured similarly varied from 1.46 to 1.49%. When limitations in growth occurred because of limited applications of one or the other treatments then variations in concentrations were greater for these elements. Fluctuations in protein are naturally greater, reflecting differences in plant activity in production of nitrogenous products through nitrogen fixation by legumes, rather than absorption only from the soil. Fluctuations in concentrations fail to reveal the larger significance of treatments in soil fertility where an inventory of total fertility harvest must be considered.

The behavior of non-essential elements lends importance to calcium activity, since analyses of these crops show reduction of silicon concentration by liming, or by increased calcium consumption by the crop. Liming alone reduced the silicon concentration but phosphate alone increased it. Such effect was about the same for legumes and nonlegumes, so that limed plants had but from two-thirds to one-half as high a concentration of iron and aluminum while lime and phosphate suggested the opposite effect.

Such results point to a role by calcium of keeping non-essential elements out of the crop as well as its aid in moving essentials into it.

Summary

A study of the forage production by redtop, bluegrass, Korean lespedeza, and sweet clover points to an importance of calcium in the utilization of phosphorus by these crops. A larger share of the applied phosphorus was recovered in the crop as the degree of saturation of the soil by calcium was greater. This greater recovery resulted more because of larger crop yields than because of higher concentration of phosphorus in the forage.

Increasing the applied phosphorus also served to increase the calcium taken from a constant soil supply and suggested a reciprocal effect by phosphorus on calcium.

When the saturation of the soil with calcium increases the phosphorus taken, it removes the so-called "phosphorus availability" from the realm of its increase by soil acidity. It makes the plant's use of calcium and phosphorus a more complex process by the plant rather than a simple solubility situation in the soil.

The saturation of one-fourth of the soil by calcium increased the phosphorus harvest by 36%, while the corresponding increase was only 10% when this same total calcium supply served to increase the amount of lime in the entire soil by only one-fourth of that necessary for saturation. The concentration of the calcium into one-fourth of the soil more than trebled the effectiveness of calcium as a means of moving native soil phosphorus into the crop. When phosphorus was applied with limestone this same effect by lime was evident. Thus liming becomes a matter of feeding calcium to the plant effectively and of aiding it in getting its phosphorus, rather than one of modifying the hydrogen-ion concentration. The question presents itself whether on some soils in the South where little lime is considered necessary because these soils are not so sour, the lime may not well be used for its effectiveness not only in supplying calcium but also in making the phosphates — and probably other fertilizer items — recoverable as crop yield increase.

The degree of saturation of a limited soil area is more significant in controlling the efficiency of the calcium recovery by the crop than is the total calcium application throughout the soil. This calcium recovery is also influenced by increased phosphorus in the soil.

The total harvest of protein also increased when increased calcium and phosphorus harvests occurred. Increases in calcium utilization by the grasses as redtop, for example, served to lower the silicon concentration, and also that of aluminum and iron. Thus, in this study, calcium played seemingly significant roles in giving increased phosphorus utilization by the crop, whether legume or nonlegume were considered.

CHAPTER 11

Carbohydrate-Protein Ratio of Peas in Relation to Fertilization with Potassium, Calcium & Nitrogen

WHILE THE INCREASED production of food is the major objective of agronomic research, such an objective does not exclude concern about the role of food in better health. In simpler terms, better health depends on better nutrition, namely, better edibles in service for growth, work, and maintenance of the vital processes. Only plants have the ability to synthesize from water and carbon dioxide the carbohydrates — stored in the plants and also transformed into fats — as the major source of food for energy. Only the plant can combine, through various reactions aided by soil fertility, the carbohydrates with nitrogen, phosphorus, and sulfur to give the amino acids. These are almost two dozen in number and are the structural units of proteins. These are the big group of nitrogenous substances essential for reproduction, growth, and repair of the protoplasmic tissues of the higher forms of life.

The carbohydrate-protein ratio has long been a factor in animal and human nutrition. Emphasis has been given to the shortage of protein and the problem of supplementing the readily procurable carbohydrates with it. Little attention, however, has been given to the fact that, in the synthetic processes of plants, the carbohydrates seem to be the common and major product on most any soils. The proteins, however, are the output by the plants growing on only the more fertile soils.

We have appreciated legumes for their high nitrogen contents. But they have not been so commonly recognized as highly dependent on the fertility for help in protein synthesis. We have therefore not looked at the problem of balancing the carbohydrates with proteins in the rations as one of managing the plant's physiology to help it grow more of the latter in place of the excessive amounts of the former by balancing the fertility to bring about that result within each of the different food and feed plants.

When calcium is commonly associated with nitrogen in provoking protein production by plants, and when potassium is associated with carbohydrates, then the balance between the amounts and activities of these three elements within the soil may be the control of the carbohydrate-protein ratio of the crop. In support of the foregoing hypothesis, the following study of the common garden peas and their contents of carbohydrates and proteins in relation to varied amounts of exchangeable potassium, calcium, and nitrogen in the soil was undertaken.

Historical

Numerous studies with peas using one or two of the three elements, potassium, calcium, and nitrogen, have been reported. Miss Day used calcium and nitrogen to show the increased crop with nitrogen, and then such increase with calcium up to a limit. Sayre used nitrogen, while Bowers and Mahoney used nitrogen, phosphorus, and potassium. Street emphasized the need by peas for both calcium and potassium.

Other studies, in addition to these, emphasize the increased yields of peas from the increases of these elements in the soil. But just how they function in the plant and what the specific role of each element is in the various physiological processes, more specifically in protein synthesis, remains to be elucidated.

Potassium has been considered essential for the formation, translocation, and transformation of carbohydrates. But how it serves is unknown. Miller considers its service to be that of transforming mono- and disaccharides into polysaccharides. The work of Street bears a similar suggestion. Hibbard and Grigsby do not believe potassium essential in photosynthesis and suggest calcium as help in changing sugar to starch and potassium in changing starch to sugar. Protein production by the plant does not emphasize a single element so much, nor is it dependent on light. Instead it is a biosynthetic performance. It demands a list of about 10 elements from the soil, among which nitrogen and calcium are commonly the most prominent. While nitrogen, phosphorus, and sulfur enter into the construction of the protein, calcium has long been recognized as required in the soil for protein synthesis by legumes. Its functions in the plant again are not wholly known though an acid neutralizing service has been suggested. In the soil, True credited it with the mobilization of other elements into the plant roots. There it may bring into the plants many other elements present only as traces and thus render more far-reaching services than now appreciated.

In the ecological array of plants, the carbon-nitrogen ratio of the forage becomes wider as one goes from the less to more highly weathered soils. Since calcium for plant service weathers out of the soil relatively more rapid than potassium, the changing calcium-potassium ratio in the soil suggests its parallelism with and cause of this change in the carbon-nitrogen ratio in the plants. There is historic basis, then, for the hypothesis that possibly the carbohydrate-protein ratio, or the food qualities of the common garden pea may be dependent on the ratios between the supplies of exchangeable potassium, calcium, and nitrogen in the soil.

Procedure and Methods

Cultural Methods

Peas of the Little Marvel variety were grown in triplicate jars with 24 different levels of fertility, involving constant amounts per jar of exchangeable phosphorus (180 m.e.), magnesium (40 m.e.), and sulfur (40 m.e.); but varied amounts of nitrogen (90 and 180 m.e.), calcium (30, 90 and 180 m.e.), and potassium (30, 90, 180, and 270 m.e.). These variables were arranged to provide triplicate jars with every possible combination. This made variable amounts of clay necessary, which were mixed with vermiculite to give suitable structure for good growth on dilution with this to the 2-gallon volume. The clay used was Putnam silt loam subsoil on to which the nutrients were absorbed from solution according to methods previously reported. The clay was mixed with the vermiculite by means of a mechanical stirrer.

The plants were grown for 60 days when harvesting of pods began. This extended through 28 days. At the end of that time, the entire plants (3 per jar) were harvested and weighed as both green and dry weights. The pods as a whole and the seeds separated were weighed in fresh from as harvested and in the final dry weight. They were used as dry seeds for the chemical determinations of the carbohydrates and the proteins.

Chemical Methods

The dried materials were ground and nitrogen determinations made according to approved methods for calculation of proteins. The carbohydrates were determined according to the official methods of the A. O. A. C., except for the use of half the specified amount of sample.

Yields of Peas

Total Vine Weights

Perhaps the major facts about the plant growth and crop yields were the response of this legume crop to nitrogen, and its emphasis on the balance between the three variables, potassium, calcium, and nitrogen, that is, these in the exchangeable form adsorbed on the clay as the only source of such nourishment. The data are assembled in Table 1. Increasing the nitrogen offered in the soil, increased the total vegetative growth in all cases except two, namely, the two highest potassium allotments in combination with the highest of calcium. There is the suggestion that this garden legume is so slow in starting its nitrogen fixation activities that the soils growing this legume successfully must provide nitrogen generously.

Calcium served in making the higher amounts of nitrogen more effective. Potassium served in making the lower amounts of nitrogen more effective as judged by the total weights of the green plants, except where the largest amounts of calcium were offered. In terms of total yields of

Table 1

Yields of Pea Vines Grown Under Various Levels of Exchangeable Potassium, Calcium and Nitrogen (Green and Dry Weights as Grams Per Treatment)

Nitrogen 90 m.e.				Nitrogen 180 m.e.			
Potassium m.e.	Calcium (m.e.)			Potassium m.e.	Calcium (m.e.)		
	30	90	180		30	90	180
	117.0*	126.8	139.0		154.4	136.2	146.0
30	24.2†	24.4	29.0	30	31.0	26.2	33.0
	150.4	132.8	127.2		162.8	178.0	152.2
90	31.4	26.2	28.0	90	33.6	26.0	33.0
	169.8	207.4	169.6		177.2	201.8	160.8
180	27.0	25.2	29.0	180	28.8	34.6	29.2
	168.2	123.2	125.8		197.4	150.0	105.6
270	23.8	19.2	20.6	270	30.0	18.8	13.0

*Green weights.

†Dry weights.

vegetative growth, the results show that (1) the growth was more closely related to the soil's supply of nitrogen, (2) it was more uniform as the nitrogen was higher in spite in variable levels of calcium, and potassium, (3) the medium application of calcium was the most effective with a medium of potassium and a high of nitrogen, (4) the plant growth response to increasing potassium allotments was most marked when both calcium and nitrogen were at high levels in the soil, and (5) the best production was obtained at high levels of nitrogen but medium levels of calcium and potassium, suggesting this as the most desirable balance of the nutrients for much vegetative output of vines and pods.

Yields of Pods (Hull and Seeds)

In terms of the production of pods as given in Table 2, the nitrogen was again outstanding, but not without relation to the levels of calcium and potassium. At low potassium levels, when the nitrogen was either low or high, then the higher calcium level, or liming, reduced the yields of pods.

Table 2

Yields of Peas (Pods and Seeds) Grown Under Various Levels of Exchangeable Potassium, Calcium and Nitrogen (Green and Dry Weights as Grams per Treatment)

Nitrogen 90 m.e.				Nitrogen 180 m.e.			
Potassium m.e.	Calcium (m.e.)			Potassium m.e.	Calcium (m.e.)		
	30	90	180		30	90	180
	125.9*	106.7	110.2		163.9	118.8	122.5
30	23.5†	20.0	20.2	30	30.4	22.3	22.8
	150.5	105.1	95.3		174.8	144.1	119.3
90	28.1	19.6	17.4	90	32.5	27.0	22.8
	140.2	171.1	112.7		126.2	151.8	117.2
180	25.6	32.0	21.0	180	23.0	28.4	22.6
	116.7	122.0	108.3		170.3	105.9	75.0
270	21.8	21.2	20.4	270	31.4	18.4	13.0

*Green weights.

†Dry weights.

But this disturbing effect of extra calcium was not so serious at higher levels of potassium provided the nitrogen level in the soil was also higher, which meant higher yields of pods.

Yields of Seeds

The yields of seeds followed the trends for the yields of pods, as shown in Table 3. Increasing the potassium had a positive effect on seed yield in combination with the medium level of calcium. It had a negative effect under high level of calcium, especially when the nitrogen was high. Heavy application of potassium was not so disturbing but gave high yields when the calcium was low and the nitrogen high.

Schedule of Production

Since daily harvests of the pods were taken, weighed, and recorded, it was possible to interpret the schedule of production according to the soil treatments.

Table 3

Yields of Pea Seeds Grown Under Various Levels of Exchangeable Potassium, Calcium and Nitrogen (Green and Dry Weights as Grams per Treatment)

Nitrogen 90 m.e.				Nitrogen 180 m.e.			
Potassium m.e.	Calcium (m.e.)			Potassium m.e.	Calcium (m.e.)		
	30	90	180		30	90	180
	59.6*	49.5	30.8		79.0	56.7	61.8
30	12.6†	11.2	10.8	30	17.0	12.6	13.0
	72.1	50.2	45.1		87.3	70.2	58.0
90	15.7	11.0	9.6	90	18.3	15.0	12.6
	64.4	83.8	57.1		60.6	75.9	57.8
180	12.8	18.4	12.6	180	13.0	16.6	12.6
	57.4	56.1	53.5		83.7	52.9	36.9
270	13.2	12.4	11.8	270	18.2	11.0	8.0

*Green weights.

†Dry weights.

In general the matter of schedule and soil treatments may be summarized by saying that (1) the production of peas was increased as the nitrogen supply was increased; (2) the period of formation of peas was longer at the higher nitrogen levels; (3) when the calcium was increased there was a tendency to shorten the period of pea formation; (4) either low or high potassium combined with high calcium shortened the period of pea formation; (5) extra potassium extended the schedule when the calcium was low; and (6) different levels of potassium were more effective at low or at high nitrogen levels. These summarizations are the same for the weights of seeds, hence the data of harvested pods serve to interpret the data for shelled peas.

Total Plant Weight

The total dry weights produced (plants, hulls, and seeds) per soil treatment serve to show the effects of the latter as presented in Table 4. From the data we may conclude that (1) the total production increased as the nitrogen supply was increased; (2) this positive effect of nitrogen was depressed at high levels of potassium; (3) the best nutritive balance was obtained at medium levels of both calcium and potassium and high levels of nitrogen; (4) the least productive treatment was that with high levels of all three varied nutrients; and (5) the effectiveness of increased potassium toward increasing the productivity of peas was clearly evident provided the nitrogen supply was high and the calcium supply was medium.

Table 4

Total Dry Matter of Peas (Vines, Hulls and Seeds) Grown Under Various Levels of Exchangeable Potassium, Calcium and Nitrogen (Grams per Treatment)

Nitrogen 90 m.e.				Nitrogen 180 m.e.			
Potassium m.e.	Calcium (m.e.)			Potassium m.e.	Calcium (m.e.)		
	30	90	180		30	90	180
30	47.7	44.4	49.2	30	61.4	48.5	55.8
90	59.5	45.8	45.4	90	66.1	63.0	55.8
180	52.6	67.2	50.0	180	51.8	63.0	51.8
270	45.6	40.4	41.0	270	61.4	37.2	26.0

The results show that potassium has very important effects on the formation of dry matter as shown by the totals of dry weights. Potassium was not correspondingly important in determining the weights of seeds, containing the proteins. Here the relation of potassium to carbohydrate production, or to bulk, stands out. It is also evident from this study that calcium and potassium have complementary effects. The favorable effects of the increasing levels of potassium were shown only when the calcium levels were also increased. Graphically portrayed, the level for each single nutrient in combination with the several variations in the other two, is shown for its total dry matter production in Fig. 1. The increments of nitrogen were increasing the total yields, those of calcium were decreasing them, while the potassium showed both increase and decrease over the range of amounts used.

All of these demonstrated the sensitivity of a crop to the supplies of nutrients when these are in the exchangeable form, or adsorbed on the clay. It suggests that if the adsorbed supplies are limited by limited amounts of clay for root zone contact the effects of variable ratios of these three

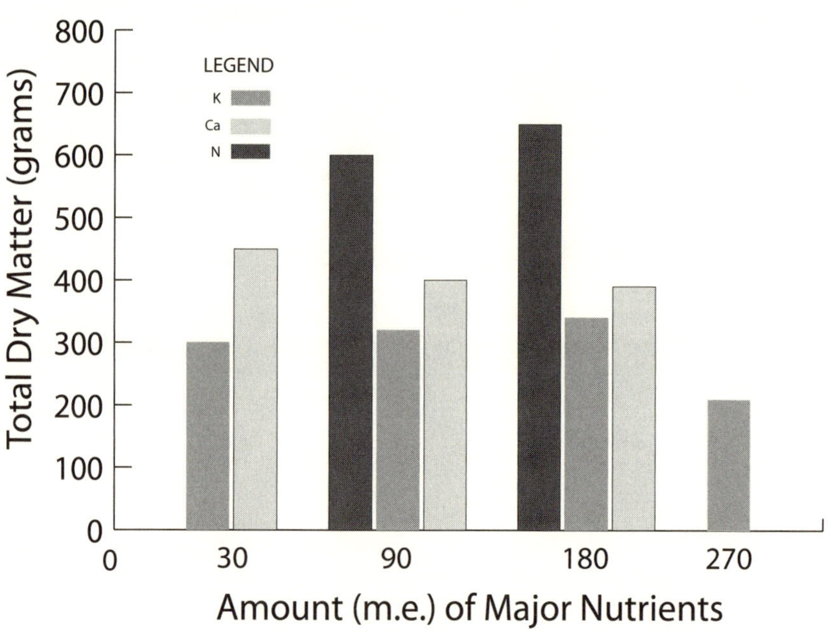

Fig. 1. — Yields as dry matter for the different levels of each separate nutrient element in combination with the several variations in the other two.

nutrient elements, nitrogen, calcium, and potassium are reflected pronouncedly in the total crop growth and its fruiting response.

Chemical Composition

Proteins

The dried pea seeds were analyzed for their total nitrogen in relation to the soil treatments. The results are given in Table 5. While nitrogen and calcium emphasized their influences on the protein concentration one cannot minimize the significance of potassium for the plant's output of this food constituent. Considering the totals of protein produced, naturally this followed the total pea yield more than any other factor. The amount of protein followed the amount of nitrogen in the soil. The influences of calcium and potassium on this were complementary, since neither one increased the total of proteins unless the other was also supplied in larger amount.

Table 5

Protein in Pea Seeds Grown Under Various Levels of Exchangeable Potassium, Calcium, and Nitrogen (as Percent of Dry Weight and as Grams per Treatment)

Nitrogen 90 m.e.				Nitrogen 180 m.e.			
Potassium m.e.	Calcium (m.e.)			Potassium m.e.	Calcium (m.e.)		
	30	90	180		30	90	180
30	24.06*	24.69	25.94	30	26.00	26.31	27.12
	3.03†	2.76	2.80		4.42	3.32	3.59
90	24.69	26.00	24.87	90	25.50	27.12	27.19
	3.88	2.86	2.38		4.67	4.07	3.42
180	24.94	25.94	25.06	180	25.75	27.25	28.00
	3.44	4.77	3.16		3.35	4.52	3.53
270	24.56	24.81	25.87	270	24.81	27.25	26.63
	3.24	3.08	3.05		4.51	3.00	2.12

**Percent of dry weight of pea seeds.*

† Grams protein per treatment.

Carbohydrates

The total sugars, starches, and hemi-celluloses of the pea seeds were determined for each soil treatment. The degree of maturity of the peas, when harvested, was an empirical matter, hence the ratios of starch to sugar were not determined. Total carbohydrates were determined with the results presented in Table 6.

In some cases the concentration of total carbohydrates was increased by increasing the nitrogen; in others the effects in this respect by calcium were more defined. Then with potassium the influence on the carbohydrates was not wthout the relation to the levels of nitrogen and calcium. It was evident that the nitrogen was a secondary element in the formation of carbohydrates. These were more directly influenced by the content of potassium and calcium in the soil. Here again in the carbohydrate production as in the total growth, the calcium and the potassium demonstrated their complementary effects. The influence of the calcium was clearly shown at low levels of potassium, and the influence of potassium was

Table 6

Carbohydrates in Pea Seeds Grown Under Various Levels of Exchangeable Potassium, Calcium, and Nitrogen (as Percent of Dry Weight and as Grams per Treatment)

Nitrogen 90 m.e.				Nitrogen 180 m.e.			
Potassium m.e.	Calcium (m.e.)			Potassium m.e.	Calcium (m.e.)		
	30	90	180		30	90	180
	36.90*	46.20	47.20		41.18	46.70	48.32
30	4.65†	5.23	5.10	30	7.00	5.96	6.28
	42.72	46.35	46.59		37.25	44.38	46.37
90	6.70	5.10	4.47	90	6.82	6.66	5.84
	40.81	48.57	46.81		41.47	48.58	45.93
180	5.63	8.94	5.90	180	5.39	8.06	5.79
	44.90	49.67	46.98		46.20	47.47	46.80
270	5.93	6.16	5.54	270	8.40	5.22	3.74

**Percent of dry weight.*
†Grams per treatment.

Table 7

Carbohydrate-Protein Ratios of Pea Seeds Grown Under Various Levels of Exchangeable Potassium, Calcium and Nitrogen

Nitrogen 90 m.e.				Nitrogen 180 m.e.			
Potassium m.e.	Calcium (m.e.)			Potassium m.e.	Calcium (m.e.)		
	30	90	180		30	90	180
30	1.53	1.89	1.82	30	1.58	1.79	1.74
90	1.73	1.78	1.87	90	1.46	1.63	1.71
180	1.64	1.87	1.87	180	1.61	1.78	1.64
270	1.83	2.00	1.82	270	1.86	1.74	1.76

clearly shown at low levels of calcium. Hence the most uniform production of carbohydrate resulted under high levels of both calcium and potassium.

Carbohydrate-Protein Ratio of Pea Seeds

Production of protein by the peas in its ratio to their production of carbohydrate is significant in this study as a demonstration of what possibility there is in making this ratio narrower through soil treatments. These ratios for different soil treatments were calculated and are presented in Table 7.

Increasing the nitrogen gave a narrower ratio, in general, and put this nutrient element up as the major control of the pea seeds. The effect by calcium on the ratio depended on the nitrogen. For potassium, the ratio was wider, in general, as the potassium in the soil was higher. However, this effect by potassium was less significant as the levels of calcium and nitrogen were higher. It is indicated that nitrogen and calcium modified this ratio through their major influence on the protein. While potassium modified the ratio somewhat by its influence on the protein, its effects were more pronounced through the carbohydrates.

Summary

Pea plants grown for seed production under variable amounts of the soil's exchangeable potassium, calcium, and nitrogen demonstrated the influences by these soil treatments not only on the vegetative growth, but also on the carbohydrate-protein contents of the pea seeds. It was clearly evident that the balance of these three nutrients was the important factor in control. The effects of increments of any one of these nutrients was dependent on the amounts present of the others. These facts held for the production of the vegetative bulk, for the total seed produced, and for the carbohydrate-protein ratio of those seeds.

CHAPTER 12

Calcium & Phosphorus as They Influence Manganese in Forage Crops

PLANT PHYSIOLOGY HAS regularly recognized the significance of the degree of acidity of the soil, but has not yet clearly interpreted its significance in plant nutrition. Emphasis on lime additions to the soil for its modification of the degree of soil acidity has overshadowed attention to calcium as a nutrient, and/or as it serves in bringing other nutrients into the plant. Because the degree of hydrogen-ion saturation of the colloidal fraction of the soil is mainly the reciprocal of the loss therefrom of calcium ions, we have been inclined, in cases of crop failure, to attribute causal significance to the wrong one of these reciprocal factors. Studies of the significance of calcium in nitrogen fixation and plant nutrition were undertaken to determine more accurately the role of calcium in crop growth. The separation of its role in changing soil reaction from that in serving as plant nutrient, and in mobilizing other nutrients into the crop, served as a challenge. Its relation in this last respect to manganese in particular, one of the micro-nutrient elements, was chosen for study.

The importance of manganese in the nutrition of plants and of animals has been established well enough to warrant attention to it in soil fertility. Its disturbed delivery to plants by soils near the neutral or alkaline reactions has been recognized. Such irregularities put the common practice of liming a soil for the sake of neutrality into the danger zone of general manganese shortage for plants in our extensive agricultural soils. Since calcium as a nutrient item, particularly for nitrogen fixation by legumes, has been separated from its effects in modifying soil acidity, the following study attempted to determine manganese movement into the crop when calcium modified the soil reaction as contrasted to that when calcium served as a nutrient without changing the reaction of the entire soil body in root contact. Phosphates were tested similarly as to their influence on the manganese.

Plan of Study

The soil used was the surface layer of a well weathered prairie soil of the Kansan glaciation, one of the planosols,[1] known as the Putnam silt loam. It is of acid reaction, pH 5.5, relatively low in organic matter and phosphorus, and developed to the point of having a marked clay concentration in the upper subsoil. Its exchange capacity is approximately 20 m.e. per 100 gms. of soil. This is usually saturated to about 50 percent with hydrogen. The more common legumes will produce only poor yields on this soil.

Amounts of treatments applied. Pot cultures were grown in quintuplicates of two legumes, sweet clover (*Melilotus alba*) and lespedeza (*Lespedeza stipulacea*), and of two non-legumes, bluegrass (*Poa pratensis*) and redtop (*Agrostis alba*). The soil treatments consisted of separate additions of calcium carbonate, of calcium phosphate and of sodium phosphate, and of joint additions of the calcium carbonate and calcium phosphate. The amounts of calcium carbonate applied to the soil were such as (a) would exchange slightly more than one-half of the replaceable hydrogen in one-fourth of the soil; and (b) would more than replace the total exchangeable hydrogen in this smaller soil portion. The phosphates were used in amounts that represented (a) liberal applications in practice, and (b) twice this amount.

Placement of treatments. The applications of calcium carbonate were made by distributing it (a) throughout all the soil in the pot, and (b) into the surface one-fourth of the soil. The calcium phosphate was applied similarly. The sodium phosphate was put into only the surface or one-fourth. The joint applications of calcium carbonate and calcium phosphate were used in the four possible combinations as amounts, and were placed into the surface or one-fourth of the soil only.

These placements of the calcium carbonate provided, in the first place, two different, but low, degrees of calcium saturation or of partial neutralization of the entire soil volume available to the plant. In the second place, they provided soils in which the surface areas alone had two different

[1] *According to* Soils and Men, *U.S.D.A. Yearbook of Agriculture, 1938.*

degrees of calcium saturation, namely one with more than 75 percent and one in excess of complete calcium saturation, while three-fourths of the soil volume remained untreated. For simplicity's sake, these distributions of the additions to the soil may be spoken of by numbers as follows:

Treatment No. 1 — Small amount throughout the entire soil volume.
Treatment No. 2 — Large amount throughout the entire soil volume.
Treatment No. 3 — Small amount through one-fourth or surface of the soil.
Treatment No. 4 — Large amount through one-fourth or surface of the soil.

The phosphate additions represented different and higher degrees of saturation by the phosphate in the surface portion of the soil, and two different, but much lower, degrees of saturation when applied throughout the entire soil body. The combinations of calcium carbonate and calcium phosphate were used in the surface portion only, and represented the higher degrees of surface soil saturation by each of them. No manganese was applied.

Analytical methods. The crops were harvested at intervals of significant top growth so as to simulate grazing. Weight records of the harvests were taken. The crops were submitted to analysis by the standard gravimetric methods for the calcium and phosphorus and to the Lundegardh spectrographic method for manganese, and account was taken of the concentrations and totals in the crops.

Results

Results from calcium carbonate. The most noticeable result was the influence of the increasing amounts of calcium carbonate throughout the entire mass of soil (Treatments Nos. 1 and 2), as they reduced the percentage and the total amount of manganese in the crop; and the influence of the increasing degree of saturation of the surface soil layer by calcium (Treatments Nos. 3 and 4), as it had the very reverse effect. The percentages of the manganese in the crop are shown in Fig. 1, and the totals of it in Fig. 2. There is such a pronounced similarity between these two figures as to testify that the manganese responds as a decided nutritional disturbance in the plant metabolism rather than as a variation in manganese amounts simply according to variable plant mass. When the manganese behaviors, as given in Fig. 1 and 2, are related to the total calcium taken by the crop, as given in Fig. 3, then this fact becomes more evident.

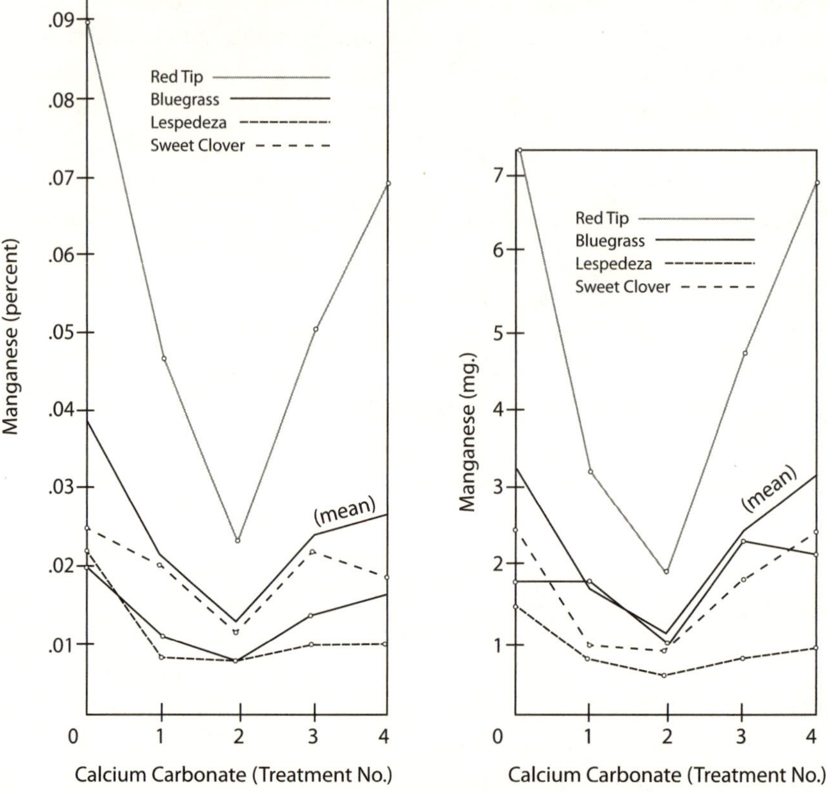

Fig. 1. (left) — Percentages of manganese in the different crops as influenced by two different amounts of calcium carbonate applied throughout the soil (Treatments Nos. 1 and 2), and into the surface soil only (Treatments Nos. 3 and 4).

Fig. 2. (right) — Total manganese in the different crops as influenced by two different amounts of calcium carbonate applied throughout the soil (Treatments Nos. 1 and 2), and into the surface soil only (Treatments Nos. 3 and 4).

In Treatments Nos. 1 and 2 by limestone, which were lessening the soil acidity to greater degrees and were giving large calcium intake by the crop, there were decided decreases in the manganese concentrations of and intake by the crop. Yet in Treatments Nos. 3 and 4, which saturated the upper portion of the soil more completely so as to change the soil reaction much more in that limited soil volume and to deliver still greater amounts of calcium into the crop, there was the reverse relation between the manganese and the calcium, and gave increasing concentrations and total amounts of manganese taken by the crop.

This suggests clearly that an increase in the amounts of calcium carbonate throughout the soil, so as to shift its reaction toward neutrality, served to decrease the movement of manganese into the crop. Increasing the delivery of calcium to the plant by means of the higher saturation in the limited surface soil zone brought increasing delivery of manganese presumably from the remaining three-fourths of the soil given no calcium carbonate. As an agent that removed soil acidity, the calcium carbonate lessened the amount of manganese going from the soil to the crop. As a fertilizer that supplied calcium to the crop, it enabled the plants to take greater amounts of manganese from the soil below the zone of calcium fertilization.

Possibly an increased or modified microbiological action as a competitor with the plant for the manganese, may be the explanation for the reduction in manganese within the crop when calcium carbonate was distributed throughout the soil. This is suggested by the fact that the smaller application (Treatment No. 1), was relatively more disturbing than the larger one (Treatment No. 2), as is shown by the graph as the mean for all four crops either as percentage or as total manganese in Fig. 1 and 2. These studies did not aim to separate the microbial from the simple chemical effects.

Such facts bring to attention the need to consider whether our use of calcium carbonate, or limestone, for the purpose of correcting soil acidity is the most effective service by this soil treatment that is now undergoing wider adoption as a regular farm practice. They suggest that calcium must be put into the fertilizer category, and that excessive applications prompted by low cost or unbridled enthusiasm may bring disappointments.

Results from phosphates. The influence of the single phosphate soil treatments on the manganese intake into the crop was wholly positive, in that as more phosphate was given, either throughout the entire soil mass or into the surface soil only, there was increasing manganese in the harvest. These data are brought together in Fig. 4, which gives the totals for manganese and for phosphorus taken by the plants per pot.

Increasing the sodium phosphate in the upper soil portion increased the manganese taken. Putting the calcium phosphate into the top soil (Treatments Nos. 3 and 4), was more effective in bringing both manganese and phosphorus into the harvest. This is shown by the highest points on the graphs at the right side where the double dosage of calcium phosphate in the surface soil is indicated. The positive relation between the total manganese and the total phosphorus in the crop is shown more clearly by the close parallelism between the graphs representing the respective means

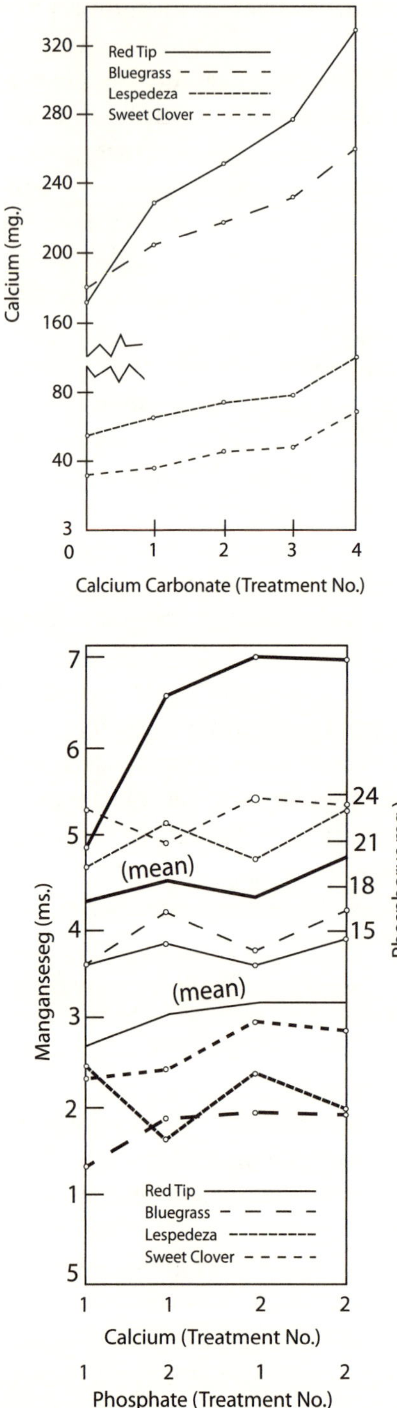

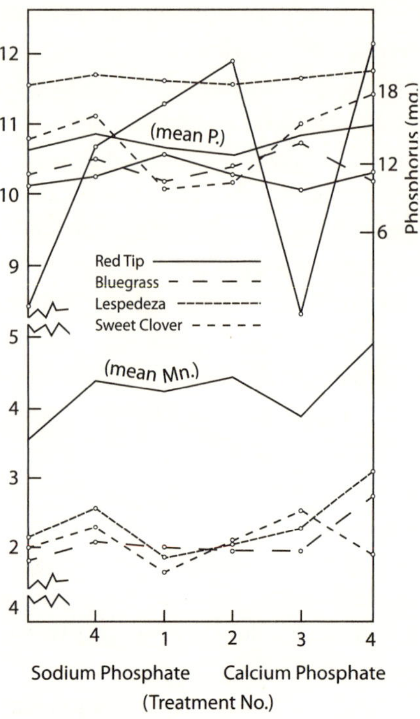

Explanation of figures 3–5

Fig. 3. (top left) — Total calcium in the different crops as influenced by two different amounts of calcium carbonate applied throughout the soil (Treatments Nos. 1 and 2), and into the surface soil only (Treatments Nos. 3 and 4).

Fig. 4. (top right) — Total manganese and phosphorus in the different crops as influenced by different amounts of phosphates applied throughout the soil (Treatments Nos. 1 and 2), and into the surface soil only (Treatments Nos. 3 and 4).

Fig. 5. (left) — Total manganese and phosphorus in the different crops as influenced by two different amounts of calcium carbonate and calcium phosphate used in their possible combinations in the surface soil. (Lighter lines = P. Heavier lines = Ca.)

for all crops. It points to an increase of manganese that was parallel with increased crop yield.

Results from calcium carbonate combined with calcium phosphate. When the joint applications of calcium carbonate and calcium phosphate are observed for their influence on the manganese harvested in the crop, this is slightly greater per unit of phosphorus taken by the crop than was the case where phosphates were applied singly. This is shown in Figure 5, more particularly in the graph for the mean of all crops combined. The offering of more of each of these soil treatments so as to grow heavier crops increased the manganese taken from the soil. This suggests that the use of the manganese was correlated with the better or increasing growth through calcium and phosphate treatments.

Seemingly, then, the manganese was not a limiting factor in this Putnam silt loam. Its consumption by the plant from this soil was hindered, in some measure, by the phosphorus shortage, but more by the calcium shortage. It was when both calcium and phosphorus were applied that the largest crops were grown, and that the larger amounts of manganese were taken from the soil.

Manganese contents of the different crops. The contents in manganese of the different crops are worthy of note. They are in agreement with analyses by others, particularly the high value for redtop, and suggest that manganese is another help in fitting crops into the general ecological array of plants according to composition. The variations in concentrations and totals in the different crops are assembled in Table 1.

In terms of concentrations of manganese within the crop, redtop is much the highest, reaching 0.14 percent on soil given calcium phosphate only, and .071 percent where this treatment was combined with calcium carbonate. It is followed in order by sweet clover with .026 percent as maximum. Then comes bluegrass with .024 percent as its highest and lespedeza with .018 percent as its uppermost concentration of manganese in these trials. When the calcium carbonate was put into the surface soil to give more calcium to the crop, then the concentration of manganese was higher in the lespedeza than in the bluegrass.

When attention is directed toward the total manganeses in the crop, then the redtop is the highest, provided it was given calcium phosphate either singly or combined with calcium carbonate. Here in the case of a crop commonly considered suitable for lime-deficient soils and commonly not given soil treatment, calcium and phosphorus play an influential role in helping it to get manganese from the soil. Sweet clover follows in

Table 1

Concentrations and Totals of Manganese in the Different Crops.
(Ranges for Different Soil Treatments)

Crops	Concentrations, percent			Totals, mg.		
	Soil treatments					
	Calcium carbonate	Phosphates	Calcium carbonate plus phosphate	Calcium carbonate	Phosphates	Calcium carbonate plus phosphate
Redtop	.023–.064	0.10–0.14	.053–.071	1.9–7.0	0.8–1.3	4.9–7.0
Bluegrass	.008–.01	0.020–0.024	.013–.018	0.6–1.0	1.8–2.8	1.3–1.9
Lespedeza	.008–.017	0.014–0.018	.011–.016	0.9–2.5	1.9–2.6	1.7–2.4
Sweet clover	.012–.022	0.020–0.026	.014–.019	1.0–2.3	1.7–3.2	2.3–3.0
Range of variation in concentration	0.56	.016	.042			

order as it did for manganese concentrations, particularly for the soil treatments of calcium carbonate and calcium phosphate used jointly. Bluegrass took the largest amounts for this crop when it was given phosphate, while lespedeza behaved similarly.

Summary

The concentrations of manganese within the crop and the totals taken by it from the soil point to a dual role by calcium carbonate in relation to this micro-nutrient in plant nutrition. When calcium carbonate, or limestone, was mixed throughout the soil so as to modify its reaction, then the concentration and total of manganese in the crops were decreased as the application to the soil and the consumption of calcium by the crop increased. When, however, the application was put into the surface soil to increase crop consumption of the calcium even more, then the reverse effect on manganese was manifested, so that the concentration and the total of manganese were increased.

When phosphate was applied to provide increasing concentrations, whether in the entire or in the limited soil volume, then the additional phosphorus for the crop gave increasing manganese harvest, roughly parallel with increased crop growth.

Combinations of lime and phosphate in the limited soil areas aided the crop in taking more manganese.

These studies emphasize the need to consider the beneficial nutritional role of calcium within the plant, on soils such as the type used, in making manganese available for the plant as reflected in the increased concentrations. Then there is need to consider the possible detrimental role of calcium carbonate as it modifies the reaction of the soil or other soil conditions and reduces the manganese taken by the crop possibly to the danger point of manganese deficiency.

CHAPTER 13

Soil Phosphorus — Activated Via Soil Organic Matter

WHEN NATURE BUILT up the fertility of our soils, she followed two major practices. First, to soils with reserve rock-minerals she added surface deposits of similar material by means of wind and water. Second, she also returned, in place, the crop residues grown there. She used only natural, organic and mineral-rock fertilizers.

In our management of soils for crop production we have associated the inorganic nutrient elements calcium, magnesium, potassium, sodium, iron, aluminum, zinc, copper, cobalt, manganese and others of positive, ionic characters with the soil's colloidal clay-humus fraction of the opposite, or negative, electrical characters. But the essential nutrient elements nitrogen, sulfur, phosphorus, boron, chlorine, iodine, molybdenum, and others of negative, ionic characters have been more empirically the organic matter of the soil.

Shall we not envision the anions, or negative, elements corrected with decay stages of organic matter, when its wider carbon-nutrient ratios serve as a source of energy, by the carbon — first to the fungi and then to the bacteria in the soil? May the negative elements not serve simultaneously in plant nutrition as chelated and larger molecular complexes of microbial origin?

It is significant to note that calcium, a cation, or positive element, is the most abundant "ash" element in warm-blooded bodies and, likewise, among those adsorbed and held by the negative, silicate clay, in form available to plants. The second most abundant ash element is phosphorus. It is a negative element, or anion, hence is not similarly held on the clay. Instead, it is associated — along with the other anions, like nitrogen, sulfur, boron, etc. — with the active soil organic matter.

According to recent research, phosphorus is connected with photosynthesis by chlorophyl, where the first step in forming glucose consists of a three-carbon chain with phosphorus at one end. This connects with a similar chain reversed to unite the carbons into a six-carbon chain by dropping out the two phosphorus elements. As another case of phosphorus in energy-source materials, or organic matter, this element is active in the cycle of reactions for the oxidation of glucose within the cell for its energy source. Phosphorus is intimately connected with both the biochemical synthesis of organic matter and its oxidation within living tissue; yet we have been emphasizing its roll in the soil as if it were performing much like the inorganic cations do.

Chemistries Used Together

"Organic materials that reach the soil," said Sing Chen Chang in 1931, "generally contain considerable phosphorus, ranging from 0.1% to 0.5%. Much of the phosphorus in the materials is in organic combinations which are not readily available to plants; the release of this great quantity of phosphorus in the form of readily available phosphate depends upon the decomposition of the organic compounds by microorganisms. From the point of view of phosphorus conservation, the farm manures, green manures and composts of various organic residues should not be considered merely as a source of nitrogen. The idea that phosphorus is completely mineralized during the decomposition of organic matter and can all be absorbed by the plant is, (also), too generally accepted."

The biological transformation of the inorganic to the organic phosphorus was reported as early as 1911 in the Russian literature by one Egorov. In similar literature a report stated that "in addition to the physico-chemical absorption of the phosphorus in the soil, there is also biochemical absorption and fixation, which increase with an increase in the amount of the organic matter (starch) added and also with the length of time." Also, Doryland, our American pioneer in emphasizing the carbon-nitrogen ratio of organic matter relative to nitrogen release as ammonia, or the fixation of the latter by organic matter's decomposition, pointed out that "molds (fungi) are active in assimilation of plant-food constituents during the first stages of decomposition of crop residues when there is a high energy-nutrient ratio; the molds may later play just as important a part as do bacteria in liberating plant-food constituents when the ratio is low."

Photo shows improved growth resulting from mixing phosphate with manure before applying them to the soil. Manure and phosphate were applied separately to the soil through a depth of 3 inches (pot 9) and 6 inches (pot 12). Manure and phosphate in combination were applied to the same depths, respectively, in pots 10 and 13.

Photo courtesy of Prof. A.B. Medgley, Vermont Agri. Ext. Sta.

In our disregard of the hastened depletion of the soil organic matter in conjunction with chemical salt fertilizers (especially nitrogen), we have known of the carbon-nitrogen ratio. But we have said nothing about the soil's supply of cabon, much less its ratio to phosphorus, to sulfur and all the others, along with nitrogen, and in the anionic category within the surface horizon of the soil where the activities of fungi (more than the bacteria) consuming the crop residues of wider ratios of the carbon to all these negative nutrient elements prevail, and function in maintaining the enhanced availabilities of phosphorus in connection with ample organic matter is the real phosphorus problem of our soil management.

Need Research Study

Phosphorus transformations within organic residues occur in connection with the higher energy supplies of these residues; with their wider carbon-phosphorus (nitrogen, sulfur, other anions) ratios; and when fungi seem to be the dominating microbial flora decomposing the organic matter to mobilize the phosphorus. Therefore, don't we need more research given to fungi in agriculture than to their therapeutic potentials in antibiotics? If the benzene ring can be split, as has been recently reported; if the use of the aliphatic carbon chain to fix atmospheric nitrogen in the soils is not a vain vision, as recent studies by Brookside Research Laboratories of Ohio attest, can we see how Nature built up nitrogen in our soil by non-legumes as well as by legumes?

Within the last year, it has been reported that the cohabitation of fungi with plant roots in what has been called "mycorrhiza" was demonstrated as symbiotic nitrogen fixation, using radioactive gaseous nitrogen in the soil to find it grown into the plant tissue. From the private laboratory of S. C. Hood, Florida, the better plant growth with mycorrhiza present suggested nitrogen fixation via symbiosis, but such improvement occurred only in the less-disturbed soils, well stocked with recent organic matter, and where commercial fertilizers were not generously applied.

From Mr. Hood's reports the theory seemed inevitable that fusarium, the scarcely visible fungus, associated with gliocladium and trichoderma in mycorrhiza, most commonly was a symbiont on the plant root in soils well-stocked with organic matter, but became the wilt parasite in the vascular, or conducting tissues, of the plants growing on soils of low organic matter, and treated with chemical fertilizers.

Chang, in his laboratory studies of composted organic matter and its transformation of phosphorus from inorganic to organic forms and vice versa, observed rhizopus, pennecillum, aspergilus, trichoderma, and chetomium, the last especially abundant, as early invaders. Later there were the many actinomycetes. These various fungi of decomposition sources seem to cover the wider front in close connection with transformations of organic matter of help, even via nitrogen fixation, as well a recycling both cationic and anionic nutrient elements.

Still Ignorant of Value

All of this merely points out that our knowledge of agriculture for its nutritional sources for feeding the strata in the biotic pyramid has not yet gone far into the area of life's unknown processes. The value of recycling residues, or the value of residues returned to the soil as organic matter, is still one of extensive ignorance in the area of soil chemistry.

CHAPTER 14

Calcium-Potassium-Phosphorus Relation as a Possible Factor in Ecological Array of Plants

PLANT DISTRIBUTION AND GROWTH depend mainly on climatic factors. The soil in which plants grow is a resultant also of climatic forces. Consequently, we may well raise the question whether the degree of soil development or extent of nutrient depletion resulting from varying intensities of the climatic forces may not serve as an index to the ecological array of plant species. With the soil development and the plant distribution both determined by the same climate, then the nature of the soil and the distribution of the plants should agree. Which of the characteristics of the soil might control such an agreement, is a question that may well challenge speculative consideration.

Nitrogen, calcium, phosphorus, and potassium represent, in general, the major portion of soil fertility, or plant nutrient supply. Since the ultimate source of nitrogen is the atmosphere, then the plant nutrients of soil origin which are more commonly limiting plant growth, at least of legumes, can be considered to consist of calcium, potassium, and phosphorus. Further, since the variations in these three elements also dominate in the degree of soil development, may we not then look to the possibility that these same variations which reflect the effects of climate on the soil might also determine the ecological array? Some evidence and suggestions in support of such a possibility will be given consideration.

Composition of Vegetation Reflects Influence of the Nutrient Dominant in the Soil

It is commonly agreed that potassium functions within the plant in carbohydrate production. In general, more potassium is required as more carbohydrate is produced. Potato tubers of almost pure starch, or carbohydrate composition, contain significant amounts of potassium. Sugar beets, sugar cane, sorghums, and other saccharine crops make a decided demand on the soil for potassium. Perhaps we should discriminate whether this demand is for excessive amounts per acre annually along with similarly large amounts for other nutrients, or whether potassium is required in possibly no excessive total amounts but mainly in large amounts in comparison to other nutrients. Potassium or lye leachings from the ash of wood are known from the ancient arts. Forest soils, in general, are considered as low in phosphorus and badly leached of calcium. Though not absolutely rich in potassium, they may be relatively so.

The functions of phosphorus are commonly associated with reproduction, cell multiplication, growth, or protoplasmic activities, all of which are centered about a proteinaceous composition. Protein is characterized roughly as though it were a carbohydrate into which phosphorus and nitrogen have been combined. Phosphorus and nitrogen are thus associated with proteins while potassium dominates in carbohydrates.

Since calcium is a component of neither of the two preceding different composition groups that serve as constituents for the major portion of all plants, it might seem but fanciful imagination to give it importance as an ecological factor operating through protein production. Recent studies have given it an important role in nitrogen fixation by legumes. We may also well raise the question whether we understand fully its role in nitrogen metabolism of non legumes when we see their increased protein content by calcium treatment explained so casually as originating in the increased nitrogen supply from improved soil nitrification by liming as a soil treatment.

Studies of the composition of grasses with increased protein brought about by liming suggest for calcium a much less indirect role in bringing about this improved activity in the production of protein. Thus, calcium may be significant in the formation of this type of nitrogenous compounds because it is connected with the process of bringing into the protein its characteristic nitrogen and possibly phosphorus. Calcium may thus be a controlling factor in ecology, and its wide fluctuation either as total supply in a soil or as saturating part of the adsorption complex may give it a larger role than is readily appreciated. Thus, if calcium functions strongly in nitrogen fixation and the consequent protein production, if phosphorus is likewise instrumental in augmenting this process, and if potassium is associated in the main with carbohydrate production, might we not expect that such soil conditions as allow one or the other of these elements to dominate in the nutrient supply will give dominance to one or the other of these corresponding functions in the flora?

Calcium-Potassium-Phosphorus as Variables with the Phosphorus Low or Almost a Constant

Three variables present difficulties of determination by means of limited numbers of equations in experimental problems. Hence, since phosphorus is usually so low in most soils as to be considered almost the common regularly limiting factor, we may roughly reduce the variables in this case to calcium and potassium. If we may consider that phosphorus is a constant in nature when it is so low in quantity, so low in chemical mobility, and roughly at such a low base level above which the other two vary so much more widely, then the equations will include but two variables, calcium and potassium, for the problem in question here. If phosphorus is constant, then the calcium-potassium relations become the controlling factors in the ecological array and will not be so difficult of study. These two, under such an assumption, will be given the main attention in this discussion.

When Arranged in Order of Decreasing Protein Content, Plants Have Decreasing Nutrient Mineral Contents

Studies of the nitrogen contents, particularly of crops and vegetable plants, have made possible an array with different plants following in the order of decreasing protein or nitrogen contents. The legumes stand at the head of the list. Beginning with alfalfa, for example, followed by red clover, sweet clover, and others, including garden legumes, these crops can be arranged according to decreasing protein contents and lowering feeding or nutritional values commonly accepted in farm and household practice. As one goes down the scale to some of the legumes grown in the southern states, and of less nutrient value, there is still lower protein content, or lower total protein production per acre, and correspondingly lower total mineral content, particularly of calcium. Thus, there is less mineral per acre taken from the soil. The crops yield less protein per acre as their mineral supply decreases. With minerals coming only from the soil, its contribution of these may thus control the protein yield by the crop.

In arranging this order of decreasing protein production per acre by the legumes, there is no great gap in going from the lower legumes to those nonlegumes of higher feeding value. This higher value is also connected with the greater nitrogen content or total nitrogen in the crop. Hays from wheat, barley, rye, oats, bluegrass, timothy, redtop, and meadow fescue arrange themselves in this order of decreasing protein composition and reflect their commonly accepted hay values in the same order.

This arrangement with reference to higher proteinaceous nature of the different species, both legume and nonlegume, might serve as a pattern against which there can be matched also the calcium-potassium requirements as concentrations within the crop or the needs per acre. Studies show the calcium decrease to go parallel with the nitrogen decrease, particularly in concentration within the plant. They reflect also different yields of total protein and nutrient minerals per acre in this general arrangement. When the potassium in the more commonly accepted field and vegetable crops is charted in this array according to decreasing calcium taken, or nitrogen delivered, by the crop, there is not the close agreement shown between calcium and nitrogen. Perhaps no great variation in the carbohydrate, or carbonaceous, part of the plant that amounts to a total of 50% need be expected even when there is a decided variation in protein of which the total content scarcely ever exceeds 5%. Sampling for nitrogen variation over so narrow a range may not represent random sampling for the potassium associated with the carbohydrate. With these feed crops already selected according to animal choice for feed significance, the range in potassium may still not be wide enough to represent its possibilities for variation. When one considers woody plants, or takes woody tissue as an illustration, the dominance of potassium as compared to nitrogen and phosphorus is characteristic. Thus, we may regard potassium consumption as characteristic for the wood producers or for plant skeleton production, and calcium and phosphorus consumption as characteristic for the producers of protein. Perhaps it might be simpler to consider that all plants use some amounts of all nutrients but that with a low phosphorus level in all soils, the protein-producing plants are more common when calcium dominates in the soil supply, while with the decline or exhaustion of calcium the potassium dominates not necessarily by magnitude but by contrast. It is then that the more carbonaceous, or less proteinaceous, vegetation prevails.

Soil Development Suggests Decreasing Exchangeable Calcium in Relation to Exchangeable Potassium

If this reasoning is sound, then the plant ecological array bids fair to be fitted into the complex picture of soil development according to climate. By accepting the colloidal clay particle as the nutrient-supplying nucleus of the soil, let us first consider it as neutral in reaction, and stocked liberally with the exchangeable cations of nutrient significance. Such a soil nucleus is characteristic of the chernozem soils produced in climatic areas where precipitation and evaporation are almost in equilibrium and temperatures are moderate. With increasing rainfall at such temperatures this nucleus exchanges the nutrient cations for the hydrogen ions of non-nutrient value. Consequently, the nucleus becomes acid. As the temperature becomes higher under liberal or excessive rainfall, this nucleus is broken down into less complex structures or compositions with less adsorptive or exchange capacity for nutrient cations. It likewise is less capable of holding exchangeable hydrogen ions or of showing significant degree of acidity. Thus, in the temperature zones, the complex nucleus of variable exchangeable calcium content is the characteristic of the soil. It usually has decreasing calcium with increasing hydrogen (and aluminium) as roughly the reciprocal under increasing degrees of leaching. In the warmer regions the simpler clay complex or nucleus carries little calcium and holds less of all nutrient contents.

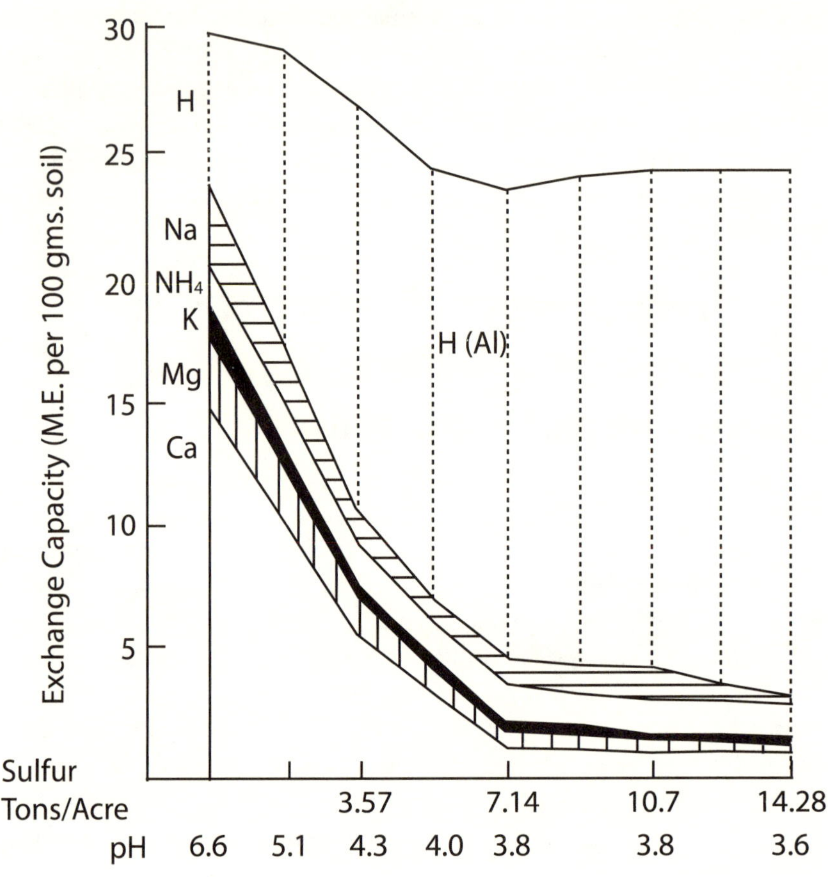

Fig. 1. — Varying relations of exchangeable cations, particularly Ca, loam weathered to different degrees by sulfur additions.

Artificially Developed Soil Shows Narrowing Ratio for Exchangeable Calcium-Potassium

As an aid in visualizing the changes within the soil colloidal complex while a soil develops or passes to higher degrees of weathering and greater nutrient loss, some research in Holland by Prillwitz may be helpful. The soil was weathered artificially through sulfur treatment and its microbiological oxidation. The change in the clay complex is shown in Fig. 1, representing the exchangeable cation variation and the loss in some of its exchange capacity. According to this scheme, one of the distinct features is the substitution for the bases by the hydrogen and aluminium. Still more distinct is the fact that the relative amount of calcium is depleted much more rapidly than any other exchangeable nutrient on the complex. With the increasing degree of soil development, the ratios of bases to each other shift, but of all the items, the calcium undergoes the greatest change. The ratio of this element to potassium shifts from approximately 11.0:1.0 at the pH figure of 6.6 to 4.0:1.0 at the pH figure of 3.8. If the anion of phosphorus is low at the outset and remains constantly so, then this shift in ratio of the calcium to potassium represents a decided change in the ratios of the nutrient offerings by a soil, even if the increasing clay content as a disturbing factor in offering of totals is disregarded. The question may then well be raised whether such shifts in exchangeable cations may not be basic for an ecological shift from proteinaceous to non-proteinaceous plant dominance, or at least to less proteinaceous vegetation, as the soils are more highly developed and the clay complex simplified to a higher degree by the increasing forces of climate in the form of more rainfall or increasing temperature.

Experimental Shifts in the Calcium-Potassium Ratio Bring Shift in Legume From Proteinaceous to Carbonaceous Production

As experimental help pointing toward the possible validity of the suggested array of dominant proteinaceous vegetation with high calcium to potassium ratio, let us note the behavior of soybeans as the calcium-potassium ratio was varied under control. When grown on a constant but low phosphorus level, a constant but liberal calcium level, and with increasing potassium, all in the exchangeable or readily available form for the plant, this legume demonstrated a suggested shift from a proteinaceous producer to a carbonaceous producer. This is shown in Table 1. When the calcium relative to potassium supply was high, this plant was a nitrogen fixer of moderate growth. When the increase in potassium was introduced so that the calcium was relatively low in relation to it, this plant grew larger, but its nitrogen-fixing activity dwindled. It consumed the offered nitrogen but diluted this with carbohydrate production. If it is true that this shift from protein to carbo-

Table 1

*Decrease in Nitrogen Fixation and Increase in Crop Weight of Soybeans with Widened Calcium-Potassium Ratio**

Exchangeable cations, m.e.			Crop weight, grams	Nitrogen		Magnesium		Calcium		Phosphorus		Potassium		K% / Ca%
Mg	Ca	K		%	mg.	%	mg.	%	mg.	%	mg.	%	mg.	
5	10	0	14.207	2.86	407	0.36	52	0.74	105	0.25	39	1.01	150	1.36
5	10	5	14.592	2.56	372	0.36	54	0.32	46	0.18	26	1.90	285	5.93
5	10	10	17.807	2.19	390	0.30	55	0.27	48	0.14	25	2.15	384	7.96

**Seed content in mg.: N = 364, Mg = 16.7, Ca = 12.2, P = 39.4, K = 171.*

hydrate follows the shift in calcium-potassium ratio in the soil in the case of a single plant species, may it not be an epitome of the evolution of the ecological array of plants in accordance with the degree of development of our soils as measured by this shift in calcium-potassium ratio?

Observations on Soil Development and General Vegetation as Possible Support of the Theory

It is commonly granted that dark soils are liberally stocked with calcium. It has been held by many that the calcium is the means of preserving the organic matter. A different significance of the calcium seems more plausible in the light of studies of nitrogen fixation. Black soils naturally rich in calcium are usually correspondingly rich in all nutrient cations and are fit media for the mineral-consuming legumes. Calcium is significant for bringing nitrogen from the air to the soil. This added nitrogen serves to hold additional carbon as organic matter of nearly constant carbon-nitrogen ratio for each climatic location. Thus, soils high in exchangeable calcium produce more and retain more organic matter even though they also have their microbiological decomposition processes favored by these liberal stocks of cations. In going from these dark soils, according to the soil classification map, or to the rainfall map, to soils of lighter color with more rainfall at constant temperature, we go from prairies to forests and follow the general array of decreasing protein production and increasing carbonaceous, or wood, content in the vegetation. Increase in leaching means a soil complex whose potassium is still offered in exchangeable form in amounts to produce carbonaceous growth, and whose calcium and phosphorus levels maintain reproduction and cell multiplication sufficient to maintain this carbohydrate manufacture, but are not high enough to bring into this plant complex the extra nitrogen and phosphorus for plant types classified as distinctly proteinaceous.

In the extreme case of the forest tree we may visualize low calcium and phosphorus supply just sufficient to maintain a reasonable leaf area in metabolic activities of carbon assimilation and annual wood production. This leaf area may remain roughly constant with slight annual increase as it maintains itself at the top of the tree, with apical growth at the expense of translocation from the disappearing branches below. The pine in the sandy soils deficient in calcium but offering little potassium may illustrate the case with tall barren trunks tipped at great height by the green, photosynthetically active top. Students of the taxonomy of prairie vegetation have also reported the apparent increase in legume species in the prairie in going from east to west in Kansas or Nebraska, for example, or in going toward less leached soils or calcium carbonate horizons of less depth in the soil profile.

Since increasing temperature encourages soil development to the extent of colloidal clay breakdown, we must expect the well-developed or more highly simplified lateritic soil complex of lower exchange capacity to offer low amounts of calcium and to fit into the scheme as suggested. If such is true, the dominance of saccharine natured crops in the South would seem logical. The southern legume crops, when carefully studied, suggest that their properties fit them into soils of lower fertility when we know that they are more promiscuous in cross inoculation and in cross pollination, both of which are properties that aid in their struggle for maintenance against low soil fertility. Soils under high temperature and moisture have always been problem soils in fertility management. An application of the low calcium-potassium ratio theory and all that goes with it in the plant array may help us to understand some of the problems of agriculture in the South.

Calcium-Potassium Ratio Theory Needs Further Testing

Attention is not invited to the theory that the calcium-potassium ratio in soils of low phosphorus content controls, in a large measure, the ecological plant array because this theory has become a proved fact, but rather because, like many theories, whether ever proved or not, it may be helpful in making order out of chaotic thinking or of seemingly unrelated facts. If such an array is correct, can we not group our list of field crops for better adaptation to soils according to soil regions or to degree of soil development? Cannot soil treatment be used to improve the composition of the crops in the lower soil fertility phase of the natural ecological array? A fuller understanding of the relation of crops to soil conditions may reduce our search for crop plants from one of ramblings over the globe for promiscuous collectings and scatterings, to one of more carefully guided transfers from and to regions of common soil characters or even transfers to improved conditions for the crop.

It is for its possible help in clearer understanding of plants in relation to soil development and fertility that the calcium-potassium ratio theory suggested herewith is offered for your speculative consideration and for criticism.

CHAPTER 15

Potash Deficiency Follows Continuous Wheat

SUCCESSFUL GROWTH of sweet clover, in contrast to its complete failure, and thereby an increase of 19 bushels of corn per acre resulted on Sanborn Field[1] in 1944 from the use of potash annually rather than biennially.

On one of the plots of this old experiment field, wheat had been grown continuously for 50 years. During the first 25 years, the soil was given six tons of manure annually. During the last 25 years, it had no treatment.

The cropping system and soil treatments were changed in 1938. This plot now has a two-year rotation of corn and wheat with sweet clover as a green manure before the corn. Limestone at the rate of two tons per acre was applied to the entire plot at the time of change. Superphosphate (20 percent) at 150 pounds and muriate of potash (48 percent) at 50 pounds per acre are now used regularly with the wheat. An additional application of 50 pounds of the muriate is given to the right half of the plot with the planting of the corn. Thus potassium is applied annually on the one half and only biennially on the other half of the plot.

The increased yield of the corn is attributed to the successful growth of the sweet clover. This increase is now demonstrating the value of this added plant food in providing the sweet clover as a green manure crop. That this 19-bushel increase is due directly to the influence of the sweet clover and indirectly to the potash was shown by the border effect, viz., the better growth of the corn in the row adjacent to the right portion of this plot as compared to the remaining corn in the left half. The marked contrast between the corn growth and yield on the two halves was as

[1] *Sanborn Field of the Missouri Agricultural Experiment Station at Columbia, Missouri.*

anticipated when the clover had previously succeeded on the one and failed completely on the other half.[2]

The response of this soil to the application of potash is attributed to its 50 years of production of wheat on this soil, and with no soil treatment during the last 25 years of that time. The removal of the straw as a concentrated carrier of potassium in addition to the removal of the grain has evidently depleted to a very low level the soil's available supply of this plant nutrient. This shortage, normally not recognized as a cause of our declining success with clover, has become evident on this soil as it affects the survival of the sweet clover stand and consequently the yield of the following corn crop.

These data indicate that potassium will require more consideration on soils well supplied with lime and phosphorus, but where clover stands are becoming increasingly hard to obtain. Heretofore lime and phosphate were considered sufficient, and when there was a clover failure the weather was always a common alibi. If we are to use legumes successfully to enrich our soils with extra nitrogen and with extra organic matter, potassium will need to be added on some of our soils.

---

[2] *Sweet clover responds to potash fertilizer: W. A. Albrecht — Better Crops With Plant Food, June 1944.*

CHAPTER 16

Red Clover Suggests Shortage of Potash

COMPETITION BY THE ASSOCIATED WHEAT as nurse crop with red clover for the limited fertility in the soil was sufficient on Sanborn Field to give a poor clover crop in the wheat stubble but a very good crop in the border of the plot where the green wheat was cut out in trimming the plot to proper size.

This poor red clover crop in the stubble occurred in the 6-year rotation of corn, oats, wheat, clover, timothy, and timothy where lime had been applied about five years ago, and where the equivalent of three tons of manure had been applied annually since 1888. In spite of rotation to reduce the rate of soil exhaustion during the past 55 years, this soil that grew clover fairly well at the outset of the experiments on this field is now so low in its delivery of fertility that the wheat, as the nurse crop, is too much competition for the red clover. The soil is no longer able to grow a wheat crop and start the clover at the same time. The elimination of the nurse crop by cutting it out of the border was the difference between a good crop of red clover in the border area and one in the stubbles that was about to be "smothered out" by the growth of weeds, if not killed out by the "bad weather."

Barnyard manure had been helping the clover in this crop rotation even before lime was used. Lime and manure had given good clover. Those facts suggest that we need to look to the low supply of potassium in the soil as partly responsible for clover failures. Barnyard manure is low in phosphorus but provides nitrogen and potassium in liberal amounts. Since clover as a legume does not suffer nitrogen shortage, the benefits by manure suggest that it is the provision of the potassium that is largely responsible for the good effects of manure on red clover. They suggest that potassium as a fertilizer may be a means of bringing back the red clover that is playing less and less a part in our cropping program of growing good forage feeds.

On Sanborn Field trials are now under way to test the wider use of potassium as a fertilizer to correct what seems the next great deficiency for clover after those of calcium and phosphorus have been met. The changes in plans at the close of 50 years of crops on the field permitted the introduction of potassium, along with the lime, phosphate, and manure treatments. Nurse-crop competition, that was removed in this case of wheat with the clover by cutting the border to result in much better clover there than in the stubble, points forcefully to potassium deficiency. Wheat straw requires 18 pounds of potassium per ton. Straw removal during the past 55 years of cropping of this plot has depleted the potash to such a degree that now the soil can give this nutrient sufficiently for clover only when the competing nurse crop is taken out. If the nurse crop and the red clover are both to be a success, more fertility must be added. Here where lime has been applied and manure that adds so little phosphorus is so beneficial, we must look to the suggestion that potassium is the deficiency holding down the red clover crop.

When competition for the soil fertility between the nurse crop and the legume crop is so keen as to kill out the legume, then we must either seed the crops separately in succeeding years or must supply the extra soil fertility needed to finish the nurse crop and carry forward the accompanying legume crop. It would seem economy to do the latter when a few hundred pounds of fertilizer is the only cost involved. It is only when we look to the mineral fertility that we can use the legumes to provide for us the nitrogen fertility from the free air.

Such demonstrations by the red clover itself suggest that very probably this valuable crop is moving toward its final extinction on the very soils where it once grew. This extinction is coming on simply because the soil has not been given the essential kind of fertility, or a sufficient form of such soil nourishment for the clover crop's survival after the nurse crop has drawn on it. Red clover on Sanborn Field is suggesting that this desirable legume cannot be a soil-builder in terms of taking nitrogen from the air unless it is given some attention by way of fertility treatments that include not only lime and phosphate but potassium as well.

CHAPTER 17

Potassium Helps Put More Nitrogen into Sweet Clover

SOME TESTS WITH sweet clover as the green manure crop in a rotation grown on Putnam silt loam on the South Farm of the Missouri Experiment Station in 1947 demonstrated that potassium as well as calcium is needed if this crop is to be a producer of considerable tonage of vegetative bulk. Potassium also demonstrated its service in raising the concentration of nitrogen in the crop, and, presumably thereby, the fixation of nitrogen from the atmosphere.

Plan of the Study

The sweet clover studied is the legume crop in a four-year rotation of corn, oats, wheat, and sweet clover. The soil treatments on the respective three plots include the basic addition of calcium in limestone at the rate of 2 tons per acre every 8 years. In addition, there is a superphosphate application of 475 pounds per rotation and a potash application of 475 pounds as a 0–20–20 fertilizer per rotation on this plot.

The crop harvests for forage yields were taken, and the plants divided into tops and roots with the customary "stubble" included with the tops by dividing at the soil surface line of the plants. The data for the crop weights according to soil treatments are given in Table 1. The weights of the tops and roots may well be compared by the ratios given in the table when calculated with the roots taken as unity. In order to measure the yields and concentration of nitrogen, the plant parts were finely ground in a special hammer mill and the nitrogen determination made on the oven-dry weights of the samples. The data are presented for the nitrogen in the plant tops and in the roots as total harvests in pounds per acre and also in

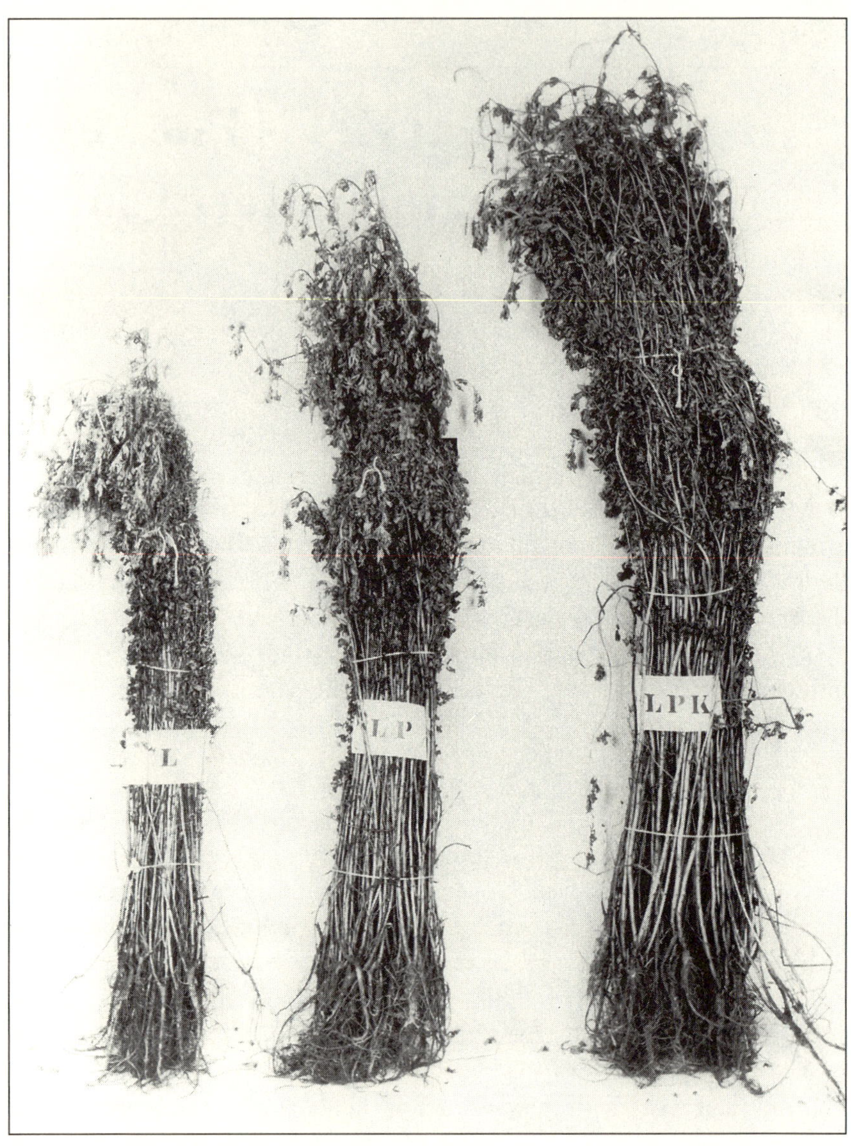

Fig. 1. — Relative yields of forage and differences in roots and stems of sweet clover varying in root-rot according to soil treatments.

terms of the concentration of the nitrogen in the vegetation as pounds per ton. Then there are given the ratios of nitrogen per acre in the tops to that in the roots, and the ratio of the nitrogen per ton of tops to that per ton of the roots.

Results

Root-Rot Less with Potassium Applied

Observations made on the sweet clover on approaching maturity showed a crop of heavier stems, more dense in growth, and taller as the additional soil treatments were applied (Fig. 1). It was especially interesting to note that the nearly mature plants could easily be pulled up from the soil where lime only was used. They were pulled up with more difficulty on the plot with lime and phosphate, but it was impossible to pull them up by their roots where lime, phosphate, and potash had been used as soil treatments.

Examination of the roots led a plant pathologist to declare that the root-rot disease was prevalent on the plants grown where the potash had been omitted, but he considered very little of this disease evident on the plants grown with the added potash. Here is the suggestion that when the plant physiology was considered and provision was made for better nutrition through the addition of potassium to balance the generous application of calcium, there was little damage from the disease.

Roots More Efficient in Making Plant Tops Because of Application of Potash

From the data in Table 1, it is evident that there are wide differences in the efficiency with which a given amount of roots made their corresponding tops under the different soil treatments. In the production of total bulk, where only lime was used, each unit of roots produced $2^1/_4$ times its weight as tops, but when both lime and phosphate were added to the soil, each unit of roots made tops about 10% more efficiently. This is shown by the ratio of 2.59 in contrast to that of 2.25. When both phosphate and potash were used along with the lime, however, each unit of roots was 50% more efficient in making tops than when lime alone was used and 30% more efficient than when lime and phosphate were used. Potash was of greater effect when added to this combination than was the phosphate under the conditions of its addition.

Table 1

Dry Matter and Nitrogen in the Tops and Roots of Sweet Clover with Different Soil Treatments

	Lime	Lime and phosphate	Lime, phosphate, and potash
Dry matter, lbs. per acre:			
Entire plant	4,950	9,035	12,190
Tops	3,435	6,515	9,385
Roots	1,515	2,520	2,805
Ratio, tops/roots	2.25	2.59	3.35
Nitrogen, lbs. per acre:			
Entire plant	92	161	234
Tops	64	123	193
Roots	28	38	41
Ratio, tops/roots	2.30	3.33	4.74
Nitrogen, lbs. per ton:			
Entire plant	37	36	39
Tops	37	38	41
Roots	37	30	29
Ratio, tops/roots	1.00	1.26	1.41

Roots More Efficient in Putting Nitrogen into Plant Tops Because of Application of Potash

There was also a wide variation in the efficiency with which a given amount of nitrogen in the roots was translocated to the tops under different soil treatments. In terms of total nitrogen per acre of roots and tops where the soil was limed, the nitrogen in the tops represented 2.3 times as much as that in the roots. Here the efficiency of the roots in putting nitrogen into the tops was about the same as the efficiency of the roots in making plant bulk, as shown by the similarity of the ratios. This is shown also by the fact that there was, coincidently, as much nitrogen in a ton of roots as in a ton of tops. When phosphate was used along with the lime on the soil, then the roots were about 50% more efficient in moving nitrogen into the tops, as shown by the ratio of 3.33 for the nitrogen in the tops to that in the roots. In terms of pounds of nitrogen per ton where lime and phosphate were used together, the figure for the roots was 30 and for the tops 38. However, when both phosphate and potash were used along with the lime, then the roots were 100% more efficient in putting nitrogen into the tops than with lime alone, as shown by the ratio of 4.74 for the former in contrast to the ratio of 2.30 for the latter. In terms of nitrogen per ton of roots grown with lime, phosphate, and potash, the figure was 29, while for a ton of tops it was 41. Potash as a soil treatment in addition to lime and phosphate made for an increase in efficiency of concentrating nitrogen into the harvested tops which was twice that for the addition of phosphate to the lime as the soil treatment.

Summary

It is significant that potash used along with calcium and phosphate had the most outstanding effect of the three soil fertility factors concerned in these trials, not only in making for more plant bulk, but also in making for more total nitrogen in the crop per acre of tops and per acre of roots. Potash was the major factor also in making for a larger concentration of nitrogen in the tops while there was a lower concentration in the roots. All of this suggests that the potassium commonly associated with carbohydrate synthesis and metabolism in the plant can scarcely be divorced from the synthesis of proteins there. The carbohydrates, or what is so commonly emphasized as the product of photosynthesis formed under sunshine energy, may well be the raw material in terms of both the starting compound and the energy supply for the products of biosynthesis such as proteins, and the many other complexes elaborated and compounded by life processes rather than by those driven under sunshine power in the leaf. Here is the suggestion that calcium is helpful in the synthesis of nitrogenous compounds or proteins in the legumes and that this synthetic process demands, in advance, the carbohydrates for the synthesis of which potash is needed. On this soil, the maximum assemblage of nitrogen in sweetclover required potash as help in this performance.

While sweet clover is commonly considered the crop that can be established on most any soil by liming alone, after other and more desirable forage legumes have failed, one dare not forget that nitrogen delivery by this crop as well as its greater production of bulk call for other fertility elements beside calcium and phosphate. There may be many elements among these, but certainly there is the suggestion from these studies on Putnam silt loam, a prarie soil and a planosol in the common soil classification, that potassium is important when the higher nitrogen content of the sweet clover crop is considered. After our soils are once heavily limed this legume as a collector of nitrogen may need extra fertility elements in the soil, with potassium well near the top of the list.

CHAPTER 18

Sweet Clover Responds to Potash Fertilizer

SOIL IMPROVEMENT by means of legumes is not merely a matter of distributing legume seeds and hoping that this kind of crop will build up the land. Legumes can take nitrogen from the air to add it to themselves only when they find plenty of their other fertility needs supplied by the soil. Lime has become well recognized as one need that we must satisfy by applying it to the soil. Phosphorus is also accepted widely as a soil treatment to improve legume crops. Sanborn Field,* with its carefully recorded experience, is indicating that we may well be putting potassium on the list with the lime and phosphate as an essential help to get stands of sweet clover for soil improvement.

On one of the plots where wheat had been grown for 25 years with manure applied annually, and then for the same number of years without manure, the cropping and soil treatments were changed in 1938 to a 2-year rotation of corn and wheat with sweet clover sandwiched in as a green manure crop for the corn. The soil treatment of lime was put on the entire plot. Superphosphate at the rate of 150 pounds per acre and muriate of potash at 50 pounds were applied with the drilling of the wheat. When the corn was planted, an additional 50 pounds of muriate of potash were put on only the right half of the plot. The seeding of sweet clover that follows the wheat is now demonstrating the value of this extra potash by the successful stand of this legume in contrast to its failure where this additional potassium was not applied.

The significance of the extra potassium as a soil treatment for sweet clover after its applications in only three rounds of the rotation is evident

This experimental field of the Missouri Agricultural Experiment Station is one of the oldest fields in the United States. It has been in service now for 55 years.

Plot 24, Sanborn Field — Late July 1943. Two-year rotation of corn, wheat, with sweet clover as catch crop to be plowed under. Fifty pounds of muriate of potash per acre applied annually on the right, with both the corn and the wheat crops, but only biennially with the wheat on the left. Lime and superphosphate are applied on the entire plot. The plot had received manure, 6 tons per acre 1888 to 1913 inclusive, but no soil treatment 1914–1938.

from the growth of this crop in the stubble in late July. Though there were small sweet clover plants where lime, phosphate, and lesser amounts of potassium were applied, the contrast between them and those where potassium was more generously used is so marked that one would not be encouraged to expect much green manure effect by the sweet clover for the corn next spring in that part of the plot where the smaller amount of potassium was applied.

With wheat grown on this plot for 50 years, with all the straw as a relatively concentrated carrier of potassium taken off annually, and with no manure going back to return potassium in the straw as bedding or in the animal urine, this plot has developed a distinct shortage in its potassium delivery for sweet clover in a 2-year rotation. This shortage occurs for a crop not commonly considered sensitive to potassium deficiencies when it may be seen growing on a pile of crushed limestone. The shortage in this plot, however, is so severe that the spring-seeded sweet clover was starved out by the first of August except where extra potassium was supplied.

Here in this plot and its soil treatment there is evidence that our legume program, which we commonly grant needs help in the form of lime and phosphate as soil treatments, may well be looking forward to other helps such as potash fertilizer if we are to nourish these legume crops properly so they can fertilize our soils by means of the nitrogen they take from the air and by their organic matter when they are turned under as green manure.

To date no studies of the chemical composition of sweet clover in relation to soil treatment have been made, such as have been carried on with lespedeza to connect the soil treatments with the improved feeding value of the forage. When potassium now used in a more limited way is tried by more farmers, their observations on animal choices of sweet clover with different fertilizers may help to make sweet clover of better feeding value, in addition to giving it the unusual green manure value it already has.

CHAPTER 19

Artificial Manure Production on the Farm

THE WELL RECOGNIZED value of barnyard manure for soil improvement and its decreased supply in this motorized age have aroused much interest in the possibilities of producing artificial manure from straw and waste materials on the farm. The production of manure (artificially) in England, by methods savoring of those used long ago in making composts, gave impetus to the idea. Since the combine thresher leaves on the land straw that is often turned under with detrimental effects on the crops following, and since accumulated straw piles of many seasons often occupy valuable land while they rot so slowly as to waste their fertility in wheat farming regions, artificial manure making is a possible means of getting this much needed organic matter and plant food content back into the soil. Experimental studies have helped to learn the requisites of this process, to reduce its laboriousness, and to test the application of it under practical farm conditions.

Principles Involved in the Process

Since rotting of vegetable matter is simply a process in which certain materials serve as food for the unseen bacteria and other microorganisms, artificial manure making may be likened to an attempt to feed the straw, leaves, and other vegetable wastes to these smaller life forms. A proper ration for these must contain: (a) material supplying energy, (b) substances producing growth, (c) essential minerals, and (d) sufficient moisture and air. In addition, proper environmental conditions must prohibit the accumulation of excessive acidity, if these invisible life forms are to multiply rapidly and consume the ration or bring about its decomposition in the shortest time. Straw, leaves, cornstalks, and similar farm wastes consist mainly of cellulose and other carbon carrying compounds which serve for energy. They are deficient, however, in the element nitrogen, which is necessary for the growth of the microorganisms. Lacking sufficient nitrogen, such materials are poor bacterial rations and will decay but slowly without its addition. They do so rapidly, however, when balanced by the addition of nitrogen according to the requirements as determined by various research workers and early suggested by the bacteriologist Omeliansky.

Cellulose and other carbon compounds must be balanced with nitrogen-carrying chemicals to give the proper ration for the microorganisms in a manner similar to that of balancing the rations for livestock by providing the proper amount of protein in purchased concentrates as supplement to the carbohydrate in corn or other grains. Thus nitrogenous chemicals are added to the straw to make it a balanced ration for the best growth and multiplication of the bacteria and to induce the consequent destruction of the straw by their rapid multiplication. Ground limestone is added to prevent the acidity, or the so-called "souring" type of rotting. The chemicals used in treating straw are fertilizer substances carrying nitrogen such as ammonium sulfate, sodium nitrate, calcium cyanamid, urea, and others, mixed with limestone. Since most farm manure should be supplemented with phosphate, this may well be added as superphosphate along with the other substances, though the process works equally well without it. Straw and other farm wastes given these supplementary chemicals and water, provide an excellent bacterial ration and conditions for the rapid decay of straw. It duplicates the manner in which animal urine acts on the bedding to produce farm manure.

Disastrous Effects from Turning Under Straw

The fact that straw is deficient in nitrogen as a bacterial ration is largely responsible for the disastrous effects on crops following closely on straw turned under. The straw in the soil begins its decay by serving as the carbon source for the microorganisms, but because of its nitrogen deficiencies they draw the soluble nitrogen from the soil. The incorporation of this into bacterial products makes it insoluble and thus reduces the soluble nitrogen supply in the soil to such a low level that crops suffer and fail. The composting of straw in the artificial making of manure escapes this danger by supplying the chemical nitrogen to balance the straw for bacterial use before it is mixed with the soil.

Various Wastes May be Used

Straw, leaves, cotton hulls, and corn stalks, both chopped and unchopped, have been used. Many forms of vegetable matter as weeds, mature sweet clover, spoiled hays, accumulated garden refuse, and numerous other kinds of materials will serve. Almost any vegetable matter, whether green or dry, can be rotted by this process by adding the chemical mixture and water with care to provide air during decay. There are many forms of farm vegetable matter left to be scattered and their fertility value dissipated, when they might well be collected into piles, treated with chemicals and water, or left for the rainfall, to bring about their decay. By this process much of such wastes will help in restoring soil fertility and maintaining the soil organic matter. Areas as large as the farm may not be necessary, but even the city lot may be big enough for use of the artificial manure method.

Garden wastes as plant tops or pea vines, when the crops mature during the season, the accumulations after the frost kills them, and lawn clippings, or weeds may be built up with the reagent and water additions for manure production. Leaves, especially, should be disposed of in this manner. There seems scarce justification for burning them. If gathered when wet, the main trouble of wetting them in the pile will be overcome. When settled in a pile they compact in such a way as to turn water readily. They must be moistened while in a loose pile, but should be preferably gathered in the moist condition after a rain. If composted then with the reagent, repiled, and remoistened occasionally, they will make an excellent manure for the garden, for the lawn, or for mulching the landscape plantings. The vegetable wastes from even a city lot may do much through the artificial manure method toward providing a suitable home-made fertilizer for the city lot.

Artificial Manure May be Composted by Hand

The material to be used, such as straw, cotton hulls, corn stalks, and others should be built up into a pile, on a level area, by 4 to 6-inch layers with a sprinkling of water on each layer to moisten it, and then a dusting of the mixture of chemical reagents. The next layer is then added similarly and this continued until a pile about 4 feet high is made. The top of the pile should be level, or low in the center, so as to collect rainfall rather than shed it.

The pile so made will soon begin to heat, tending to dry out, and may need attention by the addition of water. Repiling to mix the reagent and refuse and to incorporate air, will likewise speed the decay. Piles may be so located that water may be brought from an eaves trough, or through some other means, to facilitate making this addition to keep the pile moist. The pile may also be built up with the material left in the dry state. Decay will begin at the top of the pile as the rainfall moistens it, and will travel downward as fast as the naturally added water permits. Trenching around the pile to prohibit the leachings from draining away and to retain them in the base of the pile is advisable. This method is widely applicable where the amounts of vegetable wastes to be used are not large.

Artificial Manure Preparation from Straw During Threshing

As a means of reducing the laboriousness of making artificial manure from straw, the straw may be mixed with the chemical reagents during threshing and blown into a flat pile that will take the rain water and produce artificial manure. A mechanical attachment[1] fitted to the thresher, can be made for about $5.00 and used to deliver the reagent into the blower or stacker and will thus mix this with the straw as it is blown into the pile. This mixing is done much more effectively than can b done by hand. This attachment as shown in the drawing of Fig. 1 consists of a single section of a fertilizer drill fitted with a hopper and driven by a belt from one of the shafts on the thresher. By weighing a few loads of unthreshed grain and then noting the grain threshed therefrom — according to machine measure — the weight of straw per bushel of grain may be determined. The flow of the chemical reagent or mixture into the thresher may then be adjusted by the slide opening of the attachment so as to deliver 150 pounds of this reagent for the number of bushels representing a ton of straw.

This straw should be put into a flat pile usually not over 6 feet high, or the depth suited for the average rainfall of the late season in most parts of Missouri. With less rainfall, or greater depths of straw, more time must be allowed for the decomposition which occurs only as the moisture is provided. The straw pile can be made most receptive to rainwater by

[1] *This was designed by E. M. Poirot, Golden City, Missouri, whose help in many farm trials of artificial manure is hereby gratefully acknowledged.*

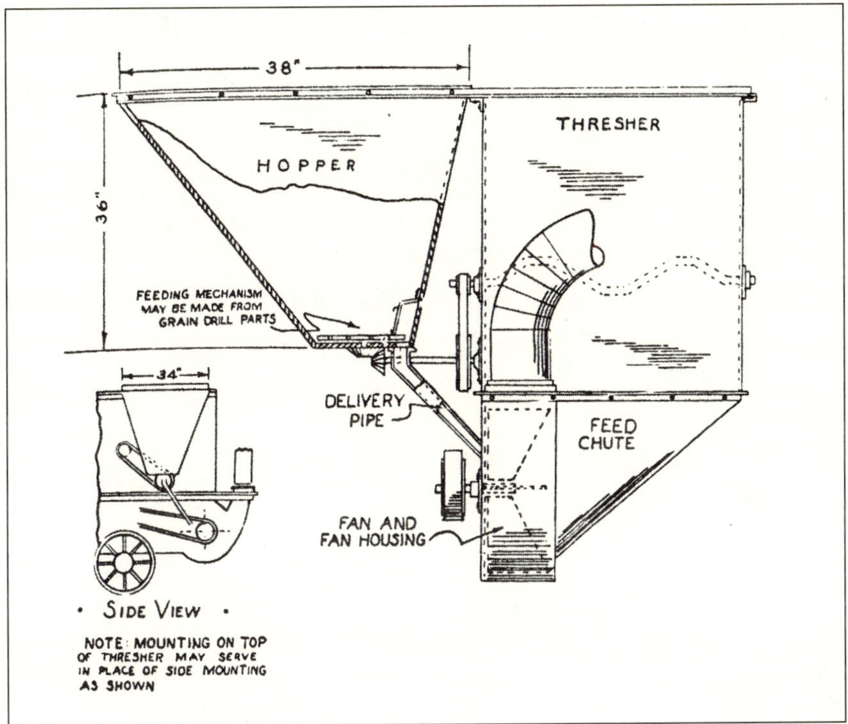

Fig. 1. — Mechanical attachment to threshing machine for treating straw with chemicals in making artificial manure.

starting it as a ridge at maximum distances from the machine with the lowered and fully extended blower or stacker in a horizontal position. By starting a ridge of straw at maximum distance and blowing the straw against the top of this ridge so that it rolls down as the pile is built toward the machine, the straw seems to be arranged in such a manner as to aid the pile in taking water rather than shedding it. This is an important item in the effective reception and use of the rainfall. With ample amounts of rainfall, decay of the straw should proceed rapidly enough to provide artificial manure for top dressing of winter wheat. Straw piles with abundance of rainfall, produced artificial manure in late November from wheat threshed in early July.

Chemical Reagents Recommended

The chemical reagent found to be effective and readily obtained, according to experimental trials, consists of the following:

Ammonium sulfate	45 parts	per 100 parts of the mixture.
Finely ground limestone	40 parts	
Superphosphate	15 parts	

This mixture should be applied at the rate of 150 pounds per ton of dry straw or other wastes and will thus add

Ammonium sulfate	67½ pounds	per ton of dry material.
Finely ground limestone	60 pounds	
Superphosphate	22½ pounds	

Other Reagent Mixtures May be Used

The reagent mixture may be made of ammonium sulfate and limestone only. These may be applied in amouts per ton of straw varying from the above figures. The use of 50 to 65 pounds of ammonium sulfate, and from 50 to 100 pounds limestone per ton of straw, will serve effectively to produce a good product. However, the lower amounts of ammonium sulfate may reduce the speed of decay. Since straw is low in phosphorus and since this element gives good returns on crops when used as fertilizer the addition of phosphorus is recommended for regular use. Barnyard manure should regularly be reinforced with superphosphate hence this fertilizer material should not be omitted from the artificial manure. Experiments suggest that some soluble potassium might be included to produce a better manure, but since straw is relatively rich in potassium, it is omitted from the reagent mixture.

Other nitrogenous materials, such as sodium nitrate, calcium nitrate, urea, or calcium cyanamid may replace the ammonium sulfate. In the case of calcium cyanamid, less limestone will be required. Trials of the different nitrogen carriers showed them to be effective in hastening straw decomosition. Complete fertilizers, high in nitrogen, mixed with the limestone have been used successfully. A wide variation in the kinds of nitrogen carrier in the reagent is permissible. Since these latter reagent mixtures are more costly than ammonium sulfate, and since it has been found to give results equal to, and in most cases superior to, other reagents, the mixture of ammonium sulfate, limestone, and superphosphate is recommended.

The ammonium sulfate and superphosphate can be obtained through fertilizer dealers, and are the materials regularly used as fertilizers. The limestone is none other than the common, finely ground agricultural limestone distributed from many stone quarries. There should be no difficulty in obtaining these materials through the usual commercial channels handling them.

No Danger to Livestock Eating Treated Straw

Of the ingredients in the reagent used, limestone and superphosphate are not harmful to animals, but are even included in mineral feed mixtures. Ammonium sulfate might be injurious to livestock if consumed in large amounts. However, should the animals eat the treated straw, the amounts of ammonium sulfate consumed would be insignificant and there needs be no alarm about the possible danger. Animals tramping over the straw will not disturb the process, and may even help it by compacting it and thus increasing moisture retention. There should be no need in this connection for special fencing around straw piles, cornfodder, or other wastes treated for artificial manure production.

Index of Completion of the Process

When decay begins, the artificial manure pile will heat much in the same manner as does fresh barnyard manure. This heating may be excessive, and can be controlled by repiling or adding water. With shallower, less compact piles depending on natural rainfall, there is little danger that excessively high temperatures will result. When the decay process has run its course, there will be a decided decrease in volume, or collapse, of the pile. No more heating will then occur. When this collapse has taken place, samples of the material twisted in the hand will break easily and the usual toughness of wet straw will be missing. The wet, strawy manure will resemble, in all respects, the strawy manure commonly produced in lots by livestock around the straw stack, or in barnyards where straw is liberally used as bedding and tramped down to form manure. The appearance of artificial manure made from straw is similar in almost every way to ordinary farm manure and handles like it. The final product will not be taken by those familiar with strawy manure.

Occasional attention should be given to the pile during decay, since repiling hastens the process. Addition of water periodically may be helpful. Whether such should be added at reasonable labor cost seems doubtful, except as an eaves trough from a building or similar simple means of watering may be used. Observations should be made on the process during decay determine its completion. Premature use and plowing under will mean some temporarily injurious effects similar to those from plowing under straw.

The use made of the manure influences its value. According to the results from Sanborn Experiment Field (Missouri Experiment Station) lighter applications of manure give it greater value per ton. On wheat as a winter top dressing one ton of barnyard manure has been found to increase the wheat yields 4½ bushels per acre as an average for a three ton application per acre. On timothy sod, the manure application has likewise been most proffitable for applications of not over six tons per acre. Ahead of corn, manure also finds a good place. Its production artificially makes it possible to top dress winter wheat or sod in the late winter or early spring with decided improvement in grain quality as shown by farm trials. In the former case it is especially helpful in establishing clover stands that might otherwise fail because of bad season or deficient fertility. Artificial manure will be more profitable as it is used in the more significant places in the crop rotation.

Economy of the Process

When manure is produced artifically by this method, its cost per ton may be taken at approximately $0.60, when only the cash outlay is considered. This estimated cost is based on ammonium sulfate at $45.00 and limestone at $3.00 per ton, with both used at the rates in the formula of the mixture previously given, and in the general experience of this and other stations as well as of farmers in producing three tons of manure from a ton of straw. This estimate of the cost of artificial manure includes no charge for the superphosphate that is introduced as a means of balancing it, since barnyard manure also should be similarly supplemented.

When measuring the cost of artificial manure, it is well to remember that such cash outlay results in the increased production of manure on the farm, the need of which is so commonly recognized. If one ton of wheat straw is produced per acre, three ton of artificial manure can be spread back for it. The use of artificial manure returns to the soil larger amounts of organic matter produced on the farm than are returned as barnyard manure. In addition it adds the amounts of nitrogen purchased in the ammonium sulfate. It carries additional phosphate so as to provide a more nearly balanced manure than the ordinary barnyard manure. Since manure can be produced by this process on any part of the farm, it is unnecessary to transport the straw to the barn and the manure back again. The artificial manure can be produced on remote parts of the farm and used there, thus manuring the neglected areas and reducing hauling costs. These and other economics must not be disregarded in estimating the economy of the process. The regular return of these larger amounts of better manure over the farm as a whole should result in an increased production and consequently more economy from the artificial manure production than cost figures might indicate.

The use of the Poirot attachment on the thresher with controlled delivery rate of reagent according to straw threshed or grain given, reduces the labor to a minimum. The costs of this cannot be estimated accurately but these will be less as one becomes more familiar with the process and brings about its better adaptation to farm conditions.

CHAPTER 20

Farm Trials of Artificial Manure

IN CONSEQUENCE OF the universally recognized value of barnyard manure and its decreased supply through motorization of farming, attention has turned toward its artificial production. The various farm wastes offer plenty of materials. The burning of wheat straw after the header or thresher, the rotting straw pile occupying valuable ground while its bulk is reduced to a few loads of almost worthless manure, or cornstalks that may need special mechanical handling in consequence of a threatening borer, all invite some artificial manure making process. This is particularly the case in regions where barnyard manure production is least extensive.

Interest has developed in artificial manure making as a result of the work of Hutchison and Richards of England, who have given the essential requirements for this process. Their method, however, is too laborious and requires too much attention to fit itself readily into the American extensive farming scheme, notwithstanding its feasibility for the market gardener or intensive farmer for whom manure has a much higher value. In view of these conditions and after study and trials of the process, some work was begun in the summer of 1926 to adopt, if possible, the artificial manure making process to general farming conditions in the Middle West.

Plan of Project

The process when applied to straw demands in the main (a) moisture, (b) a source of soluble nitrogen, and (c) neutral or alkaline conditions. With these requisites in mind, plans were made (a) to design a chemical reagent fulfilling the last two requirements, but of such simplicity that its constituents might be obtained readily and combined on the farm;

(b) to mix this material with the straw by applying it through the thresher; and (c) to test the possibility of depending on the rainfall to supply and maintain the needed moisture. The production and use of artificial manure in a farm trial were undertaken on a large farm in Lawrence County, Missouri.

Reagent Used

Since straw contains a large percentage of cellulose which serves as energy material for certain micro-organisms but is deficient in nitrogen or growth-producing substance, the reagent was designed to supplement the straw in such a way as to fulfill the requirements of the bacterial medium for cellulose fermentation as suggested by Omelianski.

Ammonium sulfate was used to supply the nitrogen. Limestone in the common 10-mesh, agricultural form was used with a view of maintaining neutrality. Superphosphate (acid phosphate) was incorporated in the formula to add phosphates to the manure. In addition, small quantities of magnesium sulfate and ordinary salt were put into the mixture, leaving the other requirements of the microorganisms to be supplied by the straw. The mixture included 45 pounds ammonium sulfate, 30 pounds limestone, 15 pounds superphosphate (acid phosphate), and 5 pounds each of magnesium sulfate and sodium chloride per 100 pounds. This, used at the rate of 150 pounds per ton of straw, added nitrogen at the rate of 0.7%, or about 14 pounds per ton, the concentration suggested by Hutchison and Richards as necessary to favor decay.

For economic reasons it seemed desirable to reduce this item, which is suggested as a possibility in the work of Halverson and Torgeson, in order to guard against a loss of nitrogen. The importance of the phosphate, magnesium sulfate, and common salt may be over emphasized by their amounts; but since the phosphates are not easily lost from and are deficient in manure, a fairly liberal quantity was used. The importance of the last two items of the reagent is being determined in some further work now under way which, to date, indicates that they may be omitted.

Applying the Chemicals to the Straw

Under farm conditions where straw accumulates as waste, the quantities are too large to permit much labor in working them over into artificial manure. Consequently, an attachment was fitted to the thresher designed to feed the reagent into the straw while passing through to the stack. This consisted of one section of a fertilizer distributor carrying a hopper and a shaft with a pulley driven by a belt from one of the straw rack shaker shafts. To adjust this to deliver the chemicals at the rate of 150 pounds per ton, the pounds of straw per bushel of grain were determined. The chemicals were then supplied at such a rate per bushel of threshed grain as to provide the proper amount per ton.

Trials of 1926

Three piles of straw were made on July 30. The first one (No. 1) was given the chemicals during threshing, while water from a nearby creek was delivered to the stack through a fish-tailed nozzle located at the end of the blower pipe and connected by a hose to a centrifugal pump driven from the blower shaft. No effort or particular attention was given to stacking the straw. It was merely left to accumulate until the pile contained about 20 tons and had a height of about 16 feet. Another pile (No. 2) was threshed in the same manner as No. 1, save that the water was omitted, and at the finish, the top of the pile was levelled so as to make it receptive to rainfall. This pile was intended to determine whether the rainfall would supply the water to initiate and maintain the process. It contained about 13 tons of straw. The third pile (No. 3), of about the same amount of straw as No. 2, was given neither chemicals nor water. Its top was also levelled to make it open to the rainfall.

Temperatures were taken as a partial index of the activities in decomposition. These, together with the rainfall by periods, are recorded in Table 1. Pile No. 1, which received both reagent and water, indicated its decomposition by a prompt rise in temperature. Pile No. 2 failed to demonstrate much change until after five successive days of rain, August 16 to 29, inclusive, totalling 4.3 inches. Periodic fluctuations in temperature occurred with subsequent additions of rainfall. The temperature of Pile No. 3, without treatment, was scarcely ever higher than that of the atmosphere.

Samples were taken at intervals and differences in decomposition noted. Both piles with chemical treatment showed highly discolored straw. This darkening of the color increased with time, while little evidence of decomposition was noticeable in the untreated straw. The pile given chemicals and water at the outset decayed in restricted but scattered areas where rainfall entered, showing that the initial application of water was insufficient. The pile receiving chemicals and the natural rainfall only decayed

Table 1

Rainfall (Inches) and Temperature (°C) of Artificial Manure in Farm Trials in 1926

Pile number and straw treatment	Temperature on dates recorded											
	August						September				October	
	1	8	15	20	22	30	5	14	23	28	2	15
No. 1 Chemicals and water added ……	44	45	54	51	70	53	38	59	59	10	32	50
No. 2 Chemicals only ….	26	26	26	47	62	54	28	51	51	9	28	30
No. 3 No treatment ..	26	25	26	24	37	38	20	38	38	7	18	22
Air temperatures …..	37	37	35	26	35	27	24	28	28	10	18	24
	Rainfall between recorded dates											
	0.45	—	0.36	4.30[a]	—	0.85	5.92[b]	3.90	—	2.24[c]	2.31[d]	3.90

[a] *Total for five successive days including date of record.*

[b] *Total for two successive days including date of record.*

[c] *Total for four successive days including date of record. Very low temperatures prevailed three days including date of record.*

[d] *Total for three of four days just preceding date of record.*

uniformly throughout. It was evident that the construction of the first pile prohibited uniform rain entrance and that the initial moistening was insufficient to continue the process. The second pile showed clearly that the rainfall could be used for the process, while the absence of decay in the check pile emphasized the importance of the chemicals.

Degree of Decomposition

Samples from the three piles, taken after 70 days, were tested for degree of decomposition by following the method of Jones. According to this method, a 6% solution of hydrogen peroxide may be used to measure the degree of decomposition, since it oxidizes partially decayed straw but does not attack the fresh material. The portion of the organic or combustible matter which was destroyed on treatment with hydrogen peroxide is shown by the data given in Table 2.

Pile No. 1, which received both water and chemicals, was so irregular in decomposition that three samples were used. The other two piles were uniform enough so that one single sample was deemed representative. It is interesting to learn from these data that the degree of decomposition was

Table 2

Degree of Decomposition of Artificial Manure After 70 Days

Pile number and straw treatment	Appearance of sample	Percentage of combustible matter removed by H_2O_2	
No. 1 Chemicals and water added	Bright strawy	11.8	
	Slightly decayed	25.5	27.5
	Very well decayed	45.3	
No. 2 Chemicals only	Well decayed		37.5
No. 3 No treatment	Bright strawy		14.3

about two and a half times as great in pile No. 2 and twice as great in No. 1, both receiving the reagent, as in No. 3 with no treatment. In the very well decayed sample of pile No. 1 the decomposition was over three times that in the check, according to this method of measurement.

The data by the Jones method agreed in all respects with general appearances. To even the casual observer the resemblance to ordinary manure and the ease with which the material could be broken up agreed with the data for the test. By early December, or about 100 days after the start of the process, the straw given chemicals only was rotted well enough to be used as manure. That given both chemicals and water had rotted in limited areas, while the untreated straw showed little or no signs of decay.

In this connection it is well to remember that the speed of the process was due, in no small way, to the excessive rainfall during the trial, as shown in Table 1. During this period of the trial the total rainfall was more than double the normal. This raised the question whether in normal seasons the rainfall would deliver enough water for the process.

Trials of 1927

To answer the above question more fully, the experiment was repeated in 1927. Three piles received the reagent applied through the thresher, while in the case of a fourth pile the reagent was applied by hand. The straw was put into flat piles about 6 feet high which was estimated to be sufficient for normal rainfall. Dependence was placed entirely on the rainfall for moisture.

Unfortunately, the 1927 season, like that of 1926, suffered excessive rainfall, and the straw in piles 6 feet deep was converted to manure by October, earlier by two months than in the first trial when the piles were as high as 14 feet. The degree of decomposition in the second trial after 60 days, as determined by the hydrogen peroxide test, was even greater than that shown in the first trial after 100 days. The material had all the appearances of and handled like manure and could have been used as a dressing for wheat land at seeding time. The pile given the reagent by hand was not as rapid nor as uniform in its decomposition and contained areas where little decay had taken place. This suggests the superiority of the method of applying the reagent through the thresher over its application by hand. Although both the 1926 and 1927 trials experienced high rainfall, the rapidity of the results suggests the possibility of varying the depth of straw to suit the normal rainfall and complete the process in a very short time.

Field Trials with Artificial Manure

If artificial manure making is to be fitted into the wheat farming scheme, for example, it should convert the straw of one crop into manure in time to serve as a winter top dressing for the next crop. Such expectations of the process are not unfair according to the results of either year of these trials. In December 1926, the rotted materials and the unrotted straw from the three treatments were spread at the rate of six loads per acre on separate parts of a field of winter wheat whose uniformity would permit such a test. Barnyard manure was used for comparison. The soil was Cherokee silt loam. This is a soil of level topography with a dark gray silt loam surface of 8 to 10 inches and a distinctly tight or impervious subsoil. The land had been limed with 2½ tons limestone per acre in July previous to the wheat seeding in October. Two hundred pounds of 20% superphosphate (acid phosphate) went on the land with the wheat. A clover mixture was seeded about the middle of March.

Observations on the growing wheat revealed to marked differences, but differences in the clover were noticeable about the time wheat was maturing. Acre yields on the wheat were not taken, but 40 heads gathered at random gave differences in both yield and quality, the latter being the more noticeable (Figs. 2 and 3). Improvements in quality resulted regardless of whether the manure was applied in December or February and some effect was evident even when used as late as April. The dry straw from the untreated stack gave no improvement in the wheat.

The differences in the clover intensified themselves after the wheat harvest. Fig. 4 shows these for sweet clover harvested in late July. Alsike clover gave corresponding differences in size of the plants.

It is interesting to note the effects of the artificial manure above those by lime and phosphate on this soil type. It gave results superior to those of straw and it is especially noteworthy that its effects on sweet clover were greater than those of barnyard manure. Manure spelled the difference in this trial between a stand of clover and no stand. It suggests that the influence of the artificial manure was not one of mere cover, since straw giving this effect failed to guarantee clover, but that probably its influence was one of available nitrogen combined with phosphates, since the latter, even in conjunction with lime, failed to give a stand of the legume comparable to that obtained when these treatments were supplemented by the artificial manure. This emphasizes the importance of the possibilities of using such manure on certain soil types on which wheat farming is common.

The spring of 1927, when the effects on the clover were observed, was one of excessive rains and low temperatures. It is well to remember that under such conditions both the supply of nitrates and the process of nitrification would be low and the effects of available nitrogen might be intensified. This does not deny, however, the beneficial effects of the artificial manure in this trial.

Discussion and Summary

Trials of artificial manure making under farm conditions suggest that this process may find a place in our more common farming schemes. The reagent should be applied at the rate of 150 pounds per ton of straw and should consist of 45% ammonium sulfate, 40% limestone, and 15% superphosphate (acid phosphate). Applying the necessary reagent through the thresher and putting the straw into flat piles of shallow depths make it possible to depend on the rainfall for moisture and to convert the straw into manure in ample time to be used with the least possible loss in bulk. This practice should encourage the utilization of common farm wastes to increase soil organic matter and to conserve soil fertility with no great expense.

With the recent decrease in price of commercial nitrogen, which is the main item of cost in artificial manure making, and in the light of prospectively lower prices, the process may well be encouraged as a means of applying both more nitrogen and more organic matter to the soil with profit. The trials of two years suggest that artificial manure making may well receive consideration as an addition to the list of better farm practices.

CHAPTER 21

Nitrate Accumulation Under the Straw Mulch

Conditions Influencing Nitrification

The literature on nitrification directs attention to the following factors; influence of temperature; effect of moisture; influence of mechanical composition, of aeration, of air-drying, of acidity, and of organic matter in the soil. In this study the acidity and organic matter as significant factors were eliminated by nitrate studies on the same soil mulched and unmulched in the greenhouse. Aeration was controlled by compressed air, and the effect of air-drying was determined by comparing the soils air-dried when put into the greenhouse with those brought in without loss of moisture. In this way it was possible to isolate the factor or factors of this group connected with the depression of nitrate accumulation under the straw-mulched soil as compared with the soil unmulched.

Nature of Soil Used

The soil used, similar to that of the previous experiment, is a brown silt loam of glacial origin with a fine friable structure, about eight inches deep and under-laid by a rather tight, mottled, silty clay loam. Three plots, with treatments given in Table 1, constituted the series used in the study. In the early trials all three plots were used, but as it was evident that the lighter mulch had effects similar to those of the heavier application but to a lesser degree, most of the data from the plot with the 2-ton mulch are omitted here, and no data were taken on this soil in the latter part of the study.

The total nitrogen in the surface soil of these plots[1] varied from 2223 pounds per 2 million in plot 6, to 2278 pounds in plot 5 — a range within the limit of error of determinations, and a difference too insignificant to account for differences in nitrate accumulation. In the spring after the mulch had been removed and the soil had become dry enough to plow (April 17, 1923), these plots contained the amounts of moisture and nitrate shown in Table 2.

Table 1

Treatment of Soils

Plot Number	Spring Treatment	Summer and Winter Treatment
5	Mulch of 1922 removed, plowed and harrowed, 6 tons straw mulch applied April 24, 1923	Weeds pulled, no crop, no cultivation, mulch undisturbed
6	Mulch of 1922 removed, plowed and harrowed, 2 tons straw mulch applied	Weeds pulled, no crop, no cultivation, mulch undisturbed
7	Plowed and harrowed as were nos. 5 and 6, April 17, 1923	Surface scraped, no crop

Table 2

Moisture and Nitrate Nitrogen in Soils at Outset

Plot Number	Treatment	Water-Free Soil	Water Loss	Water Loss	Nitrogen as Nitrate
		gm.	*gm.*	*percent*	*pounds per 2 million*
5	Mulched 6 tons	86.33	13.66	15.82	13.7
6	Mulched 2 tons	84.41	15.58	18.46	14.5
7	Unmulched	84.68	15.32	18.09	10.4

[1] *The total nitrogen determinations were made according to the method modified for nitrates, salicylic acid and sodium thiosulfate being used.*

According to the colorimetric hydrogen-ion determinations, made by following the method suggested by Gillespie, these soils have the following degree of acidity expressed as pH:

	pH
Plot 5	5.8
Plot 6	5.6
Plot 7	5.2

Using the Comber test for soil acidity, these plots showed an order of arrangement similar to that above, giving an appreciably lesser degree of acidity with mulch application.

So far as the "lime need" in terms of soluble iron, and the degree of acidity are concerned — if they are large enough to be of influence on nitrification — they would be expected to favor nitrification in the mulched plot rather than hinder it, since this plot has a lower hydrogen-ion concentration, and a lower "lime need" than the unmulched plot, both conditions favoring nitrate production. Apparently no condition innate to the soil was responsible. According to these suggestions, the depressing effect by the mulch must have come with the mulch, and was probably only temporary.

Every 2 weeks nitrate determinations were made in triplicate on the field soils on composite samples of twelve borings per plot of 15 by 40 feet. To test whether nitrogen was being transformed in the soil, regular ammonia determinations were made from early May through the season, in addition to those for nitrates made during most of the year.[2] These were all based on moisture-free soil, and careful study of the moisture content was made. The data for the ammonia are presented as graphs in Fig. 1, those for nitrates in Fig. 2, and those for soil moisture in Fig. 3.

It is evident that the supply of ammonia under the mulch is not so low as to limit nitrification, since that in the mulched soil giving little nitrification is consistently higher than that in the unmulched where nitrates accumulated. The ammonia content and the nitrate content show no consistent relation, indicating that the conditions inhibiting nitrate accumulation

---

[2] *Nitrate determinations were made on oven-dried samples. These were extracted with 0.0625N hydrochloric acid, the extract made alkaline, boiled to expel the ammonia, the volume replaced, De Varda's metal added, and distilled into standard acid.*
Ammonia was determined by distilling 100 gm. of soil with magnesium oxide by means of steam and air.

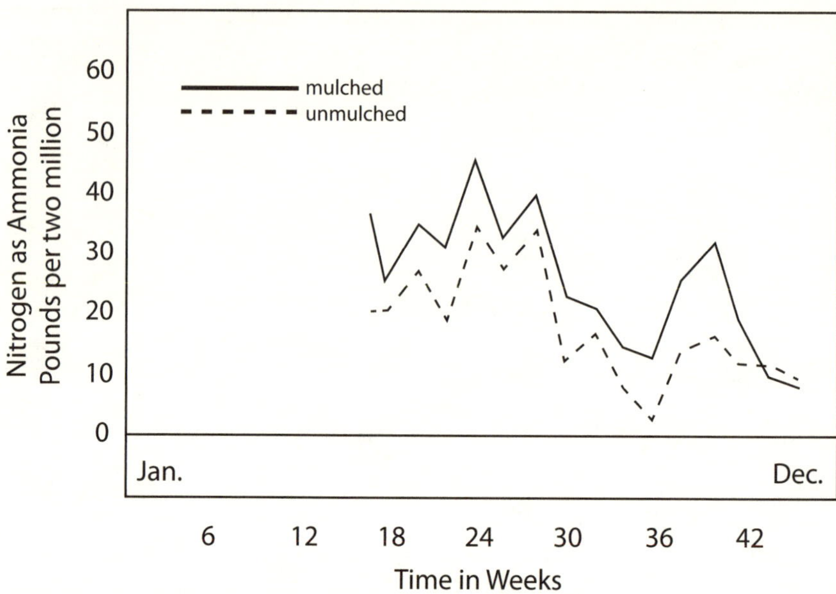

Fig. 1. —Ammonia accumulation in straw mulched and unmulched soils (May to December).

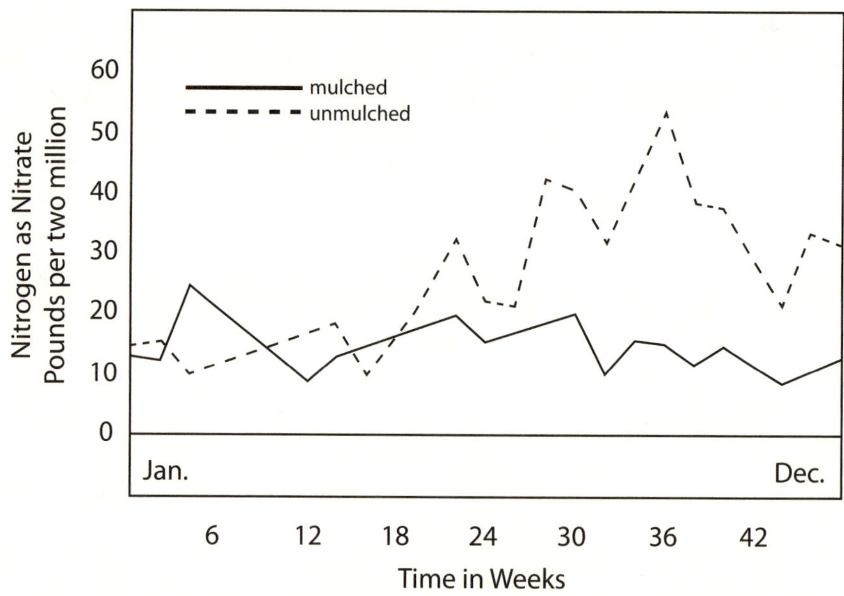

Fig. 2. — Nitrogen as nitrate in straw mulched and unmulched soils (January to December).

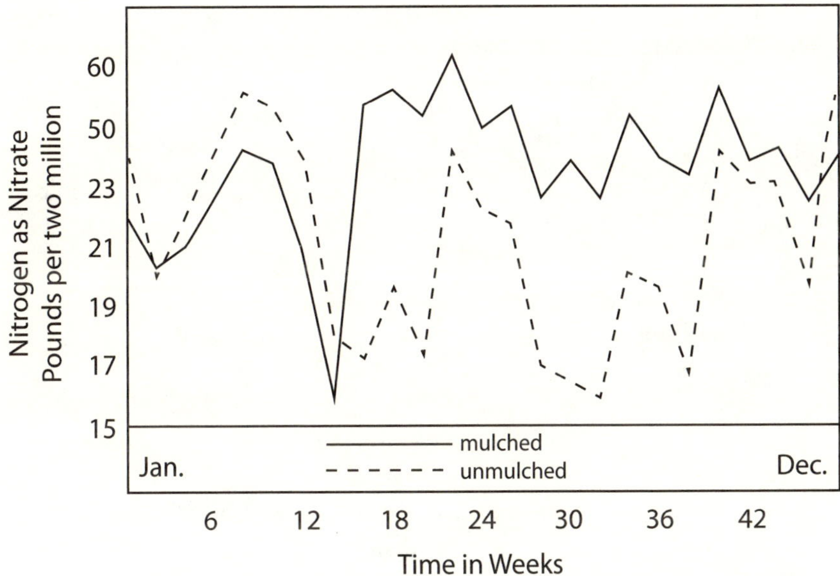

Fig. 3. — Moisture in straw mulched and unmulched soils (January to December).

Table 3

Average Temperatures

Plot	Treatment	Temperature (°C)
5	Mulched 6 tons	24.6
6	Mulched 2 tons	25.5
7	No mulch	27.8

under the mulch do not accomplish it by inhibiting ammonia production. It is evident from the graphs in Fig. 3 that under the mulch the moisture is regularly higher that in plot 5 being, as an average, 2.5 percent higher than that in plot 7. There is further, as previous data have shown, a suggestion of inverse relation between moisture and nitrate accumulation in plot 5 under the mulch. The variations in moisture in many cases, however, were so small as compared to nitrate fluctuations, that this can scarcely be considered as the factor solely responsible for the depressing effect of the mulch on nitrate accumulation.

Increased moisture under the mulch gave lower soil temperatures. Data on temperatures recorded by thermometers at depths of 3 inches were usually the same on the mulched and unmulched plots in the early part of the day, or after a rain, but differed widely at 5 o'clock in the afternoon. The averages of weekly temperatures for daily readings at this time during June, July, August and September are given in Table 3. The data emphasize the importance of the higher moisture under the mulch as a means of keeping the soil from warming as much during the day.

While the field studies were being made, physical differences in the mulched and unmulched soils were apparent. With equal proportions of moisture in both soils, that from beneath the mulch was plastic, sticky, and of poor tilth, but the unmulched soil worked well. The former seemed more solid, more run together, and of much poorer tilth.

The data and observations pointed out that temperature differences in the two soils were not wholly responsible for the differences in nitrate accumulation; that the greater accumulation of ammonia under the mulch suggested poor nitrification but not poor ammonification; and that a poor physical condition of the soil resulted under the mulch carrying higher moisture.

Pot Experiments

As a result of the suggestions given in the data, some of the soils from the unmulched and the heavily mulched plots were brought into the greenhouse for a careful study of the possible causes of the low nitrate under the mulch. The unmulched soil in the field had an average moisture content for the previous summer seasons of 19 percent, and the heavily mulched, 25 percent. These figures were adopted as "normal" for these soils during the experiment. The soils were mixed by sifting, were put into 1-gallon jars, and moisture was maintained as near normal as possible. Part was thoroughly air-dried, and remoistened to test the effect of a single air-drying treatment on the nitrate accumulation; the rest was used with as little moisture loss as possible. At the outset these soils contained 15.9 pounds and 26 pounds nitrogen as nitrate, per 2 million pounds of soil for the mulched and unmulched plots respectively. The following treatments were used in duplicate pots.

Treatments

1. Fresh soil, check.
2. Fresh soil, ammonium sulfate.[3]
3. Soil air-dried, remoistened to normal moisture.
4. Soil air-dried, ammonium sulfate, remoistened to normal moisture.
5. Soil air-dried, remoistened to 25 percent when normal was 19 or vice versa.
6. Soil air-dried, remoistened to 25 percent when normal was 19 or vice versa, and previously unmulched soil mulched,[4] previously mulched soil left unmulched.

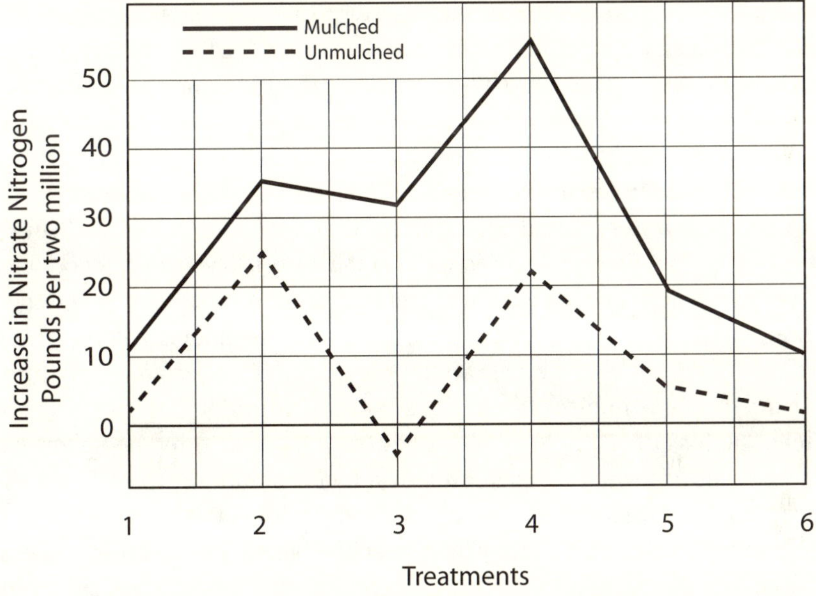

Fig. 4. — Increase in nitrate nitrogen in straw mulched and unmulched soils in pots.

[3] *Ammonium sulfate was applied in solution at the rate of 3 mg. of nitrogen per 100 gm. of soil.*
[4] *Straw was applied at the rate of 25 gm. per pot about 7 inches in diameter.*

Nitrates were determined at the time the pots were set up, and then again at intervals of 6, 10, and 17 weeks to determine the accumulation of nitrogen as nitrate under these conditions. The gains in nitrate nitrogen during the 17 weeks for the treatments on these two soils are shown in Fig. 4.

The general outstanding feature of these results is the marked difference in response in nitrate production by the soils from the mulched and unmulched plots. In the soil from the mulched plot, nitrate accumulation was greater under every treatment, indicating that this soil, put under different treatments, had even greater nitrate-producing power than the soil not mulched. Especially significant are the facts (a) that drying the mulched soil but once gave an increase in nitrate almost as large as that given by adding ammonium sulfate without drying; and (b) that air-drying and holding the moisture at 19 percent, instead of the normal 25 percent, also gave significant nitrate accumulation. In the unmulched soil the addition of ammonium sulfate was the only treatment that gave significant nitrate increases in the pots during the 17 weeks.

A marked difference in physical condition persisted in these soils, even after a single air-drying treatment at the outset. These differences are shown in plate 1. The soil under the mulch seldom froze at this latitude, consequently freezing and thawing as factors in maintaining good structure were little active. Alternate wetting and drying were also less significant in structural improvement, since the mulch prohibited, to no small extent, the loss of water;[5] nor was a new supply of air often being drawn into the soil, following the water removal by evaporation, which fact may be of great importance in explaining the irregularity in the accumulation of nitrates under the mulch. It may have been the beneficial effects in respect to structure and aeration that contributed to the marked improvement in nitrate accumulation in the mulched soil following a single air-drying.

Aeration Studies

As a result of the correlation between improved physical condition and increased nitrates in the mulched soil after air-drying, and to learn whether possibly the mulch was holding down nitrification through poor aeration caused by the high moisture and bad physical condition, the soils

[5] *For every gram of water lost from the unmulched soil there was a loss of but 0.4 gm. from the mulched soil. The mulched soil, air-dried, remoistened, and left unmulched, lost 13.4 percent more water than the same treatment without air-drying.*

were put into tubes about two inches in diameter and eight inches deep through which air could be forced. Air was forced first through water to prevent drying of the soil and then through each tube separately, sometimes through the soil from the top downward and then from the bottom upward. The tubes were filled with the equivalent of 320 gm. oven-dry soil, a series each from the mulched and unmulched plots, and given the various treatments together with daily aeration for 45 days. The results in nitrate increase are shown in Fig. 5. The initial content of nitrate nitrogen for the mulched soil was 15.9 pounds per acre when fresh, and 9.8 pounds when dried; and for the unmulched soil it was 26.0 pounds when fresh, and 31.1 pounds when dried.

The outstanding result of this trial is the discovery of the influence of aeration in increasing the nitrate formed in both soils, whether mulched or unmulched, but especially in the former. This suggests that the deficiency in aeration may have been a factor responsible for the low nitrate accumulation in the mulched soil. The most significant increase resulted in the mulched soil, which was air-dried, brought again to its "normal" or high moisture content of 25 percent, and then aerated. In this case the increase in nitrate nitrogen was 97.1 mg. in 320 gm. dry soil in the period of 17 weeks. This suggests that aeration of this soil helps nitrate accumulation, but that this effect is much greater when the soil is first dried, restored to its moisture, and then aerated.

Since aeration gave marked results in connection with these soils, especially with the higher moisture content and after air-drying, another series of tubes was set up as before so that the effect of drying the soil, and the effect of raising the moisture content of the unmulched soil from 19 percent (average in this plot) to 25 percent (average in the field for the mulched plot), and of reducing it in the mulched soil from 25 percent (average in this plot) to 19 percent (average in the field for the unmulched plot) might be noted. This test was run for 45 days during the winter. Although it did not give the gross increases as did the previous test, it gave differences comparable for treatments (Fig. 6).

As in the previous test, aeration had a significant influence: it raised the nitrate content of the soil from the mulched plot to that in the unmulched soil, and gave the greatest increase in the soil previously mulched, but air-dried, remoistened and aerated.

That the moisture in connection with the physical condition is significant in holding down nitrate accumulation under the mulch is shown by

Treatments

1. Soil from field, not aerated.
2. Soil from field, aerated.
3. Soil from field, aerated, ammonium sulfate.
4. Soil from field, not aerated, ammonium sulfate.
5. Soil air-dried, normal moisture, aerated.

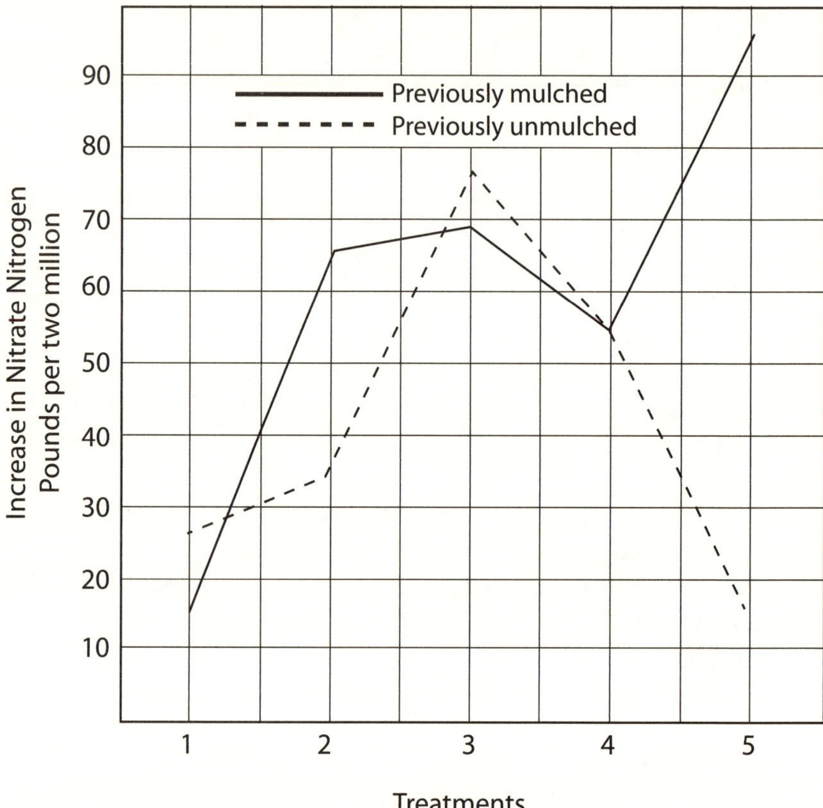

Fig. 5. — Increase in nitrate nitrogen in soils in aeration tubes (first trial).

three things; (a) the low nitrate content that occurred in the unmulched soil when the moisture was raised to that of the mulched soil (25 percent), (b) the significant nitrate increase in the previously mulched soil without aeration when its moisture was reduced, and (*c*) the nitrate increase when the previously mulched soil was merely dried and restored to its original moisture. The previously mulched soil gave especially high nitrates when in addition to the last treatment it was also aerated.

Treatments

1. Soil from field, not aerated.
2. Soil from field, aerated.
3. Soil from field, moisture changed to 25 percent when normal was 19 percent or vice versa, not aerated.
4. Soil from field, moisture changed as in treatment 3, aerated.
5. Soil air-dried, normal moisture, not aerated.
6. Soil air-dried, normal moisture, aerated.

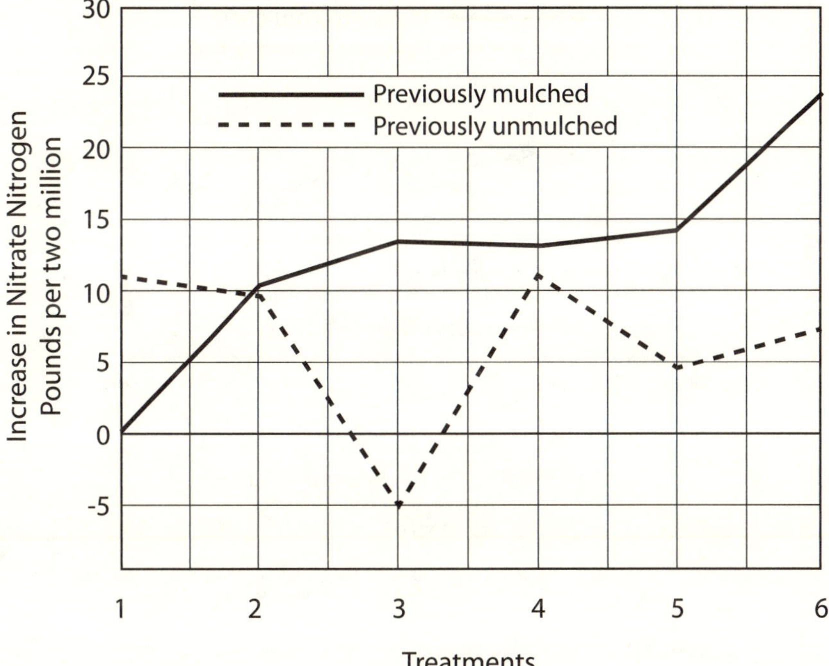

Fig. 6. — Increase in nitrate nitrogen in soils in aeration tubes (second trial).

The marked responses by these soils under the above condition suggest that mulching raised the moisture content of the soil and brought on a physical condition that slowed down nitrate accumulation. Forcibly aerating the soil, lowering its moisture, or drying it once to alter its physical condition increased the nitrate accumulation very markedly. It is well to remember that this soil had been under a straw mulch of about six tons per acre for almost four years, with the mulch removed in the spring only long enough to permit drying and plowing of the plot. When the mulch was removed and this soil plowed it showed poorer granulation and, in

Table 4

Average of Temperature Readings

	Previously Mulched (From Plot 5)				Previously Unmulched (From Plot 7)			
	Unmulched		Mulched		Unmulched		Mulched	
Depth (inches)	0	3	0	3	0	3	0	3
Temperature, °C	22°	20°	21°	21°	22°	21°	22°	22°

Table 5

Nitrate Accumulation in Soil as a Result of Mulching or Removing Mulch (Pounds Nitrate Nitrogen per 2 Million Water-Free Soil)

Flat Number	Treatment	Start	After 5 Weeks	Gain	After 10 Weeks	Gain	After 17 Weeks	Gain
Soil Previously Mulched (Plot 5)								
1	No mulch	10.97	15.24	4.27	21.63	10.66	19.54	8.57
2	Mulch	10.97	15.08	4.11	13.42	2.45	12.03	2.06
Soil Previously Unmulched (Plot 7)								
3	No mulch	34.78	24.99	–9.79	30.53	–4.25	25.69	–9.09
4	Mulch	34.78	25.31	–9.47	30.19	–4.59	15.59	–19.19

general, poorer tilth. The regularly high moisture content as a result of the cover and the failure of the mulched plot to undergo alternate wetting and drying, or alternate freezing and thawing — all of which provoke bad structure — may be responsible in no small measure for the differences in the nitrate accumulation between this soil and that left unmulched.

Soils in Greenhouse Flats

The next step in the study consisted in reversing the conditions in the mulched and unmulched soils by bringing each of these soils into flats in the greenhouse, and giving each the treatment of a mulch and no mulch. Four flats, each 2 feet square and 1 foot deep were used, two with the soil from the previously unmulched plot and two from the mulched plot.

Table 6

Nitrification of Solutions when Inoculated from Mulched and Unmulched Soils (32-Day Test)

Greenhouse Treatment	Inoculation from Flats Mulched in Field		Inoculation from Flats Unmulched in Field	
	Nitrogen as Nitrate	Nitrogen Oxidized	Nitrogen as Nitrate	Nitrogen Oxidized
	mg.	*percent*	*mg.*	*percent*
No mulch........	2.59	25.9	2.89	28.9
Mulch............	2.04	20.4	1.98	19.8

One of each pair was given a straw mulch similar to that in the field and the other of the pair was left unmulched. In the field, the mulched plot commonly had a much lower temperature than the soil unmulched. In the greenhouse this was obviated, since the temperature records on these flats over the period of 29 days (Table 4) show the average of readings about the same on all four flats, or no difference in favor of either the presence or absence of the mulch. Nitrate determinations were made on the flats at intervals of 5, 10, and 17 weeks with the results given in Table 5.

The data show clearly the effect of removing the mulch as a means of increasing the nitrates, and the effect of adding the mulch as a means of depressing their accumulation. As bringing the soil into the greenhouse represents a different temperature condition and a different rate of moisture loss, some irregularities may have been caused by these. The soil from the unmulched plot never increased its total supply of nitrates whether mulched or unmulched; on the other hand, a significant decrease in nitrate nitrogen resulted when the mulch was applied and left for 17 weeks.

Here again the mulched soils, whether previously mulched or unmulched in the field, had the lower nitrates and also the higher constant moisture. The soils in all cases were brought up to the same moisture twice weekly. The soil having a mulch in the field lost 2.55 pounds of water when unmulched in the greenhouse, as compared to 1 pound when mulched. The soil not mulched in the field lost 2.39 pounds as compared to 1 pound for the above respective treatments in the greenhouse.

Studies with Nitrifying Solutions

These same soils were sampled after 10 weeks and inoculations made from them into sterile solutions in the laboratory, in order to test the change of 10 mg. of nitrogen as ammonia to nitrates in 32 days. In each case, the change to nitrates was greater in flasks inoculated with the unmulched soil, as shown in Table 6. The ammonia nitrogen was more slowly oxidized when inoculations were made from soil under the mulch. This suggests that the presence of the mulch influences the nitrifying flora so that their activity is lessened possibly through decreased numbers or lessened virulence.

Summary

A careful study in the field and in the greenhouse of the causes of low nitrate accumulation in a soil under straw mulch as compared with the nitrate accumulation in the same soil without mulch has shown that:

1. The failure of nitrates to accumulate is not due to a shortage of ammonia nitrogen, since this is present in larger quantities under the mulch than in soil not mulched.
2. Aerating the mulched soil increased nitrate accumulation.
3. Modifying the structure of the mulched soil by air-drying and remoistening gave a marked increase in nitrate accumulation.
4. Air-drying and remoistening coupled with aeration, gave the highest nitrate accumulation.
5. Applying the mulch increased the soil moisture content and brought on a marked change in soil structure, with less granulation and poorer tilth.
6. Soil, used as inoculum, from the plot under the mulch had a much lower nitrifying efficiency as measured by change of ammonia to nitrate in solution.
7. Reducing the moisture content of the soil under the mulch to that of the soil without mulch gave a slight increase in nitrates, while raising the moisture of the unmulched soil to that of the mulched gave a decided decrease in nitrates. This decrease, however, was prevented by aeration. This emphasizes that the mulch exerts some force on depressing nitrate accumulation through lessened aeration as a result of increased soil moisture.
8. Removing the mulch gave a marked increase in nitrate accumula-

tion after 2 months, while its application to a previously unmulched soil brought on a marked decrease in the same time even though the moisture remained unchanged.

Conclusions

These facts all indicate that the straw mulch, in applications as heavy as 6 tons per acre, cuts down evaporation, thereby increasing the moisture, lowering the temperature and preventing the normal exchange of air, all of which induce a poor physical condition and unfavorable environment for nitrate accumulation.

Accompanying these physical changes there may be some significant chemical factors, as change in solubilities as a result of drying as shown by Gustafson, or other factors, since Lebedjantzev believes that the yielding power of a soil is maintained by alternate wetting and drying; but nevertheless, the mulch brings on the changed physical conditions which depress the nitrate accumulation, and the removal of which restores the normal nitrate activities.

CHAPTER 22

Organic Matter for Plant Nutrition

IT WAS THE FAMOUS ZOOLOGIST and geologist, Agassiz, who suggested that we "Study Nature not books." Then, with similar suggestions that we put "Nature before man," there was a poem in the ancient Latin, entitled (in translation) "For Nature Will be Conquered Only by Obeying." That thought set up in rhyme was widely quoted several decades ago as "The Riddle of the Sphinx." Science started as, and in truth still is, the organization of knowledge of natural phenomena. Unfortunately, we study technology, now, more than "natural" science.

The so-called "natural" gardeners and farmers are given to practices founded on empiricism or on the knowledge that those practices readily serve. Why their methods succeed is not yet interpreted by either science or sales literature. Natural gardeners use organic matter for the return of plant nutrients and the mobilization by decomposition and "chelation"[1] of both the active and the reserve mineral elements as nutrients, to say nothing of newly synthesized organic compounds for higher qualities in the vegetable crops. Because by those gardening and farming practices, they try to duplicate the natural environment through which climax crops are grown in man's absence rather than under a synthetic environment by this technological management, they have been derided by methods which in public debate are called "Argumentum ad hominem," a personal attack on the opponent and not on the subject.

Adherence to the belief that soil organic compounds are essential in plant nutrition is claimed by pseudo-scientists and their sophisticated science to be a case of "clinging to a myth." Those claims are often prompted

[1] *A combining of the inorganic elements into a large non-ionized organic molecule.*

by some bias for sales promotion. They forget that much that is "professional" in practice and of extensive service is no more than empiricism. It is by starting with empirical knowledge, however, that we are prompted to search for causes, and become scientific. Hence, we can still wisely use empiricism. We still do so extensively. The physiology of relief by taking aspirin, a drug consumed annually by the tons, is still a scientific *unknown.* Its use in medical practice may be also called a "myth" when it is founded on no more than the grinding of swamp-willow bark and using the extract of this as medicine.

Consequently, when the inorganic or mineral parts of plant nutrition are so widely emphasized and promoted, but the organic parts of the nutritional support are neglected, it might be well to tabulate some of the reasons for the undue emphasis of the inorganic and to present some of the un-familiar "organic" facts of natural plant growth. It would be helpful to prevent some of the unfortunate tactics of useless debate about plant nutrition as commercially practiced. It might be more helpful to study crop growth in Nature without man's management, but on fertile soils and according to particular climatic settings responsible for these.

The Dead Ash, Not the Living Organic Substance is Emphasized

When some of the pioneer botanists[2] studied plant growth in the very dilute aqueous solutions of highly-ionized and chemically active salts, they were aiming at an accurate determination of the different elements required for plant growth. Research today is still using that method to determine the essentiality of various micro-nutrients or "trace" elements not yet so catalogued. But even that method is, seemingly, not refined enough to measure the small amounts of chemical substances to which the life processes of plants respond.

But nutrient solutions will supply plants over but a short period of time. Their use cannot enlighten us on the ratios of the amounts of elements taken in, or what amounts in combination of them would be considered a "balanced" plant diet. Such solutions require frequent changes or supplementations by a few elements. Unlike the soil growing plants naturally,

---

[2] *Among the formulators of nutrient solutions were the early names of Sachs, 1860, and Knop, 1865, of Germany, and the later name of Hoagland, 1948, of California.*

they cannot supply, at the outset, the growing season's total supply within the volume of root-reach.

As for the ratios of the dozen or more inorganic elements in any nutrient solution, those relations are determined by solubilities and the necessary prevention of their precipitation out of solution as insolubles and unavailables. Hence, solutions do not enable one to determine the effects on the plant's chemical composition by variable ratios between two, three or more nutrient elements. Those effects by natural soil variations in such ratios are widely demonstrated by differences in the amounts or ratios of elements absorbed on, and exchanged to, the root by the soil's clay or humus fractions. Those effects can now be readily demonstrated and measured by the colloidal technique which uses organic compounds both natural in the soil and synthesized in commerce, as well as by the finer fractions of colloidal clay.

The nutrient solution technique of the laboratory, or its commercial application as "hydroponics," does not permit variation in ratios offered to meet the needs of different plants. Instead, it demands a dilution to the degree of expecting the inorganic ions to behave more nearly according to the laws of mixtures of gases (behaving independently of each other) rather than according to interchanges and reactions with precipitation out of solution complete enough to duplicate conditions accepted for quantitative chemical analyses. When the use of only the soluble inorganic salts for plant nutrition as a technology falls so far short of duplicating the growth of crops rooted in the soil as were Nature's methods during the ages of plant evolution for their healthy survival — and when the major crops are grown where rainfall exceeds evaporation to wash soluble salt out of the soil — shall we chide the unsophisticated gardeners and farmers for trying to fit their soil and crop practices more nearly to what they call the "natural," and what they have found successful during the centuries rather than what is only a recent technology? For them, the nutrients for all life coming from the soil are still "insoluble but available" to the crops by natural methods. They still speak of "A Living Soil" and according to their successes, "natural" farming is no myth.

Knowledge Comes Slowly

The development of our scientific information about plant nutrition and crop production naturally depended on the advances of chemical science. That consisted of only inorganic chemistry for many years. That early science was given to "ash" analyses. By combustion, those procedures eliminated, at the very outset, what is organic and what makes up about twenty times as much of the crop bulk as the inorganic parts do.

Then, also, we learn chemistry by beginning with the inorganic aspects including now about one hundred elements. Even that beginning phase of chemical science proves highly lethal to any further interest of a high percentage of students of that science. All too many of them fail to arrive at the organic phase of it. They do not learn of its many synthetic processes representing at this date about a half million different known compounds resulting mainly in connection with the life processes dependent initially on the organic synthetic processes of plants.

The study of soil as plant nutrition began by matching plant ash with its list of inorganic elements against the similar list of the ignited soil's composition. When organic chemistry came along so late to become a synthetic science in place of mainly an analytical one in only recent decades, it should not be surprising that agricultural practices have not become concerned about organic compounds taken from soils by plants for their nutrition.

But it should be surprising (to say nothing of poor faith to his students) to see the reported claim of a chemist-agronomist of an experiment station that "Before the plant foods contained in compost, manure and other organic matter can be used by plants, they must be broken down by bacteria into simple *mineral* compounds which the plants assimilate, and there is no difference between these minerals and those processed in fertilizer factories."[3]

For one content with such a naive concept of plant nutrition which limits "plant foods"[4] to the inorganic substances of mineral (rock) origin even in the use of composts, the sight of a mushroom crop and its rapid growth would not be impressive, even when it grows by feeding on the organic compounds released by decomposing manure at only a certain stage in that natural process. Perhaps the teachings of the above type and the neglect to teach so many other basic and natural truths are reasons why the crop's growth on soil by means of many organic compounds, as well as of the inorganic elements — both assimilated by the roots — remains a myth in

---

[3] *Reader's Digest, July, 1962, p. 104.*

[4] *The term "plant foods," according to botanical usage, refers to substances synthesized particularly by the leaf processes and taken up as organic compounds by the cells. Those substances serve in the metabolic processes within the cells. The inorganic elements taken from the soil are considered as "nutrients", since they do not supply energy in plant nutrition.*

the classroom where it might better be interpreted as Nature's contribution through which man attempts to manage plant nutrition.

Seemingly, our teachings are limited to thinking only of inorganic salts and their plant service, or only as the very beginnings of chemical science envisioned them. Apparently the botanical science of plant physiology also is not studied extensively in agricultural production to learn the natural plant processes of organic compounds involved, when the tests of the use of only inorganic elements in plant nutrition on most any soil are undergirded by commercial grants to subsidize them.

Fertilizer Inspection Uses Dual Criteria

Inspection of commercial fertilizers by states also abets our ignorance of the role of soil organic matter in plant nutrition, while it helps the manufacturers see the chemical compositions of their competitors' goods determined by the state inspection. That is a special service to the fertilizer manufacturers, even though it is claimed to be such to the farmers who pay the costs of it. That inspection uses water solubilities as the criteria for the amounts of nitrogen and the potassium in the erroneous belief that such a quantity *outside* of the soil is an index of their availability to, or absorption by, the plant roots for fertilizers *within* the soil.

But for inspecting the phosphorus guaranteed in the fertilizer, which element is taken by plants from mineral compounds too insoluble for solution in water to approach their availability to plants from soil, the criterion is solubility in an organic solution viz. ammonium citrate. This suggests that it is a chelating solution of the phosphorus by means of an organic substance and, unwittingly, makes a close approach to the methods by which we now know plants mobilize the inorganic nutrients both from the soil and within themselves. By accident, not by science, one-third of the service, namely the test for one of the three inspected elements, is unknowingly using what is *natural* and has only recently been recognized within that aspect by our thinking.

Chelation, Nature's Mobilization of the Inorganic Elements by the Organic Molecules

Within the last decade or two the significance of the soluble salt aspect and the ionization of its inorganic elements in plant nutrition has been reduced decidedly. Instead, their role in non-ionized union within larger organic molecules has become magnified and extensive in Nature. Now the chemistry of plant growth (and of other life forms) is spoken of as "molecular biochemistry." Reactions are between large molecules, as illustrated by magnesium in chlorophyll during the past ages. That inorganic element within the immense chlorophyll molecule is not rendering service in photosynthesis by ionic behaviors of the magnesium as we have been comprehending most inorganic behaviors. We do not know just how the magnesium serves.

Now that some organic compounds, produced in the laboratory, take from solutions and hold the inorganic elements by what seems much of a duplication of their adsorption (and exchange) by the inorganic clay minerals, we speak of that organic behavior toward the inorganic as "chelation" of the latter by the former. The commercial organic compound ethylene diamine tetra-acetic acid (EDTA) is an illustration used extensively in recent experimental work. It adsorbs, or chelates, many different inorganic parts with improved nutritional services by the latter as a consequence of the uptake by the root and activities within the plant of that combination of the inorganic as an integral and non-ionizing part of the larger organic molecule. This is a service by the soil organic matter, or humus, in ways even more complex than those corresponding helps rendered by the clay fraction of the soil when it adsorbs and exchanges to the roots, the calcium, magnesium and other ions which are insoluble yet available because of that natural phenomenon.

One of the significant demonstrations of this natural phenomena was made by one of the naturalists among scientists, Professor Midgeley of Vermont, years ago. He studied the effects on the crop by phosphates and barnyard manure applied separately to the soil in contrast to mixing them before their application. The latter gave much better plant growth and made so much more phosphorus available as shown by plant composition, than the former method.

Drs. Hopkins and Whiting of Illinois, gave similar demonstration of the higher availability of phosphorus from rock phosphate when that was plowed under along with red clover as a leguminous green manure in a kind of sheet composting performance within the soil.

But more recently Vernon E. Renner of the Missouri Experiment Station, introduced radioactive phosphorus into the soil for use by young barley. That crop was harvested, carefully analyzed and used as an organic manure for a soybean crop on a soil high in its inorganic phosphorus, according to soil test. The application of the organic manure at the rate of a ton per acre mobilized its phosphorus into the soybean crop with an efficiency just a hundred times that of the movement of the inorganic soil phosphorus along the same biochemical course for crop production.

Methods of Teaching May Need Modification

The separation of inorganic chemistry from organic chemistry, in our methods of learning that science, has magnified unwittingly that former phase as if it were more important than the organic one in crop production. This has been unfortunate, when in Nature there is no such separation. The research into the biochemistry of photosynthesis by Melvin Calvin,[5] which won the Nobel prize recently, emphasizes phosphorus active in the first carbon compound in the production of sugar by photosynthesis. That first compound is not a six-carbon sugar. Instead, it is a three-carbon compound containing phosphorus. Then, two of those unite by splitting out the phosphorus to result in the six-carbon sugar — formerly considered the first stage in photosynthetic action — and releasing the phosphorus to repeat its service in synthesizing the three-carbon compounds into six-carbon ones.

Thus, there are natural exhibitions in which the so-called anionic phosphorus coming from the soil is chelated and combined into most improved molecular biochemistry of growth. We are gradually appreciating the similar services by cationic elements such as magnesium in chlorophyll, iron in hemoglobin of blood and copper in the similar life fluid of the crustaceans, like the lobster. We are viewing similarly many other enzyme-like performances in which the extensive list of inorganic macro- and microelements of the soil as either cations or anions are doing wonders within large molecules with a ratio of their ash to organic part that duplicates the ratios of those in living tissues. The arts of the pioneer practicioners of empiricism, i.e. the trial and error methods aiming to duplicate Nature's behaviors, have long preceded what is now technology and the science supporting it. The latter is, unfortunately, coming along all too slowly when potential commercialization rather than curiosity about the natural is the major stimulus for research.

[5] *Melvin Calvin. The Path of Carbon in Photosynthesis. Science 135:879–889, 1962.*

Agronomic Science Becoming More Organic-Minded

Textbooks of botany and bulletins of some years ago reported the uptake of organic compounds for their nutritional service.[6] Amongst those reported as improvers of plant growth were such complex ones as coumarin, vanillin, pyridine, quinoline, asparigin, nucleic acids, and, in fact, some in each group of carbohydrates, organic acids and nitrogenous compounds. In entomological work, commercial research by the Boyce-Thompson Institute of near two decades ago reported that some three hundred and more organic compounds — aimed to be "systemic" insect poisons within the plants — were taken into the plant roots from the soil.[7] Apparently such reports have not registered as cases of soil organic matter serving as large organic molecules moving into the plants from the soil. Research at the Missouri Experiment Station by Dr. George Wagner, working with seedlings under sterile conditions, has been demonstrating sugars and proteinaceous substances taken as nutritional values for them.

But it remained for P.C. de Kock of Scotland to combine science and empiricism for attention by both the agronomists and the so-called "Natural" practitioners, when in 1955 he reported his exhibition of the curative effects on chlorotic plants offered and taking up the commercial organic compound, ethylene diamine tetra-acetic acid (EDTA, molecular weight 380.20) and thereby mobilizing iron from the soil; and when he duplicated the same beneficial effects by substituting for the EDTA the organic matter extracted from the soil. Thus natural organic matter demonstrated its activities in moving the essential mineral nutrient for plants, namely, iron in chelation possibilities just as was demonstrated for the commercial organic EDTA.[8]

Only very recently was it demonstrated that an inorganic element fed to plants through the roots in chelated union with EDTA is no longer under control of that organic chelating agent by the time it is moving up through the stem. When samples of the exudate from the cut stem were examined, the organic element initially controlled by EDTA was chelated with other compounds, mainly the simpler malic (apple) acid (molecular weight 158.11) and malonic acid (molecular weight 104.06).[9] This indicates the

[6] *Edwin C. Miller. Plant Physiology. McGraw-Hill, 1938.*

[7] *Annual meeting Amer. Assn. Adv. of Science, St. Louis, Missouri.*

[8] *P. C. deKock. Influence of Humic Acids on Plant Growth. Science 121:474, 1955.*

[9] *L.O. Tiffin and J. C. Brown. Iron Chelates in Soybean Exudates. Science 135:311–313, 1962.*

possibility that many organic compounds within the plant are operating to reduce the ionic activities of inorganic elements and are moving them about within the plants as parts of larger organic molecules. It is the latter, then, that dominates the former. The "ash" contributions from the soil come under control of *molecular biochemistry.*

Now that we find the natural behavior duplicating what we have done by laboratory techniques, we as agronomists are more ready to accept possible functions in plant nutrition by soil organic matter with more credence. The way is now open for many forthcoming research projects on soil organic matter for plant nutrition. This highly neglected half or more of past plant nutrition bids fair to be elucidated in the near future. But when the essentiality of inorganic elements is still an unfinished task that involves a list of no more than a hundred in total, then by what names might he not be called who will suggest a research project even under federal funds to determine the essentiality of the many organic compounds, of which but a half million are characterized or catalogued to date?

Discriminating Animals May Aid Research in Organic Compounds

The use of animals as bioassayers of feeds demonstrates that they recognize the dangerous, or beneficial, effects within what they will consume because of organic compounds taken directly by the plants from the soil. Animals respond to effects also from organic compounds in the soil as manures or organic fertilizers of the crops fed. Livestock has not taken readily to pasturing green sweet clover. If confined to a field of such, the various animals will first clean up the fence rows, water courses and areas of vegetation other than the sweet clover. Their reluctant taking of any sweet clover suggests such as only an act of desperation. They apparently recognize in the dicumerol, synthesized by that crop, its anti-coagulating effects on the blood and its cause of bleeding to death on injury or surgical treatment of the animals.

Hogs, given choice of corn grain grown with sweet clover as the preceding crop turned under for leguminous organic manure on plots given increasing combination treatments of calcium in lime, phosphorus and potassium, discriminated sharply amongst four simultaneous offerings of the grains. Those choices differed according to whether the sweet clover was turned under green in spring, or merely as the residue of a

Natural chelation is suggested when phosphatic fertilizer and barnyard manure applied separately are not biochemically as effective (Pots 9 and 12) as when applied to the soil in a mixture (Pots 10 and 13, with three inches of soil treated in case of the first numbers and six inches, the second.)

crop grown for seed the preceding year. In case of the organic manure of sweet clover residues from its use as seed crop on the four plots, the hogs chose to eat more of the grain according as more inorganic fertilizers were applied, or as more yield of corn per acre resulted. However, when sweet clover was turned under green ahead of the corn planting, the hogs decided to choose exactly in the reverse order. For them the less green, sweet clover used to fertilize the corn, the better. They preferred no green sweet clover as organic fertilizer for the production of their corn (maize) as feed.

No chemical data were taken to tell us whether dicumerol, or organic compounds suggesting it, were in the corn grain. The hogs merely reported that organic matter from green sweet clover, used to fertilize corn, carried organic effects in the grain which they refused. On the contrary, sweet clover used as dried, matured residue carried organic effects into the grain of their highest choice. While many folks may be deriding organic farming, the hogs vote for it. But they are not speaking of it in general. Even they report that judgment must be exercised as to the kinds of organic farming one is talking about, and that associated with attention to the inorganic essentials.

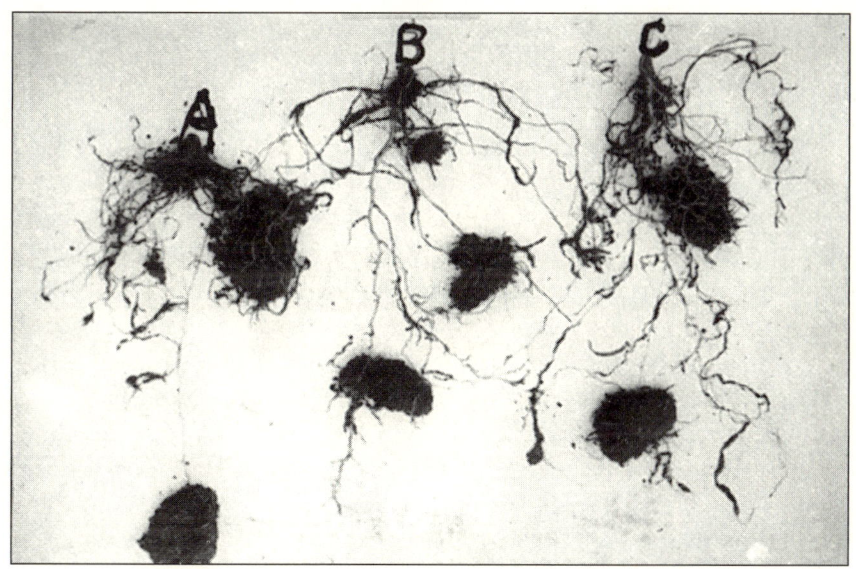

The phosphate-manure mixture plowed under in the field grew clumps of roots in the buried clumps of manure, even though it was but a delicate root that searched out those root-growing fertility centers. Lower photo of three plants, A, B, C, carefully dug from the soil.

(Photo courtesy of Prof. A. R. Midgley, Vermont Experiment Station.)

It is not common knowledge that the organic compounds of well known, specific, chemical structure giving the fecal odor, namely, indole and skatole, will be taken up by a plant like the white dwarf bean of Michigan fame. But it was demonstrated by Dr. F.M. Pottenger, Jr., of California, that those odorous organics as taken may be either stored in the seeds with the scent emanating from them, or may be converted into the well known growth-hormone, indole-acetic acid. That was suggested when fertilization of the soil by cat dung from raw milk fed the cats converted the dwarf beans to pole beans in two cat pens but corresponding dung or manure from cooked milk fed the cats in six pens did not violate their growth behavior claimed by their pedigree as dwarf plants.

Composting Pulverized Minerals is Natural

Nature's management of soil for extended maintenance of its high productivity of crops as nutrition for all other life forms consists of two major practices. The first is the regular applications by wind (loess, dusts, etc.) and by water (alluvium, inwash, etc.) of deposits of unweathered, finely pulverized rock-mixtures on the surface of the soil. The second is the regular covering of the soil surface by organic matter as crop residues.

By the latter, as energy and sustenance for the microbial flora, its life processes decomposing the finely pulverized minerals represent an active development of a new stratum of surface soil where the earth and the atmosphere with its meteorological forces meet. The surface phenomena there are the dynamics by which Nature's composting processes are combining the organic matter with the rock-mineral fertilizers to make those insoluble inorganic soil elements become available plant nutrition (not salts) through their union with the conserved organic nutrient compounds, or through Nature's blending in support of microbes and plants. Unfortunately, our in-organic salt concepts, magnified by their commercial potential, have kept us blinded from Nature's more efficient management of production to support all that lives.

The reported "Healthy Hunzas," isolated in the high Himalayas have not been viewed as a case of a climax human crop dependent on their complete adoption of the practices by which the soil productivity is naturally maintained for climax crops (and live-stock) of domestication with the Hunzas as a corresponding climax human crop included.

Nature's Part is Still the Major Unknown Factor in Technological Agriculture

Of course, we talk about and teach only what we know. Hence, if we don't know that crops are nourished by organic compounds taken from the soil — a fact demonstrated as early as the first climax crops in the course of their evolution before domestication — we are just *naturally* content to believe that crops are nourished only by what has been "broken down by bacteria into simple mineral compounds." Then, too, "we are just *naturally down on* what we are *not up on*." With limited information of nature's performances, our discussions and debates about our managements of those in what we include in agriculture may miss the truth widely and become illustrations of “argumentum ad hominem.” We need to study Nature, not only books.

Concerning the Influence of Calcium on the Physiological Function of Magnesium

A paper William A. Albrecht considered so important he caused it to be circulated to his students follows. This title by Professor Oscar Loew from the German journal, *Die Ernahrung der Pflanze* (Plant Nutrition), XXVII, (No.3): 97-101: (No. 6), 121-122, March 1&2, 1931 was translated by Albrecht in 1970 as *Concerning the Influence of Calcium on the Physiological Function of Magnesium.*

The Albrecht equation depended on the above connection more than most of the miscellany supporting the nourishment of plants.

Antagonisms Between Calcium and Magnesium

Numerous observations lead to the following conclusions:

1. Besides their own physiological functions, the magnesium salts exercise poisoning effects on all plants, including the higher Algae and higher species.
2. This poisoning effect by magnesium rests mainly on the displacement of calcium from its important place in the cell nucleus.
3. The poisoning effects by magnesium are wholly prevented by the presence of ample amounts of calcium salts.
4. A distinct excess of calcium salts lowers the function of the magnesium which manifests itself in reduced plant production.
5. The nuclear substance of the lower algae and fungi is calcium-free.

The above statements will be given more specific elucidations in the following paper.

Many chemo-physiological questions can be answered most simply by observing the cells of algae. The Spirogyra group serves to answer specific questions. The chlorophyll's particular arrangement takes form as a band of lobes embedded spirally in the cytoplasm. A thread of Spirogyra consists of many such similar cells. For observing the cell nucleus, the *Spirogyra majuscula* serves best, since, in this variety, the spiral of the chlorophyll is so flat that the cell nuclei are nicely observed hanging from the middle of the cell. A perchance poisoning effect on the cell nucleus can be observed when the salts, precipitating the calcium, exhibit their calcium-disturbing effects; not only those alkaline ones of oxalic acid, but also those of hydrofluoric acid as well as of pyro-and metaphosphoric acids. When the algal threads are laid into 10 cc-50 cc of solutions of 1.0 to 0.1% concentrations, one observes — according to concentration — in 10–15 minutes, that the nucleus contracts into a bullet-shaped structure — but to a thinner, irregular thread when higher concentrations of various salts are used for their immersion. Later, one sees sinuated edges formed of the chloroplasts, becoming sharply pointed and soon disappearing; then the entire chloroplast shrinks in length and width. Then in one or two hours the cytoplasm dies, as does the cell, in consequence of its shrinkage and turgor loss. Since the entering salt, precipitating the calcium, must first pass through the cytoplasm, though yet this latter dies last, the order is arranged so that their single deaths are a sequence started in the nucleus and chloroplasts but not in a direct order as of poisoning.

It is of special interest that free oxalic acid in a dilution of 0.01 to 0.001%, exercises poisoning effects on the nucleus of the cell when the Spirogyra strand is laid into 100 cc of the above solution. Also germinated seeds and isolated leaves are favorable objects for study of the similar poisonous effects.

The simplest explanation of these poisonings is the fact of a loss of calcium from some very important positions in the nucleus and the chloroplast. This loss is evidently tied up with a lessening of the water content so that a general break down in the finer cell structure results, which occasions chemical changes in constituent nucleo-proteids, since the living protoplasms are labile (unstable) structures of labile (unstable) materials.

More significantly, it was shown by additional studies that the *lowest forms of algae and fungi behave indifferently toward salts precipitating calcium*. I conclude, there-from that for the simpler construction of those cells no calcium-containing protein substances are necessary, a fact (thesis) which has fine support from Molisch's observation, that the *lowest forms of algae can grow and multidy in nutrient solutions without a trace of calcium.*

It seems most unusual that magnesium, unconditionally necessary for every cell, *can exercise poisoning effects on plants from the higher algae and those higher, but not on the lowest algae or the fungi.* There is the analogy here also of the cells to the calcium-precipitating salts. We can conclude that *where no calcium is needed, magnesium cannot be poisonous.* My observation shows further agreement, namely, that poisoning effects by magnesium can be prevented only according as sufficient soluble calcium is present. Also if magnesium removes calcium out of the nucleus, accordingly calcium from solution can be restored again before injury results.

The first observation which I have made of concern here was the following: Some threads of Spirogyra were put into the following solutions in glass-distilled water and examined daily as bits of threads under the microscope with the following results:

Concentration	*Observation*
Calcium Chloride 0.2%	Fully healthy for 5 months
Magnesium Chloride 0.2%	All cells dead in 4 days
Combination of above two	Fully healthy for months

These results were "controls" for tests of other salts. Potassium salts, in essential degree, retarded the poisoning effects but did not prevent them. Perhaps these results rest on the possible so-called forming of "Double Salts."

From the confirmations of each antagonism some had been mentioned. Hansteen had established the following for cereal plant roots: with use of the calcium-magnesium mixture, there must be for each two parts magnesium at least one part calcium to combat the poisoning by magnesium. The root system develops most fully when relatively more calcium is used, so that for one part magnesium from 1 to 2 parts calcium are added. More calcium reverses the beneficial effects. Hansteen found further, that the root hairs, the vital organs of absorption, developed most fully by each favorable Ca-Mg ratio. Warthiadi reported the root weights of six wheat plants as only 7.2 gms, by a Ca:Mg ratio of 0.3:1.0, while with the ratio of 1:1 the weights of roots were 12.7 gms. Also the root hairs were best developed under the latter ratio.

Also, from observations in the field, a case of magnesium poisoning may be presented. It was observed at the Research Station of North Carolina that on low-calcium soils a treatment of but 12 pounds of magnesium sulfate per acre injured the tobacco plants. The observer added: "It is often difficult to distinguish whether the poisoning by magnesium is more prominent than the calcium deficiency." This fact is really characteristic since the poisoning effect rests on the fact that calcium is crowded out of its important combination. Also both phenomena are simultaneous.

Also in animals, the crowding out of calcium by excess of magnesium has been pointed out. The calcium concentration in urine is increased by taking of known amounts of magnesium salts. But also the poisoning effect by magnesium has been prevented by addition of calcium salts in animals. Meltzer and Auer of the Rockefeller Institute gave a rabbit so much magnesium sulfate that lameness resulted. Thereafter the rabbit in deep unconsciousness, given a few cubic centimeters of a 3% calcium chloride solution, intravenously, was brought out wide awake in a few moments. The same authors cited my observations on algae.

The Calcium-Magnesium Ratios and Phosphoric Acid

Whilst a specific mass of calcium salt must be present for magnesium to function without acting as a poison, this function is reduced when the calcium is increased over that of magnesium. This last relation is easily comprehended if we examine the function of magnesium. If magnesium and calcium are present in the soil in relatively lesser amounts, then the phosphoric acid of the soil solution eventually — via help of the acidic root secretion according to the law of mass action — will be equally divided between the two cations; magnesium phosphate, after uptake by plants, can give off its phosphate for assimilation. The free magnesium will then react with phosphates in the cells so this newly formed magnesium phosphate finds use. But if calcium is present in much larger amounts than magnesium, then the calcium will take larger amounts of phosphate than the magnesium gets. Accordingly, the magnesium can function less, which exhibits itself in slowed development of plants and lessened yield. It becomes clear that the available calcium dare not be significantly higher than the magnesium, whereby the available phosphorus can be most fully used. In fullest agreement with our observation is the fact established by Gehring, namely, that the magnesium phosphate is a particularly favorable form which magnesium fertilizing brings about. This fact confirms the observation of Roessler and Wrangells.

Just what effects the variable calcium-magnesium ratios have on plant development we learned from our many researches in water, sand and soil cultures at the Agricultural Institute, University of Tokyo, in company with colleagues and advanced students. Those have shown that the best calcium-magnesium ratio plays between 1:1 and 3:1, according to the ratio from weight of sprout to seed weight since, in the leaves calcium prevails well over magnesium while in the seed the reverse ratio prevails. I shall mention here some reported well-established observations. Thomas and Frear observed that the best calcium-magnesium ratio is 3:1.

Portheim and Semec of Botanic Institute in Vienna published a work with sprouts of *Phaseolus vulgaris* (beans) saying, "If the plants were given calcium nitrate combined with magnesium nitrate, their growth was damaged according to the varied ratios, and the duration of their growth." "Only when the calcium factor was 2.78 was the growth of the beans with the combination of the two as mixture the best.

According to Snowden, fruit trees thrive best when the soil contains at least 3.2 parts calcium per one part magnesium. The consequent effects of relatively more magnesium exhibit themselves very noticeably."

Lenz has shown that the more productive soils in Bavaria exhibit the narrower favorable ratios between calcium and magnesium.

L. Bernardini, in cooperation with Corso and Siniocalchi had a series of researches with water, sand and soil cultures. In one the calcium was held constant while the magnesium was varied; in another, the two cations as nitrates varied so that their sums of the molecules of cations remained constant. In spite of these conditions there were similarities in results: By cereal plants the most favorable ratio of calcium to magnesium was 1:1; by maize, spinach and cabbage, it was 2:1; and by peas it was 3:1.

An unfavorable calcium-magnesium ratio in the soil can appear, to a certain degree, in the root and the leaf because of regulated uptake under osmotic laws and through the transpiration stream contributing certain amounts of mineral nutrients. For the same reasons there can be variations in ash analyses. When we brought the calcium-magnesium ratio of 1.2:1 of a neutral, humus-clay soil to a ratio of 10:1 by the admixture of calcium carbonate, we observed the following ratios of calcium to magnesium.

	In the Soil	In the Roots	In the Leaf	Harvest of Oats
Soil Untreated	1.2:1	2:1	2.5:1	301 gms
Soil Given $CaCo_3$	10:1	3.7:1	4:1	106 gms

The above data, resulting from the calcium carbonate put into the soil to widen the calcium-magnesium ratio, exhibit clearly the increased unfavorable ratio occurring in the leaf. The seed was not chemically tested since the resulting ratios were less wide.

In recent times Gehring concerned himself with investigations of the magnesium question and the narrower ratios of the supplies of calcium and magnesium of the soil in numerous field studies. These profitable works have been cited under comments in the "Ernahrung der Pflanze, 1930. Nos. 21 and 22."

Disturbances in Field and Pot Cultures

Many authors have arrived at contradictory results in research attempts to establish the level at which a certain calcium-magnesium ratio in different soils can influence the yields. Therefrom we note by liming the sour, heavy, or the humus-rich soils with consequent soil improvement, one so significant increase in the yields can follow that another change in ratio of calcium to magnesium cannot be effectual. It is to be noted, further, that the degree of availability of calcium, magnesium and phosphoric acid of the soil cannot be determined with precision. It appears though that, according to the proposal by Ulbricht, the extraction of the soil with 10% hydrochloric acid gives the best results. We have used that method.

The research of Soederbaum is very instructive in this connection. He extracted a clay soil and a humus one with 2% hydrochloric acid during 48 hours at room temperature. In spite of successive complete washings each later outflow of the traces of acid showed the soil unusable for plants, which rested evidently only on the acidity produced in the soil, which, then, only after the addition of calcium carbonate had neutralized it, permitted plant growth without additional fertilizing.

Barley on the clay soil yielded 41.4 gms harvest, in contrast to 73.4 gms on the original soil; and the humus soil yielded 18.4 gms in contrast to 45.5 gms for the original soil.

Soederbaum stressed that "The Extraction with 2% hydrochloric acid could dissolve out of the soil's total only a part of available plant nutrients." It demanded that a more concentrated acid must be used.

The pot cultures bring on another disturbing moment: it is the reduced function of the plant's roots because of their cramped condition. Anyone who has observed critically the root mat (like felt) in the bottom of the pot must recognize therein the reason for the delayed growth of pot cultures. I have stressed for a long time that three points must be recognized to get reasonably reliable results with pot-cultures.

1. The number of plants must be limited according to the size of the pots; one per 1–2 Kilos of soil.
2. The seeds dare not be put too near the pot wall to prohibit root extension.
3. The fertilizer for pots must be 3–6 times the concentration of that used in the field, so that the roots in the soil can increase their function which is cramped, or reduced, in the part of the root along the pot's wall and the bottom. It was this point which was emphasized by Wagner-Darmstadt.

When these research regulations are unheeded, one points out that in the first periods of plant development under different calcium-magnesium ratios the marked differences in plants disappear and the harvest shows that no plants have attained a normal development in weight.

The water culture, according to Knop's system with relatively few plants per container excludes the disturbances. The collective nutrients are present in similar degrees of availability, and the amounts of nutrients build no great differences. One can use calcium and magnesium in the nitrate forms and in amounts so that the molecules of both cations, by the changes of relations, give the same sums so the uptakes of nitrogen are not altered. One can use added sulfur as potassium sulfate. Knop recommends that iron be given as a trace of iron chloride. Because of its strong acidic reaction, a small amount of iron sulfate or ferroammonium sulfate should be preferred. Krone's declaration that Knop's nutrient solution produces only pale plants depends on his use of too much and a very sour iron chloride solution. Every one who uses water cultures properly can establish the law of the calcium factor with the greatest of ease.

How Shall the Law of the Calcium Factor in Practice be Stated?

From the very beginning it was very clear that with respect to the calcium factor in practice we are dealing with mainly pronounced differences in calcium and magnesium contents of the soil. *If the magnesium exceeds the calcium which is prominent in the subtropical and tropical regions (deserts excluded) then the calcium fertilization shows itself more important. But should the calcium content be noticeably higher than three magnesium, accordingly the latter as application may well be tested. It may be a question of needing a magnesium sulfate fertilizing which in yield production surpassed all other magnesium fertilizers.* According to our researches in Tokyo, there are 4.8 parts crystallized magnesium sulfate as capable for work as 100 parts pulverized magnesite for barley culture. But when magnesium sulfate is applied as top-dressing, one part is sufficient. At the research station of North Carolina it was observed that calcium-rich soil with 0.4% magnesium showed symptoms of magnesium deficiency by tobacco. But an application of 20 to 30 lbs. magnesium sulfate per acre could remove the symptoms of magnesium deficiency. Often it is convenient to combine the magnesium with the potassium fertilization. The potassium-magnesium-sulfate has established itself brightly in this case.

BIBLIOGRAPHY

Potassium in the Soil Colloidal Complex and Plant Nutrition.

Albrecht, Wm. A., Graham, E. R., and Ferguson, C. E., Plant growth and the breakdown of inorganic soil colloids. Soil Sci. 47: 455–458, 1939.

Albrecht, Wm. A., and Schroeder, R. A., Plant nutrition and the hydrogen ion: I. Plant nutrients used most effectively in the presence of a significant concentration of hydrogen ions. Soil Sci. 53: 313–327, 1942.

Alexander, I. T., Byers, H. G., and Edgington, G., A chemical study of some soils derived from limestone. U. S. Dept. Agr. Tech. Bul. 678, 1939.

Allen, D. I., Differential growth response of certain varieties of soybeans to varied mineral nutrient conditions. Doctoral thesis, University of Missouri, Columbia, 1942. [unpublished]

Brown, I. C., and Byers, H. G., Chemical and physical properties of certain soils developed from granite materials in New England and the Piedmont, and of their colloids. U. S. Dept. Agr. Tech. Bul. 609, 1938.

Converse, J. D., Gammon, N., and Sayre, J. D., The use of ion exchange materials in studies on corn nutrition. [unpublished]

Ferguson, C. E., and Albrecht, Wm. A., Nitrogen fixation and soil fertility exhaustion by soybeans under different levels of potassium. Missouri Agr. Exp. Sta. Res. Bul. 330: 1–52, 1941.

Graham, E. R., Magnesium as a factor in nitrogen fixation by soybeans. Missouri Agr. Exp. Sta. Res. Bul. 288: 1–30, 1938.

Graham, E. R., Calcium transfer from mineral to plant through colloidal clay. Soil Sci. 51: 65–71, 1941.

Hough, G. J., Gile, P. S., and Foster, Z. C., Rock weathering and soil profile development in the Hawaiian Islands. U. S. Dept. Agr. Tech. Bul. 752, 1941.

Jenny, H., Factors in soil formation. McGraw-Hill Company, New York, 1941.

Kansas State Board of Agriculture. Pre-harvest wheat survey. Topeka, Kansas, 1940.

Marshall, C. E., The layer lattices and the base exchange clays. Ztschr. Krist. (A) 91: 433–449, 1935.

Schantz, H. L., The natural vegetation of the Great Plains. Ann. Assoc. Amer. Geogr. 8: 81–107, 1923.

Vanderford, H. B., and Albrecht, Wm. A., The development of loessial soils in central United States as it reflects differences in climate. Missouri Agr. Exp. Sta. Res. Bul. 345, 1942.

Wehmer, C., Die Pflanzenstoffe, botanisch systematisch bearbeitet, bestandteile, und zusammensetzung der einzeln pflanzen und deren producte. G. Fischer. Jena, 1929–1931.

Whitney, M., Soil and civilization. D. Van Nostrand Company, New York, 1925.

Unpublished data of E. O. McLean and W. J. Pettijohn.

Saturation Degree of Soil and Nutrient Delivery to the Crop.

Graham, Ellis R., Primary minerals of the silt fraction as contributors to the exchangeable base level of acid soils. Soil Science.

Jenny, Hans, and Overstreet, R., Cation interchange between plant roots and soil colloids. Soil Sci. 47: 257–272, 1939.

Albrecht, Wm. A. and Klemme, A. W., Limestone mobilizes phosphates into Korean lespedeza. Jour. Amer. Soc. Agron., 31: 284–286, 1939.

Adsorbed Ions on the colloidal Complex and Plant Nutrition.

Albrecht, Wm. A., Inoculation of legumes as related to soil acidity. Jour. Amer. Soc. Agron., 25: 512–522, 1933.

Albrecht, Wm. A., Physiology of root nodule bacteria in relation to fertility levels of the soil. Soil Sci. Soc. Proc., 2: 315–327, 1937.

Albrecht, Wm. A., Some soil factors in nitrogen fixation by legumes. Intern. Soc. Soil Sci. Third Comm. Trans., 1939.

Albrecht, Wm. A. Calcium-potassium-phosphorus relation as a possible factor in ecological array of plants, Journal Amer. Soc. Agron., 32: 411–418, June 1940.

Albrecht, Wm. A., and Jenny, H., Available soil calcium in relation to "damping off" of soybeans. Bot. Gaz., 92: 203–278, 1931.

Albrecht, Wm. A., and Klemme, A. W., Limestone mobilizes phosphate into Korean lespedeza. Jour. Amer. Soc. Agron., 31: 284–286, 1939.

Graham, Ellis, R., Magnesium as a factor in nitrogen fixation by soybean. Mo. Agr. Exp. Sta. Res. Bul. 288, 1938.

Horner, Glenn M., Relation of the degree of base saturation of a colloidal clay by calcium to the ground nodulation and composition of soybeans. Mo. Agr. Exp. Sta. Res. Bul. 232, 1935.

Hutchings, Theron B., Relation of phosphorus to growth, nodulation and composition of soybeans. Mo. Agr. Exp. Sta. Res. Bul. 243, 1936.

McCalla, Thomas M., Behavior of legume bacteria in relation to the exchangeable calcium and hydrogen ion concentration of the colloidal clay fraction of the soil. Mo. Agr. Exp. Sta. Res. Bul. 256, 1937.

Ravikovitch, S., Anion exchange. I. Adsorption of the phosphoric acid soil. Soil Sci., 38: 219–239, 1934. II. Liberation of the phosphoric acid adsorbed ions by soils. Soil Sci., 38: 279–290, 1934.

True, R. H., The significance of calcium for higher plants. Science, 55: 1–6. 1922.

Surface Relationship of Roots and Colloidal Clay in Plant Nutrition.

Bradfield, R., Chemical nature of a colloidal clay. Missouri Agric. Exper. Sta. Res. Bul. 60, 1923.

Dittmer, Howard J., A quantitative study of the subterranean members of the soybean. Soil Conservation VI: 33–34, 1940.

Ferguson, Carl E., and Albrecht, Wm. A., Nitrogen fixation and soil fertility exhaustion by soybeans under different levels of potassium. Missouri Agric. Exper. Sta. Res. Bul. 330, 1941.

Graham, Ellis R., Primary minerals of the silt fraction as contributors to the exchangeable base level of acid soils. Soil Science 49: 277–281, 1940.

Graham, Ellis R., Calcium transfer from mineral to plant through colloidal clay. Soil Science 51: 65–71, 1940.

Jenny, H., and Overstreet, R., Contact effects between plant roots and soil colloids. Proc. Net. Acad. of Sci. Washington 24: 384–392, 1938.

Marshall, C. E., The chemical constitution as related to the physical properties of the clays. Trans. Ceramic Soc. 35: 401–411, 1936.

Marshall, C. E., Studies in the degree of dispersion of clay. IV. The shapes of clay particles. Jour. of Phys. Chem. 45: 81–93, 1941.

Magnesium Depletion in Relation to Some Cropping Systems and Soil Treatments.

Albrecht, Wm. A., Calcium and hydrogen ion concentration in the growth and inoculation of soybeans. Jour. Amer. Soc. Agron. 24: 793–806, 1932.

Albrecht, Wm. A., Inoculation of legumes as related to soil acidity. Journal Amer. Soc. Agron. 25: 512–522, 1933.

Albrecht, Wm. A., and McCalla, T. M., The colloidal clay fraction of soil as a cultural medium. Amer. Jour. Bot. 25: 403–407, 1938.

Albrecht, Wm. A., Adsorbed ions on the colloidal complex and plant nutrition. Proc. Soil Sci. Amer. 5: 8–16, 1940.

Albrecht, Wm. A., Plants and the exchangeable calcium of the soil. Amer. Jour. Bot. 28: 394–402, 1941.

Baver, L. D., and Bruner, F. H., Rapid soil tests for estimating the fertility needs of Missouri soils. Missouri Agr. Exp. Sta. Bul. 404, 1939.

Ferguson, C. E., and Albrecht, Wm. A., Nitrogen fixation and soil fertility exhaustion under different levels of potassium. Missouri Agr. Exp. Sta. Res. Bul. 330, 1941.

Garner, W. W., et al., Sand-drown, a chlorosis of tobacco due to magnesium deficiency, and the relation of sulfates and chlorides of potassium to the disease. Jour. Agr. Res. 33: 1–30, 1923.

Graham, E. R., Magnesium as a factor in nitrogen fixation by soybeans. Missouri Agr. Exp. Sta. Res. Bul. 288: 1–30, 1938.

Graham, E. R., Soil development and plant nutrition: II. Composition of sand and silt separates in relation to the growth and chemical composition of soybeans. Soil Sci. 55: 265–273, 1943.

Harris, H. L., and Drew, W. B., The establishment and growth of certain legumes on eroded and uneroded sites. Ecology. [In press.]

Whitt, D. M., The role of blue-grass in the conservation of the soil and its fertility. Proc. Soil Sci. Soc. Amer.: 309–311, 1941.

Whitt, D. M., and Swanson, C. L. W., Effect of erosion on changes in fertility of the Shelby loam profile. Jour. Agr. Res. 5: 283–298, 1942.

Calcium in Relation to Phosphorus Utilization by Some Legume and Nonlegumes.

Albrecht, Wm. A., Some soil factors in nitrogen fixation by legumes. Trans. Third Com. Intern. Soc. Soil Sci. A: 71–84, 1939.

Albrecht, Wm. A., and Klemme, A. W., Limestone mobilizes phosphates into Korean lespedeza. Jour. Amer. Soc. Agron., 31: 284–286, 1939.

Ferguson, Carl E., Possible decomposition of colloidal clay by plant growth. Thesis, University of Missouri, 1939.

Horner, Glenn M., Relation of the degree of base saturation of a colloidal clay by calcium to the growth, nodulation and composition of soybeans. Mo. Agr. Exp. Sta. Res. Bul. 232, 1935.

Carbohydrate-Protein Ratio of Peas in Relation to Fertilization with Potassium, Calcium, and Nitrogen.

Albrecht, Wm. A., Calcium potassium-phosphorus relation as a possible factor in the ecological array of plants. Jour. Amer. Soc. Agron., 32: 411–418, 1940.

Albrecht, Wm. A., Colloidal clay culture—Preparation of the clay and procedures in its use as a plant growth medium. Soil Sci., 62: 23–31, 1946.

Bowers, J. L., and Mahoney, C. H., The influence of nitrogen, calcium, and potassium on the yield of Alaska peas grown on soils of known fertility level. Amer. Soc. Hort. Sci. Soc., 37: 707–712, 1939.

Day, D., Some chemical aspects of calcium deficiency effects on Pisum sativum. Plant Physiol., 10: 811–81, 1935.

Hibbard, R. P., and Grisby, B. H., Relation of light, potassium, and calcium deficiencies to photosynthesis, protein synthesis and translocation. Mich. Agr. Expt. Sta. Tech. Bul. 141, 1934.

Loew, O., The physiological role of mineral nutrients on plants. U. S. Dept. of Agr. Bul. 45. 1903.

Miller, E. C., Plant physiology. New York and London: McGraw-Hill Book Company, Inc., 1938.

Murneek, A. E., and Heinze, P. H., Speed and accuracy in determination of total nitrogen. *Missouri Agr. Exp. Sta. Res. Bul.* 261, 1937.

Sayre, C. B., Nitrogen improves quality, increases yields of peas. *N. Y. State Expt. Sta. Bul.* 121: 8–9, 1946.

Schroeder, R. A., Some effects of calcium and nitrogen upon peas. *Amer. Soc. Hort. Sci. Proc.*, 41: 375–377, 1942.

Stark, R. N., Environmental factors affecting the protein and oil content of soybeans and the iodine number of soybean oil. *Jour. Amer. Soc. Agron.*, 16: 636–646, 1924.

Street, O. E., Carbohydrate-nitrogen and base element relationships of peas grown in water culture under various light exposures. *Plant Physiol.*, 9: 301–22, 1934.

True, Rodney, H., The function of calcium in the nutrition of seedlings. *Jour. Amer. Soc. Agron.,* 13: 91–107, 1921.

Calcium and Phosphorus as They Influence Manganese in Forage Crops.

Albrecht, Wm. A., Nitrogen fixation as influenced by calcium. Proc. 2nd. Int. Congr. Soil Sci. 3: 29–39, 1930.

Albrecht, Wm. A., Calcium and hydrogen-ion concentration in the growth and inoculation of soybeans. Jour. Am. Soc. Agr. 24: 793–806, 1932.

Albrecht, Wm. A., Inoculation of legumes as related to soil acidity. Jour. Am. Soc. Agr. 25: 512–522, 1933.

Albrecht, Wm. A., Calcium-potassium-phosphorus relation as a possible factor in the ecological array of plants. Jour. Am. Soc. Agr. 32: 411–418, 1940.

Bertrand, G., The role of infinitely small amounts of chemicals in agriculture. Am. Fert. 37: 37–38, 1912.

Bloin, D. W., Manganese content of grasses and alfalfa in grazed plots. Jour. Agr. Res. 48: 657–663, 1934.

Brown, P. E. and Minges, G. A., The effect of some manganese salts on ammonification and nitrification. Soil Sci. 2: 65–85. (Iowa Res. Bul. 35.), 1916.

Cooper, H. P., Barnes, W. C., Wallace, R. W. and Smith, R. L., Irish potato fertilizer experiments. South Carolina Exp. Sta. 50th Ann. Rep., pgs. 152–154, 1937.

Daniels, Amy L. and Emerson, Gladys J., Relation of manganese to congenital debility. Jour. Nutr. 9: 191–203, 1935.

Gerretsen, F. C., The effect of manganese deficiency on oats in relation to soil bacteria. Trans. 3rd. Int Congr. Soil Sci. 1: 189–191, 1935.

Gilbert, B. E., Normal crops and the supply of available soil manganese. Rhode Island Sta. Bul. 246, 1934.

Haas, A. R. C., Injurious effects of manganese and iron deficiencies of the growth of citrus. Hilgardia 7: 181–206, 1932.

Hopkins, E. F., Manganese an essential element for green plants. N. Y. (Cornell) Mem. 151, 1934.

Jones, J. S. and Bullis, D. E., Manganese in commonly grown legumes. Jour. Ind. and Eng. Chem. 13: 524–525, 1921.

Kemmerer, A. R., Elvehjem, C. A. and Hart, E. B., Studies on the relation of manganese to the nutrition of the mouse. Jour. Biol. Chem. 92: 623–630, 1931.

McHargue, J. S., Manganese in plant growth. Jour. Ind. Eng. Chem. 18: 172–174, 1926.

McLean, F. T. and Gilbert, B. E., Manganese as a cure for chlorosis in spinach. Science 61: 636–637, 1925.

Schaible, P. F., Bandemer, Selma L. and Davidson, J. A., Manganese content of feed stuffs and its relation to poultry nutrition. Mich. Exp. Sta. Tech. Bul. 159, 1938.

Calcium-Potassium-Phosphorus Relation as a Possible Factor in Ecological Array of Plants.

Albrecht, Wm. A., Nitrogen fixation as influenced by calcium. Proc. 2nd Intern. Congress of Soil Sci., 3: 29–39, 1930.

Albrecht, Wm. A., Inoculation of legumes as related to soil acidity. Jour. Amer. Soc. Agron., 25: 512–522, 1933.

Albrecht, Wm. A., Nitrate production in soils as influenced by cropping and soil treatments. Mo. Agro. Exp. Sta. Res. Bul. 294, 1938.

Albrecht, Wm., A., Some soil factors in nitrogen fixation by legumes. Trans. Third Com. Intern. Soil Sci., A: 71–84, 1939.

Graham, Ellis R., Magnesium as a factor in nitrogen fixation by soybeans. Mo. Agr. Exp. Sta. Res. Bul. 288, 1938.

Horner, Glenn M., Relation of degree of base saturation of a colloidal clay by calcium to the growth, nodulation and composition of soybeans. Mo. Agr. Exp. Sta. Res. Bul. 232, 1935.

Parker, F. W. and Truog, E., The relation between the nitrogen content of plants and the function of calcium. Soil Sci., 10: 49–56, 1920.

Prillwitz, P. M. H. H., Die invloed van den basentoestand van den grond opde ontwikkeling van de theeplant. (Dissertation Wagening 1932.) Die ernahrung der pflanze, 30: 386–387, 1934.

Smith, N. C., and Albrecht, Wm. A., Calcium in relation to phosphorus mobilization by some legumes and grasses. Soil Sci. Soc. Amer. Proc. In press, 1940.

Farm Trails of Artificial Manure.

Halverson, W. V., and Torgerson, E. F., Production of artificial farmyard manure by fermenting straw. Jour. Amer. Soc. Agron., 19: 577–584, 1927.

Hutchison, H. B., and Richards, E. H., Artificial farmyard manure. Jour. Min. Agr. Great Britain, 28: 398–411, 1921–23.

Jones, G. A. G., Notes on the action of hydrogen peroxide on farmyard manure in different stages of decomposition. Jour. Agr. Sci., 27: 104–108, 1927.

Omelianski, W., Ueber die Garung der Cellulose. Centbl. Bakt. II, 89: 225–231, 1913.

Nitrate Accumulation Under the Straw Mulch.

Albrecht, Wm. A, Nitrate accumulation under straw mulch. Soil Sci., 14: 299–305, 1922.

Andrews, F. M., and Beals, C. C., 1919 The effect of soaking in water and aeration on the growth of Zea Mays. Bul. Torrey Bot. Club., 46: 91–100, 1919.

Beaumont, A. B., Studies in reversibility of colloidal condition of soils. N. Y. (Cornell) Agr. Exp. Sta., Mem. 21, 1919.

Bizzell, J. A., Some conditions effecting nitrification in Dunkirk clay loam. Jour. Amer. Soc. Agron., 1: 222–228, 1910.

Blair, A. W., and Prince, A. L., Variation of nitrate nitrogen and pH values of soils from the nitrogen availability plots of New Jersey. Soil Sci., 14: 9–17, 1922.

Comber, N. M., A qualitative test for sour soils. Jour. Agr. Sci., 10: 420–444, 1920.

Gainey, P. L., and Metzler, L. F., Some factors affecting nitrate accumulation in soil. Jour. Agr. Res., 11: 43–64, 1971.

Gillespie, L. J., Calorimetric determination of hydrogen-ion concentration without buffer mixtures, with especial reference to soils. Soil Sci., 9: 115–136, 1920.

Gustafson, A. F., The effect of drying soils on the water soluble constituents. Soil Sci., 13: 173–214, 1922.

Hall, T. D., Nitrification in some South African soils. Soil Sci., 18: 219–235, 1924.

Jensen, C. A., Relation of nitrification to field factors. U. S. Dept. Agr. Bur. Plant Indus. Bul. 273. 1910.

Klein, M. A., Studies in drying soils. Jour. Amer. Soc. Agron., 7: 49–77, 1915.

Lebedjantzev, A. N., Drying of soil, as one of the natural factors in maintaining soil fertility. Soil Sci., 18: 419–447, 1924.

Lipman, J. G., Blair, A. W., Owens, I. L., and McLean, H. C., Factors relating to the availability of nitrogenous plant-foods. N. J. Agr. Exp. Sta. Bul. 251, 1912.

Lipman, J. G., and Brown, P. E., Moisture conditions affecting the formation of ammonia, nitrite and nitrate. N. J. Agr. Exp. Sta. Bul. 251, 1908.

Lyon, T. L., and Bizzell, J. A., Formation of nitrates in soil after freezing and thawing. Jour. Amer. Son. Agron., 5: 45–47, 1913.

Murray, T. L., The effect of straw on biological soil processes. In Soil Sci., 12: 233–259, 1921.

Palladin, V. I., Palladin's Plant Physiology, Ed. 2, p. 67–68. P. Blakston's Son & Co., Philadelphia, 1923.

Rahn, O., Effect of drying soils on their physiological condition. Centbl. Bakt. (etc.), Abt. 2, 20: 38–61, 1907.

Ritter, G. W., Das Trocken der Erden. Centbl. Bakt. (etc.), Abt. 2, 33: 116–143, 1912.

Scott, H., The influence of wheat straw on the accumulation of nitrates in the soil. Jour. Amer. Soc. Agron., 13: 233–258, 1921.

Sievers, F. J., The maintenance of organic matter in soils. Science, 58: 78–79, 1923.

Stephenson, R. E., The effect of organic matter in soils. Soil Sci., 12: 145–162, 1921.

White, J. W., Nitrification in relation to the reaction of the soil. Pa. Agr. Exp. Sta. Ann. Rpt. 1913–1914, p. 70–71, 1914.

Whiting, A. L., and Schoonover, W. R., Nitrate production in field soils in Illinois. Ill. Agr. Exp. Sta. Bul. 225, 1920.

Organic Matter for Plant Nutrition.

Calvin, M., The Path of Carbon in Photosynthesis. Science. 135: 879–889, 1962.

Miller, E. C., Plant Physiology. McGraw-Hill, 1938.

DeKock, P. C., Influence of Humic Acids on Plant Growth. Science, 121: 474, 1955.

Tiffin, L. O. and Brown, J. C., Iron Chelates in Soybean Exudates. Science, 135: 311–313, 1962.

Publisher's Note

This bibliography contains reference works that Dr. William A. Albrecht used for research when working on many of the papers contained in this book. Some selections are not available from works that have been obtained from Dr. Albrecht's personal papers.

INDEX

THE OTHER SIDE OF THE FENCE – HISTORIC DVD

William A. Albrecht. In this 1950s-era film, Professor Albrecht's enduring message is preserved and presented for future generations. With introductory and closing remarks by *Acres U.S.A.* founder Charles Walters, Prof. Albrecht explains the high cost of inadequate and imbalanced soil fertility and how that "dumb animal," the cow, always knows which plant is healthier, even though we humans don't see a difference with our eyes. A period film, dated in style but timeless in message. Perfect for a group gathering. *DVD format, 26 minutes. ISBN 978-0-911311-87-4*

ECO-FARM – AN ACRES U.S.A. PRIMER

Charles Walters. In this book, eco-agriculture is explained — from the tiniest molecular building blocks to managing the soil — in terminology that not only makes the subject easy to learn, but vibrantly alive. Sections on NP&K, cation exchange capacity, composting, Brix, soil life, and more! *Eco-Farm* truly delivers a complete education in soils, crops, and weed and insect control. This should be the first book read by everyone beginning in eco-agriculture . . . and the most shop-worn book on the shelf of the most experienced. *Softcover, 476 pages. ISBN 978-0-911311-74-7*

WEEDS – CONTROL WITHOUT POISONS

Charles Walters. For a thorough understanding of the conditions that produce certain weeds, you simply can't find a better source than this one — certainly not one as entertaining, as full of anecdotes and homespun common sense. It contains a lifetime of collected wisdom that teaches us how to understand and thereby control the growth of countless weed species, as well as why there is an absolute necessity for a more holistic, eco-centered perspective in agriculture today. Contains specifics on a hundred weeds, why they grow, what soil conditions spur them on or stop them, what they say about your soil, and how to control them without the obscene presence of poisons, all cross-referenced by scientific and various common names, and a new pictorial glossary. *Softcover, 352 pages. ISBN 978-0-911311-58-7*

SCIENCE IN AGRICULTURE

Arden B. Andersen, Ph.D., D.O. By ignoring the truth, ag-chemical enthusiasts are able to claim that pesticides and herbicides are necessary to feed the world. But science points out that low-to-mediocre crop production, weed, disease, and insect pressures are all symptoms of nutritional imbalances and inadequacies in the soil. The progressive farmer who knows this can grow bountiful, disease- and pest-free commodities without the use of toxic chemicals. A concise recap of the main schools of thought that make up eco-agriculture — all clearly explained. Both farmer and professional consultant will benefit from this important work. *Softcover, 376 pages. ISBN 978-0-911311-35-8*

HANDS-ON AGRONOMY

Neal Kinsey & Charles Walters. The soil is more than just a substrate that anchors crops in place. An ecologically balanced soil system is essential for maintaining healthy crops. This is a comprehensive manual on soil management. The "whats and whys" of micronutrients, earthworms, soil drainage, tilth, soil structure and organic matter are explained in detail. Kinsey shows us how working with the soil produces healthier crops with a higher yield. True hands-on advice that consultants charge thousands for every day. Revised, third edition. *Softcover, 352 pages. ISBN 978-0-911311-59-4*

HANDS-ON AGRONOMY VIDEO WORKSHOP (DVD)

Neal Kinsey teaches a sophisticated, easy-to-live-with system of fertility management that focuses on balance, not merely quantity of fertility elements. It works in a variety of soils and crops, both conventional and organic. In sharp contrast to the current methods only using N-P-K and pH and viewing soil only as a physical support media for plants, the basis of all his teachings are to feed the soil, and let the soil feed the plant. The Albrecht system of soils is covered, along with how to properly test your soil and interpret the results. *80 minutes. ISBN 978-0-911311-96-9*

THE BIOLOGICAL FARMER

A COMPLETE GUIDE TO THE SUSTAINABLE & PROFITABLE BIOLOGICAL SYSTEM OF FARMING

Gary Zimmer. Biological farmers work with nature, feeding soil life, balancing soil minerals, and tilling soils with a purpose. The methods they apply involve a unique system of beliefs, observations and guidelines that result in increased production and profit. This practical how-to guide elucidates their methods and will help you make farming fun and profitable.*The Biological Farmer* is the farming consultant's bible. It schools the interested grower in methods of maintaining a balanced, healthy soil that promises greater productivity at lower costs, and it covers some of the pitfalls of conventional farming practices. Zimmer knows how to make responsible farming work. His extensive knowledge of biological farming and consulting experience come through in this complete, practical guide to making farming fun and profitable. *Softcover, 352 pages. ISBN 978-0-911311-62-4*

ADVANCING BIOLOGICAL FARMING

Gary F. Zimmer & Leilani Zimmer-Durand. One of the leading authorities on biological farming, Zimmer is recognized for improving farming by restoring soils. Arguing that an optimally productive soil contains a balance of inorganic minerals, organic materials and living organisms, he relies less on modern improvements than on "the things we've learned by improving fertility in a natural, sustainable way over many years." This book offers invaluable scientific support for committed organic farmers as well as conventional farmers who'd like to reduce chemical inputs and use natural processes to their advantage. *Advancing Biological Farming* updates and expands upon Zimmer's classic, *The Biological Farmer.* Technically precise yet written in friendly language, this book is for everyone who wants a future in biological farming. *Softcover, 244 pages. ISBN 978-1-601730-19-0*